Trade Like Chuck!

How to Create Income in ANY MARKET!

By Chuck Hughes

This book is dedicated to the memory of my Dad, Charlie, who taught me, along with life's lessons, the importance of investing.

And to all my children, may the next generation of investors please step up to the plate!

TABLE OF CONTENTS

INTRODUCTION

Legacy Publishing LLC

The Legacy Publishing Team

Welcome to the exciting world of stock market investing! Your *Legacy Publishing Team* has a combined total of over 60 years of investing experience and more than 25 years of experience teaching investors how to trade stocks successfully.

We have taught thousands of people from all walks of life and backgrounds with no investing experience to trade the *Legacy Publishing* stock market strategies ... everyone from high school dropouts to college professors, from cab drivers and construction workers to attorneys and doctors.

Team member Lee Ridilla has helped people in over 30 countries from Australia to Venezuela learn how to implement the *Legacy Publishing* stock trading strategies. Lee's teaching expertise and guidance gives people with little or no experience the resources for becoming successful traders. The knowledgeable and helpful *Legacy Publishing Team* is here to answer any questions or concerns you may have about learning to trade stocks. We have but one goal. That goal is your success. We measure our success by your success!

Real People . . . Real trades . . . Real Profits

The *Legacy Publishing Team* "practices what they preach". The Team is in the trenches every trading day successfully profiting from every type of market condition from severe bear markets to highly volatile, non-trending type markets.

Copies of our brokerage account statements presented in this book show that the *Legacy Publishing* trading strategies have produced $5,291,774.74 in **actual**, documented profits and cash income over the past 5 years.

Team members Ryan and Chuck Hughes were awarded a total of 13 International Trading Championship trophies including eight first-place, four second-place and one third-place finish. The International Trading Championship is a highly competitive, real money trading contest in which competitors from around the globe display their trading skills trading real money. All profit results are audited by CPAs before being posted on the sponsor's website.

Despite the difficult market conditions in 2014, Chuck had a 339.8% real time return trading the *Legacy Publishing* strategies with a second-place finish in the trading contest. He then won first-place in 2015, earning his eighth championship with a 305% real time return. Chuck has more first place finishes in the trading contest than any other trader in the history of the competition.

We like to use actual trade examples and profit results in our publications. We do not show you profit results to "brag". The reason we're showing you is to build your confidence in the *Legacy Publishing* strategies. Because they really do work... and there is no reason they can't work for you as well. We are showing you actual profit results so you can feel comfortable and confident that you are learning from someone who knows what they're talking about!

Stock Market Trading Strategies

The *Legacy Publishing Team* utilizes three different stock trading strategies designed to profit in any type of market condition including bear markets. In this book we would like to introduce you to these simple strategies that are easy to implement using indicators readily available on the internet.

Strategy #1 - *PowerTrend*

PowerTrend is our trend following system that can help identify stocks and ETFs with the best profit potential. We have been using *PowerTrend* successfully for more than 30 years. *PowerTrend* was very profitable during the last two severe bear markets in 2008 and 2001 as you will see shortly. It only takes a few minutes to qualify trades using *PowerTrend*.

The key to success for *PowerTrend* is the ability of the system to find low risk entry points for our stock trades. With the vast majority of our stock trades, the stock price does not decline much from our entry price. This helps avoid being 'stopped out' of our stock trades and this leads to a high percentage of winning trades.

Historical results for a portfolio of diversified ETFs show that our basic trend following system has produced 40 consecutive years of profits.

$1.1 Million in Actual Profits

In Chapter 2 we list our closed trade stock/ETF profits over the past three years using the *PowerTrend* system to select stock/ETF trades. The trade by trade listing shows $1,175,384.12 in closed trade profits with 70% profitable trades demonstrating the ability of *PowerTrend* system to select profitable trades.

The Most Important Investing Principle Is Not What You Think

In Chapter 2 we will explore a simple portfolio risk management principle for stock investors that allows them to manage risk and maximize profits. Actual stock trades presented in this chapter show that we only need to profit on one out of every ten trades in order to have a profitable portfolio.

Discover how portfolio risk management can give you the edge you need to succeed as a stock investor regardless of which technique or indicator you use to select stock trades. As successful investors we always want to think in terms of investing with limited downside an unlimited upside.

Strategy #2 – Stress Less Stock Investing

PowerTrend has produced a lot of winning trades over the past several decades.

When you purchase a stock or ETF and the trade is profitable, you are always faced with a dilemma. Do you take profits on your stock in case the stock declines in price and turns a profitable trade into a losing trade? Or do you hold the trade in case the stock continues to move up in price and produce additional profits?

We know from experience that it is very difficult to watch a winning trade develop into a losing trade. This is very hard on your psyche as a trader and can help you lose confidence in your ability to be a successful trader.

Fortunately, we have found a way to avoid this dilemma by purchasing 'insurance' on our profitable stock trades. This insurance helps protect you against loss in the event the stock declines in price. At the same time, purchasing the insurance does not limit the upside profit potential if your stock continues to increase in price.

As we will discover shortly, this trade insurance can even guarantee that your stock trade will be profitable!

Purchasing trade insurance transforms stock investing from a risky investment to one of the lowest risk investments in the investment universe.

Once you buy the insurance protection for your stock investment, you can forget about your stock trade! There is no need to place a protective stop as your stock is already protected. You can place the trade and take a vacation! No need to monitor the markets or world events. Bad earnings reports or severe market selloffs don't matter.

This strategy delivers limited risk and at the same time unlimited profit potential for stock traders resulting in Stress Less Investing.

We will also look at ways to help pay for the cost of this stock insurance including a method that can cover the complete cost of the insurance guaranteeing a profit on your trade.

Strategy #3 – Income Strategy

This little understood strategy allows you to collect weekly or monthly cash income from your stocks. This strategy has regularly delivered a better than 100% 'cash on cash' annual return regardless of the price movement of the underlying stock.

When you receive a 100% cash on cash return, a lot can go wrong with your stock trade and it can still be profitable. Your timing on entering the trade can be bad and you can still profit. The underlying stock price can decline substantially and you can still profit. The strategy can also help you avoid being stopped out of your trade with volatile price moves in the stock.

The Income Strategy is a low risk way to generate steady cash income in your stock brokerage account. The strategy is also ideal for generating income in retirement accounts just as we do here at *Legacy Publishing* in our retirement accounts.

Legacy Team Member Chuck Hughes used this income strategy to win the International Trading Championship with a 122% annual return. And Team Member Ryan Hughes took second place in the competition utilizing this income strategy.

The Income Strategy can also allow you to pay the 'insurance' premium that protects your stock mentioned in Strategy #2. If the Income Strategy covers the cost of the insurance premium then all risk is eliminated from your stock trade. And you are guaranteed to profit regardless of the price movement of the stock even in the unlikely event the stock price declines to zero.

$4 Million in Actual Cash Income

Our brokerage account Transaction Reports presented in the Appendix show that we collected $4,068,824.22 in actual cash income over the past five years utilizing the Income Strategy. This resulted in over $67,000 in cash income per month.

CHAPTER 1
PowerTrend Investing

In this Chapter we are going to explore the *PowerTrend* system that can help select stock and ETF trades with the best profit potential. *PowerTrend* has a long history of profitability in any type of market condition. This simple but powerful strategy uses a trend following system that tells us if we should be buying or selling stocks.

The concept behind trend following is very simple. When the trend is up, we buy stocks. When the trend is down, we sell stocks.

PowerTrend is universal in nature and has a long history of profitability in a broad spectrum of investments including stocks, Exchange Traded Funds (ETFs), stock indexes, fixed income investments, mutual funds, sector funds, commodities and currencies.

Two-Tiered Approach
With decades of investing experience, we have found that investing with the trend when used in conjunction with risk management is the best overall approach for profitable investing. This two-tiered approach has worked well in all types of markets and has stood the test of time.

In 2008 during the worst financial crisis since the Great Depression, *PowerTrend* not only signaled to exit stocks, it also produced enormous profits from short positions and turned wealth destruction into wealth creation.

During the last bear market, the broad based S&P 500 Index lost 56% of its value but then staged a powerful comeback with a 171% rally more than doubling its value.

During this powerful comeback rally, the airwaves were cluttered with negative opinions about the outlook for the stock market. Pundits warned of double dip recessions, slow growing global economies, the European debt crisis, quantitative easing by the Fed and the rise of gold to $3,000 an ounce with the impending boom in inflation.

If you had heeded these negative forecasts you would have missed out on the 171% rally in stocks and what could be one of the most powerful rallies in our lifetime. *PowerTrend* not only profited when it went short stocks in 2008 but it also reversed and bought stocks in the Spring of 2009 and has captured most of the comeback rally in stocks since then.

We think the average investor is much better served by following a simple trend following system like *PowerTrend* than listening to the forecasts of analysts and market gurus.

To the average investor the stock market can seem complicated and confusing. Stocks can go up or down for no apparent reason. Apple reports great earnings but the stock plummets. The price of oil drops and the inflation report is tame but the major stock market indexes dive. Pfizer reports terrible earnings but the stock rallies. The Friday Employment Report is dismal but the Dow Jones Industrial Average soars.

When it comes right down to it, the reason **why** stock prices are going up or down seems to be anybody's guess. You might as well try to read tea leafs.

Highly paid analysts would have us believe that a company's fundamentals drive stock prices. Yet how many times have you seen the stock of companies with good fundamentals crash while those with terrible fundamentals soar?

But none of that matters for one simple reason. At the end of the day, if there are more buy orders than sell orders the price of the stock will go up. And if there are more sell orders than buy orders, then the price of the stock will go down. It's just that simple. Everything else is just noise.

Successful trade selection can be reduced to two simple rules:

1. Buy investments if the buying pressure exceeds the selling pressure
2. Sell investments if the selling pressure exceeds the buying pressure

To make real money in the market you don't need to know why a stock price rises or falls, you just need to know in advance which way it's most likely to go. If you can quantitatively measure the buying and selling pressure of a stock using a trend following system, then you will know in advance whether the price is likely to rally or decline.

Follow the Price Trend Instead of Trying to Predict It

The truth is that it is very hard to try to predict the future with any type of consistency. We learned early in our investing careers that it is better to invest with the trend than trying to predict the trend.

One of the most effective ways to measure the price trend is to use technical analysis to quantitatively measure the price movement of a stock. Technical analysis is a market discipline that quantifies stock price movement with the goal of identifying repetitive price patterns.

For example, if the price of a stock is increasing then the buying pressure is exceeding selling pressure and the stock should be bought. If the price of a stock is decreasing then the selling pressure is exceeding buying pressure and the stock should be sold.

Moving averages are a simple method for tracking the current price trend of a stock and allow us to 'trade with the trend' instead of trying to predict the future price movement of a stock.

For example, the price chart below depicts the monthly price movement for Home Depot stock along with its 10-Month Simple Moving Average (SMA). We can clearly see from the price chart that the 10-Month SMA for Home Depot is sloping up indicating a price up trend and that buying pressure is exceeding selling pressure.

Buying Pressure is Exceeding Selling Pressure

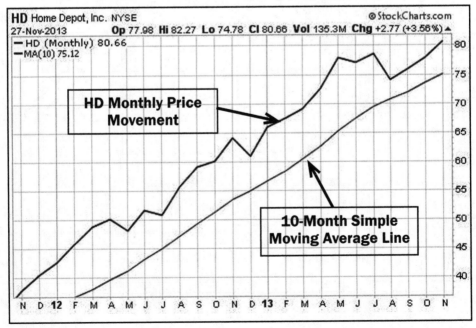

And the price chart below depicts the monthly price movement for
Microsoft stock along with its 10-Month Simple Moving Average (SMA). We
can clearly see from the price chart that the 10-Month SMA for Microsoft
is sloping down indicating a price down trend and that selling pressure is
exceeding buying pressure.

Selling Pressure is Exceeding Buying Pressure

Moving averages give us a 'picture' of the price trend of a stock and enable us to know instantly if buying pressure is exceeding selling pressure or if selling pressure is exceeding buying pressure.

Let Price Movement Determine When You Should Buy or Sell

Through experience we learned that you want to purchase a stock only if the buying pressure exceeds selling pressure as indicated by the stock being in a price up trend. Buying a stock in a price down trend is risky as it requires you to correctly predict when the stock will 'bottom out' and resume a price up trend.

Buying a stock because it is cheap and predicting that the price has bottomed out can be nearly impossible to forecast correctly on a regular basis. This 'crystal ball' type of approach is risky as you must correctly predict the future price movement. A safer approach would be to wait until a stock is in a price up trend before buying. A stock's price reflects all of the known information about a company so let the price movement of the stock tell you when you should buy and sell.

Similarly, you don't want to take a short position in a stock unless the stock is in a price down trend. Taking a short position in a stock in a price up trend requires you to correctly predict when a stock will top out and start a price down trend.

Quantitatively Measuring Buying and Selling Pressure

There are many variations of moving averages that can be used to determine the price trend. In our experience, the 1-Month Price of a stock in relation to its 10-Month Simple Moving Average (SMA) is an excellent way to quantitatively identify the price trend of a stock. Identifying the price trend allows us to know in advance the most likely future price movement of a stock.

If the 1-Month Price (shorter-term) is above the 10-Month SMA (longer-term) a bullish price trend is indicated.

And if the 1-Month Price is below the 10-Month SMA a bearish price trend is indicated. This simple system has been very effective in correctly identifying bullish and bearish price trends.

PowerTrend System 'Buy' Signal
1-Month Price is Above 10-Month SMA

PowerTrend System 'Sell' Signal
1-Month Price is Below 10-Month SMA

The goal of the *PowerTrend System* is to determine whether a stock is in a price up trend or down trend. This has to be established before you buy a stock. Investing with the trend is a basic principal that is essential for successful investing.

If we can quantify the price movement of a stock we can determine the price trend and the most likely future price movement of a stock. Many times the major price trend continues in the same direction and can persist much longer than you might expect.

For example, the price chart below depicts the monthly price movement and the 10-Month SMA for Mastercard (symbol MA) stock. In the lower left hand corner of the chart we can see that the 1-Month price of Mastercard stock closed above its 10-Month SMA (circled) triggering a 'buy' signal for Mastercard.

This buy signal indicated that the most likely future price movement for Mastercard is up and the stock should be bought. Mastercard stock has advanced steadily since this buy signal rewarding investors with more than a 500 point profit since the buy signal was issued (prices do not reflect the subsequent 10 for 1 stock split for MA).

When the 1-Month price of MA closed above the 10-Month SMA around the 240 price level, it was hard to imagine the stock would rally more than 500 points. This is a good example of why it is better to follow the price trend instead of listening to analysts' predictions.

1-Month Price Closed Above 10-Month SMA = Buy

Example of a Sell Signal

Let's now take a look at an example of *PowerTrend* 'sell' signal. The price chart below depicts the monthly price movement and the 10-Month SMA for Caterpillar stock (symbol CAT). In the upper left hand corner of the chart we can see that the 1-Month price of CAT stock closed below its 10-Month SMA (circled) triggering a 'sell' signal for Caterpillar.

This sell signal indicated that the most likely future price movement for CAT is down. If you owned CAT stock you should consider selling your stock.

Selling CAT stock when this *PowerTrend* sell signal was issued would have prevented a painful 66% price decline in the stock.

1-Month Price Closed Below 10-Month SMA = Sell

It's important to note that the *PowerTrend* system takes both bullish and bearish trades. Bearish trades profit if the underlying stock or index declines in price. During the last two severe bear markets when the S&P 500 Index lost more than 50% of its value we actually profited handsomely from buying bearish ETFs. Taking bearish trades can actually diversify and reduce the risk in your portfolio.

Profiting in Bear Markets

Let' now take a look at how the *PowerTrend* system profited during the last two severe bear markets.

The price chart below depicts the monthly price movement and the 10-Month SMA for the S&P 500 Index ETF (symbol SPY) over a five year period from the Fall of 2004 to the Fall of 2009. We can see the SPY 1-Month price was above the 10-Month SMA signaling a buy signal from the fall of 2004 to November of 2007. This buy signal caught most of the bullish move for the Index during this period.

In the upper center of the chart we can see that the 1-Month price of the SPY ETF closed below its 10-Month SMA (circled) triggering a 'sell' signal for the SPY ETF near the 1310 level.

This sell signal indicated that the most likely future price movement for SPY is down. We don't know of any analysts or market gurus who predicted the S&P 500 Index would drop more than 50% in a short period of time. We think investors are better served by following a simple trend following system like *PowerTrend*.

The *PowerTrend* system issued similar signals for global equity, bond, commodity and currency markets. We started to take bearish positions in these global markets by purchasing bearish ETFs and profited on the way down turning wealth destruction into wealth creation.

Turning Wealth Destruction into Wealth Creation

On the following page we included a snapshot of our investing portfolio on September 15th 2008. That day will go down in history as the beginning of the worst financial crisis in the United States since the Great Depression.

Due to the Lehman Brothers and Fannie Mae bankruptcy, the Merrill Lynch buyout and the AIG insurance company insolvency, that day could be considered one of the worst global financial storms in history. Some called it a Financial Armageddon. Over thirty trillion dollars of highly leveraged mortgage securities that went bad caused a financial meltdown that froze global credit. The loss of people's dreams and financial security became palpable.

Fortunately, the *PowerTrend* system had already positioned us in bearish positions for the global currency, commodity and equity markets. By the end of the day the Dow Jones Industrial Average had lost over 500 points in ONE day. But our trading accounts *had a positive return for the day*.

The copy of our brokerage account Profit/Loss Report that follows shows $14,987.22 in closed trade profits from bearish positions on September 15th. Our open trades had a 14.5% return for the day. Our advisory service portfolios had similar returns. We locked in solid profits that day.

Many investors consider short positions high risk which they are if not done correctly. If you short a stock or ETF you incur unlimited risk if the stock or ETF moves up in price.

We take limited risk short positions by purchasing bearish ETFs. Purchasing an inverse or bearish ETF is a bearish strategy as the short ETF increases in value as the underlying ETF goes down in price. We can't lose more than we invest regardless of the price movement of the underlying stock or ETF.

The Number One Rule of Investing

The number one rule of investing is not to risk more than you invest. If you are short a stock or ETF, it only takes one unforeseen event to create an adverse market move that can wipe out your account and possibly cause a margin call which you would be legally obligated to pay. This can and does happen as we know fellow traders who were wiped out when they were on the wrong side of the 1987, 2001 and 2008 bear markets.

14.5% Return in One Day While Dow Dropped 504 Points

Account Reports: Profit/Loss Report

🖨 PRINT

Give your accountant a break. View profits/losses for all trades executed on one specific date or during a range of dates. Track by position, whether it's closed, or still opened. Download to a spreadsheet for easy manipulation, processing and tax reporting.

Trade date: [»] **9/15/2008** [SELECT DATE]

Trade date: [»] [SELECT DATE]

Symbol: [▲] Submit

Guide to the Profit/Loss Report

*To see all transactions within specified date range leave symbol blank

☐ Show detailed unrealized positions

Click here to download data

Realized P&L on Closed Positions

Sept 15th Closed Trades

Symbol	Date Bought	Date Sold	Shares	Cost Basis	Sales Price	Gain-loss
+EWYMH	8/27/2008 3:35:11 PM	9/15/2008 10:52:32 AM	4	$6,302.00	$7,093.95	$791.95
+EWYMH	8/27/2008 3:35:11 PM	9/15/2008 10:52:41 AM	1	$1,575.50	$1,778.49	$202.99
+FLNOD	9/8/2008 2:57:00 PM	9/15/2008 10:51:53 AM	5	$10,727.50	$10,032.43	-$695.07
+FLNOD	9/11/2008 11:38:18 AM	9/15/2008 10:51:53 AM	5	$11,227.50	$10,032.43	-$1,195.07
+JIKOH	9/3/2008 3:27:07 PM	9/15/2008 10:34:02 AM	5	$9,827.50	$11,622.42	$1,794.92
+RSXWX	9/15/2008 3:51:00 PM	9/15/2008 9:58:34 AM	5	$6,527.50	$9,572.43	$3,044.93
EEV	8/26/2008 2:39:36 PM	9/15/2008 9:46:40 AM	100	$9,681.50	$11,910.13	$2,228.63
EEV	8/26/2008 2:39:36 PM	9/15/2008 9:46:40 AM	100	$9,701.50	$11,910.13	$2,208.63
EEV	8/26/2008 2:39:36 PM	9/15/2008 9:46:40 AM	100	$9,681.50	$11,920.13	$2,238.63
EFU	8/26/2008 2:32:13 PM	9/15/2008 9:44:26 AM	236	$25,458.42	$28,890.29	$3,431.87
EFU	8/26/2008 2:32:13 PM	9/15/2008 9:44:26 AM	64	$6,903.98	$7,838.80	$934.82

Total Realized Gain-Loss: **$14,987.22**

Unrealized P&L on Open Positions

Open Trade Profit

Symbol	Description	Position	Avg Price	Cost Basis	Market Value	Type	Unrealized Val.
+EEVLD	Proshares Tr Ultr Shrt Msci Dec 2008 120.00 Call	-3	$19.9182	$5,975.45	-$10,080.00	Stock Option	-$4,104.55
+EWYMH	Ishares Inc Msci S Korea Jan 2009 60.00 Put	5	$17.5550	$8,777.50	$9,800.00	Stock Option	$1,022.50
+JIKOH	Claymore Exchange Traded Fd Tr Bny Bri&c Ptf Mar 2009 60.00 Put	5	$21.4550	$10,727.50	$12,650.00	Stock Option	$1,922.50
+RSXWX	Market Vectors Etf Tr Russia Etf Nov 2008 50.00 Put	5	$16.0550	$8,027.50	$11,500.00	Stock Option	$3,472.50
EEV	Proshares Tr Ultr Shrt Msci	300	$107.0817	$32,124.50	$42,240.00	Equities	$10,115.50
EFU	Proshares Tr Ultr Shrt Msci	300	$114.0817	$34,224.50	$40,059.00	Equities	$5,834.50

Total Unrealized Gain-Loss: **$18,262.95**

Downloading the 1-Month/10-Month SMA Charts

The 1-Month Price and 10-Month SMA charts can be downloaded from
www.stockcharts.com with the basic subscription. First type in the ***Symbol***
for the stock you want to examine. Then under the ***Period*** drop down
menu click "Monthly" to display the monthly price.

In the ***Overlays*** section select "Moving Avg (simple)" and under
Parameters select "10" to display the 10-Month SMA.

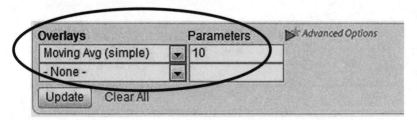

Click ***Update*** to create the price graph.

Here is an example chart using the settings outlined:

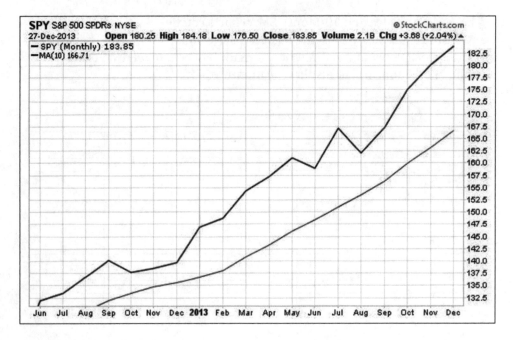

These settings can be saved as a favorite or book mark.

Determining a Buy Signal

With the *PowerTrend* system we only look at the stock/ETF price on the last trading day of the month and ignore all other trading days. It only takes about 10 minutes a month to look at the closing price to determine if we buy, sell or hold.

> *If the price on the last trading day of the month closes above the 10-Month SMA the stock is on a 'buy' signal. We can either buy the stock that day or use the Keltner Channels to help time a low risk entry. We will look at timing our entry with the Keltner Channels later in this chapter. If you already own the stock/ETF then hold the stock and check the closing price on the last trading day of the following month.*

In the price chart below, the vertical lines above **Nov, Dec** and **Feb** represent the price on the last trading of the month. The vertical line above **2012** represents the price on the last trading day in January.

We can see that on the last trading in **Nov** and **Dec** the SPY price was below the 10-Month SMA so no action was required. On the last trading of January (2012) the SPY price did close above the 10-Month SMA and SPY was on a 'buy' signal.

Buy Signal on Last Trading Day of January (2012)

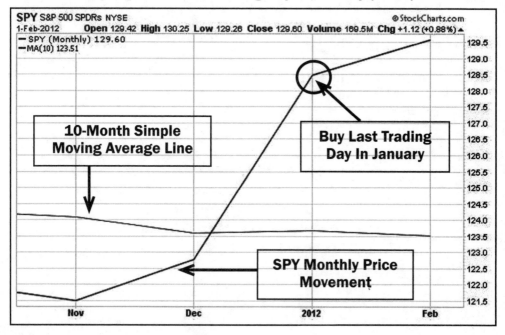

Determining a Sell Signal

Let's now take a look at how a sell signal is determined. As previously noted, with the *PowerTrend* system we only look at the stock/ETF price on the last trading day of the month and ignore all other trading days.

If the price on the last trading day of the month closes below the 10-Month SMA then the stock is on a 'sell' signal. If you own the stock you should consider selling the stock.

The price chart below displays the 1-Month price and 10-Month SMA line for Boeing stock. The 1-Month price closed below the 10-Month SMA triggering a sell signal for Boeing (circled). This sell signal occurred at the 81 dollar level. Boeing subsequently declined to 28.19.

The price chart below displays a more detailed look at the Boeing sell signal. The 1-Month price closed below the 10-Month SMA triggering a sell signal for Boeing (circled). This sell signal occurred at the 81 dollar level. Boeing subsequently declined to 28.19.

In the price chart below the vertical lines above **Sep, Oct, Nov** and **Dec** represent the price on the last trading day of the month. We only look at the stock price on the last trading day of the month and ignore all other trading days.

We can see that on the last trading day in **Sep** and **Oct** Boeing stock price was above the 10-Month SMA and was on a buy signal. On the last trading in **Nov** Boeing stock price closed below the 10-Month SMA and Boeing was on a sell signal. If you owned Boeing stock then Boeing should be sold.

Sell Signal on Last Trading Day of November

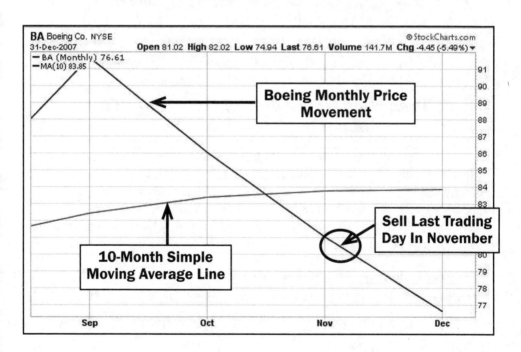

Measuring Price Movement Is the 'Key' To Selecting Profitable Trades

Stock prices are in a constant state of flux. The constant up and down price movement of a stock makes it difficult at times to see the real price trend of a stock. That is why it is important for investors to monitor the price trend of a stock.

The position of the 1-Month Price in relation to the 10-Month SMA can give us a quick and accurate overview of a stock's current price trend. We can instantly see if a stock is in a price up trend or price down trend. Sometimes a stock's price movement is 'flat lined' and there is no clear trend.

In order to be a successful investor we do not have to know what an analyst's rating is for a stock or if there is 'insider' buying. All of that information is already reflected in a stock's price movement which can be quantitatively measured by the 10-Month SMA. Following a discipline of buying stocks in a price up trend and selling stocks in a price down trend can help you become a successful investor.

We've been using trend following successfully for 30 years. A trend following system eliminates emotional decision making and subjectivity and allows us to follow the trend instead of trying to predict it.

"Prediction is very difficult, especially if it's about the future."– Nils Bohr

The *PowerTrend* System has a long history of being very effective in selecting profitable stocks. Historical studies show that price trends tend to continue in the same direction and can continue on longer than one may initially expect. The position of a stock's 1-Month price in relation to its 10-Month SMA allows us to know in advance the most likely future price direction of a stock.

Advantages of *PowerTrend System*

- Uses a moving average to quantitatively measure price trend
- Allows us to instantly know if we should be buying or selling a stock
- Simple to implement and totally mechanical
- Only takes about ten minutes a month to implement
- Not optimized and works across a wide variety of markets . . . stocks, bonds, ETFs, indexes, currencies, metals
- You can change the 10-Month SMA parameter to 6-Months, 8-Months or 12-Months and the system still works

Timing Our Stock Purchase

As noted previously, when the price of a stock on the last trading day of the month closes above the 10-Month SMA, the stock is on a 'buy' signal. We can either buy the stock that day or use the Keltner Channels to help us time a low risk entry. This allows us to purchase a stock after a *PowerTrend* buy signal. If we purchase a stock after a *PowerTrend* buy signal occurs, we still use the risk management guidelines discussed later in the next chapter.

The Keltner Channels function as an overbought/oversold indicator. The goal is to purchase a stock that is on a *PowerTrend* buy signal but is temporarily oversold. This helps us to enter a stock after it has already moved up in price with a low risk entry.

The Keltner Channels can quickly and easily be downloaded from investing websites such as www.StockCharts.com. Steps for down loading the Keltner Channels follow.

Overbought is a term used to describe a stock that has been increasing in price over a period of weeks or months with very few price pullbacks. Oversold is a term used to describe a stock that has been decreasing in price over a period of weeks or months with very few prices increases.

Stocks on a *PowerTrend* buy signal do not advance in a straight line. There are always price corrections or retrenchments along the way. Like the tide there is an ebb and flow in the price movements in stocks. This is the natural order of the markets . . . stocks advance and then the price declines inevitably as profit taking occurs.

Stocks can remain on a *PowerTrend* buy signal as these price declines occur as long as the price decline is not severe enough to cause the 1-Month price to close below the 10-Month SMA which indicates a reversal to a sell signal.

The Keltner Channels are a valuable timing tool as the channels can help us prevent buying stocks when they are in an overbought condition. When stocks become overbought they are vulnerable to profit taking and minor price declines within the context of remaining on a *PowerTrend* buy signal. The Keltner Channels can help us avoid buying stocks when they become overbought and instead buy stocks and call options when they become oversold.

When you avoid buying stocks that are overbought and instead buy stocks when they are oversold (but still on a buy signal) you greatly increase your odds of selecting a profitable trade.

Let's take a look at an example of the Keltner Channels and how they can help us select our entry point. The price chart below displays the daily price movement for Apple stock along with the three Keltner Channels (prices do not reflect the subsequent 7 for 1 stock split for Apple). There is an upper channel, middle channel (which is the dotted line) and a lower channel.

When a stock trades near the upper channel it is an indication the stock is becoming overbought and will most likely encounter selling pressure and then trade back down towards the middle or lower channel.

When a stock trades near the lower channel it is an indication the stock is becoming oversold and will most likely encounter buying pressure and then trade back up towards the middle or upper channel.

If you are considering buying Apple stock, you don't want to buy if the stock is trading near the upper channel as there is a good chance the stock will encounter selling pressure near the upper channel and then decline in price.

It is better to wait until the stock trades near the middle or lower channel before buying. This results in a better entry as the stock most likely will trade back up towards the upper channel.

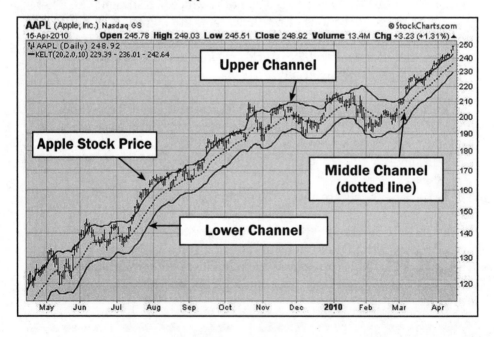

Circled below are examples of Apple stock trading above the upper channel. When a stock is trading above the upper channel it is better to wait for the stock to decline towards the middle or lower channel before buying.

When a stock is trading near the middle or lower channel there is a good probability that it will rally back towards the upper channel.

In each of these examples, after the stock traded above the upper channel it declined back towards the middle or lower channel within a week or two except for the example that occurred in mid-July. In this example the retracement took a little longer as the stock traded near the upper channel in mid-July and did not retrace back to the middle channel until mid-August. This happens occasionally in strong bull markets.

Apple is trading above the upper channel and has stayed above the upper channel for several weeks not presenting any buying opportunities. In our experience this is very rare. Apple stock would have to decline to about 236 before it touches the middle channel.

Don't Buy When a Stock Is Trading Near the Upper Channel

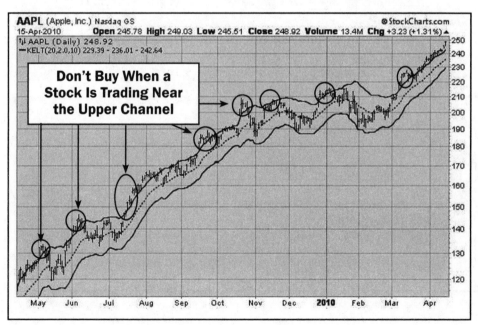

Identifying the Keltner Channel Price Levels

Whenever you download a Keltner Channel price chart, the price chart will list the price levels for the Lower, Middle and Upper Channel. The Lower Channel price level is 229.39 (circled below). The Middle Channel price level is 236.01 and the Upper Channel price level is 242.64 (circled below).

Note: Prices do not reflect the subsequent 7 for 1 stock split for Apple.

Lower Channel Currently at 229.39 Price Level

Middle Channel Currently at 236.01 Price Level

Upper Channel Currently at 242.64 Price Level

If you are considering buying Apple stock, you would want to wait until the price of the stock declines to the middle or lower channel price level which is the 236.01 to 229.39 price level in this example.

Actual Trade Examples Using the Keltner Channels

Our brokerage account trade confirmations below list purchases we made for Apple stock. The confirmations list the date of purchase and purchase price.

Transaction History				Alerts | Transfer Money | Bill Pay | Help
Transactions	Check Summary	Deposit Summary	Categories	Reports
Date	Type	View	Description (show categories)	Amount ($)
11/04/09	Bought		400 of AAPL @ $193.38 (Order #1687)	-77,359.99
12/09/09	Bought		100 of AAPL @ $197.40 (Order #1801)	-19,747.99
02/16/10	Bought		400 of AAPL @ $203.40 (Order #1883)	-81,367.99
02/18/10	Bought		400 of AAPL @ $203.65 (Order #1889)	-81,467.99

We used the Keltner Channels to help select our stock purchase entry point. We bought Apple stock when the stock was trading near the middle or lower channel which lowers our entry risk of buying stock when it is overbought and due for a price correction. These actual entry points are circled below.

You can see from the price chart that Apple stock did not decline in price much below our entry points. Using the Keltner Channels to help time our entry points reduced the risk of our stock purchases. By mid-April, Apple stock was trading near 249 giving us a substantial profit on the stock purchases.

We Bought AAPL Stock When It Was Trading Near the Middle or Lower Channel

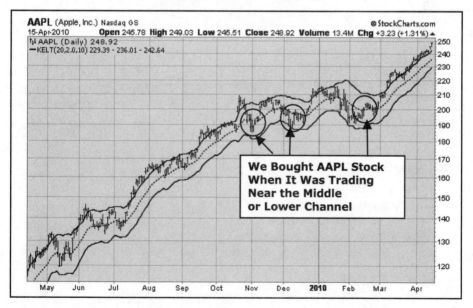

We have found the Keltner Channels to be a valuable timing tool that help us select a low risk entry point for our stock purchases.

Buying a stock when it is trading near the lower or middle channel can help prevent buying stocks when they are in an overbought condition and are vulnerable to price declines.

Buy Stocks When They Are Trading Near the Lower or Middle Channel

We like to buy a stock when the stock is trading near the middle or lower channel and is oversold but still on a *PowerTrend* buy signal. When a stock is oversold there is a good probability that it will rally back towards the upper channel providing us with a lower risk buy point.

We try to avoid buying a stock when it is trading near or above the upper channel and is overbought. When stocks become overbought they are vulnerable to profit taking and will most likely encounter selling pressure.

The Keltner Channels can help us avoid buying stocks when they become overbought and instead buy stocks when they become oversold lowering the overall risk and increasing the profit potential of stock investing.

High Probability Buy Signals

The price chart below displays the Keltner Channels for Baidu stock. Occasionally the price of a stock will become very oversold even though the stock is on a *PowerTrend* buy signal and will actually close below the lower Keltner Channel. Notice how the price of Baidu stock closed below the lower Keltner Channel (circled).

This oversold condition normally sets up a very powerful rally! If you purchase a stock or call option when it closes below the lower Channel there is a high probability that your trade will be profitable. Our brokerage confirmation below shows that we purchased 200 shares of Baidu at 98.17 when the stock closed below the lower Channel.

Bought 200 Shares BIDU @ 98.17

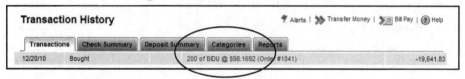

Buying Baidu stock when it closed below the lower Keltner Channel produced a nice return. These high probability signals do not occur very often. We are always on the lookout for these type of high probability signals.

The Keltner Channels are a very valuable timing tool that allows us to select lower risk entry points that have a high probability of being profitable. Some additional high probability trade examples taken over different time periods follow.

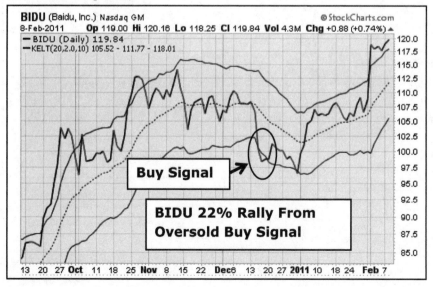

High Probability Buy Signals

Our brokerage confirmations that follow show that we have been buying stocks and ETFs on a *PowerTrend* buy signal after the stock or ETF closed below the lower Keltner Channel. Notice how these stocks and ETFs did not decline much after the high probability buy signal which created low risk entries.

Bought 100 Shares Nasdaq ETF @ 81.48
Bought 400 Shares Nasdaq ETF @ 81.89

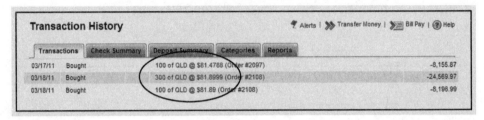

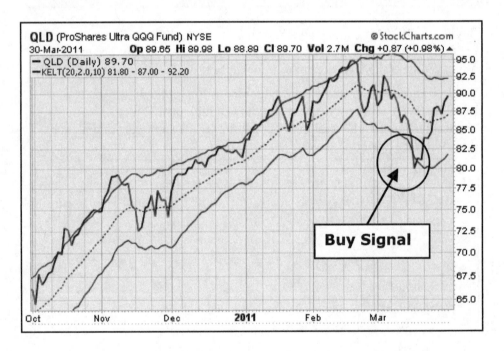

High Probability Buy Signals

Bought 100 Shares AAPL @ 333.00
Bought 100 Shares AAPL @ 333.01

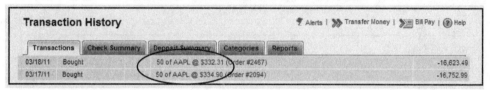

Date	Transaction	Action (Buy, Sell)	Symbol	Quantity	Price	Principal Amount
☐ 03/18/2011	06950341682	Bought	AAPL	100	333.00	33,300.00
☐ 03/18/2011	06950339263	Bought	AAPL	100	333.01	33,301.00

Bought 50 Shares AAPL @ 332.31
Bought 50 Shares AAPL @ 334.90

Transaction History   🔔 Alerts | ≫ Transfer Money | ≫ Bill Pay | ⑦ Help

| Transactions | Check Summary | Deposit Summary | Categories | Reports |

03/18/11	Bought	50 of AAPL @ $332.31 (Order #2467)	-16,623.49
03/17/11	Bought	50 of AAPL @ $334.90 (Order #2094)	-16,752.99

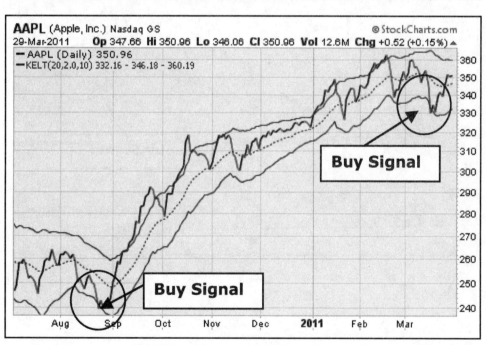

High Probability Buy Signals

Bought 1,000 Shares S&P 500 ETF @ 49.04
Bought 400 Shares S&P 500 ETF @ 49.96
Bought 1,000 Shares S&P 500 ETF @ 49.96

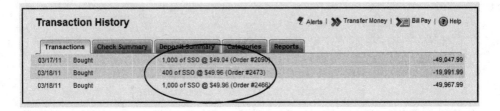

High Probability Buy Signals

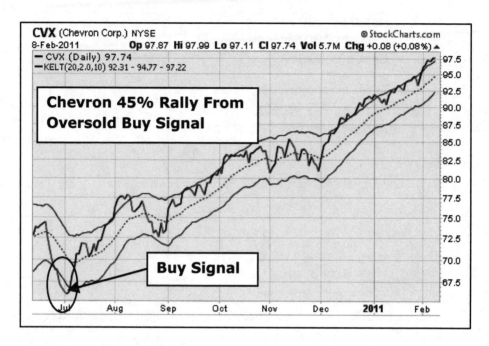

High Probability Buy Signals

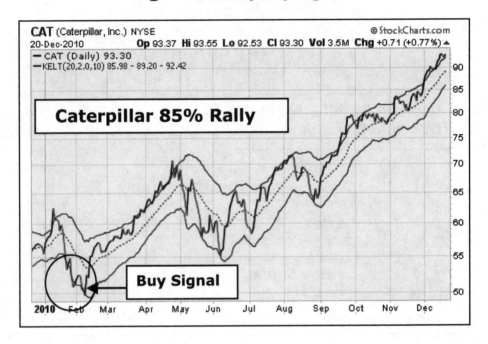

Caterpillar 85% Rally

Buy Signal

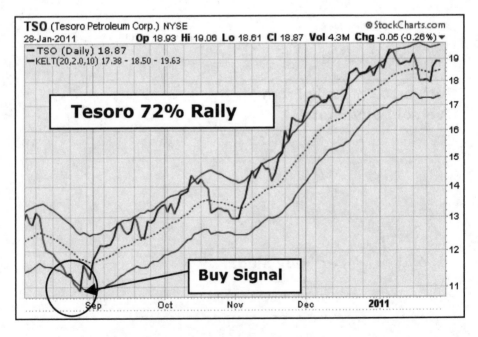

Tesoro 72% Rally

Buy Signal

"I can see clearly now, the rain is gone,
I can see all obstacles in my way.
Gone are the dark clouds that had me blind.
It's gonna be a bright (bright), bright (bright)
Sun-Shiny day"

–Johnny Nash

Yes, the Keltner Channels clear the clouds of confusion and pave the way to clear decision making. Once you understand the channels of success it will become very clear when you should buy stocks.

The Keltner Channels are a great tool that can help you establish low risk entry points for your stock purchases which in turn can increase the profit potential and accuracy of your trades.

On the following page we will show you how to download the Keltner Channels and make them yours! For us they are a very helpful tool in selecting trade entries. Learn it, embrace it, and use it!

Downloading the Keltner Channels

The Keltner Channels can be easily downloaded from www.StockCharts.com. On the home page type in the stock symbol and click "Go". In this example we typed in the symbol for Apple stock AAPL.

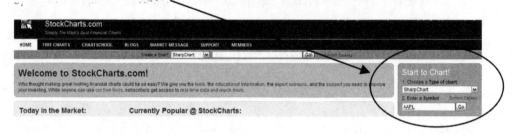

Once you click "Go" the default chart for Apple will appear. Below the default chart for Apple select "Daily" under **Periods** and "1 Year" under **Range**. Under **Overlays** select "Keltner Channels". The default **Parameters** are 20,2.0,10.

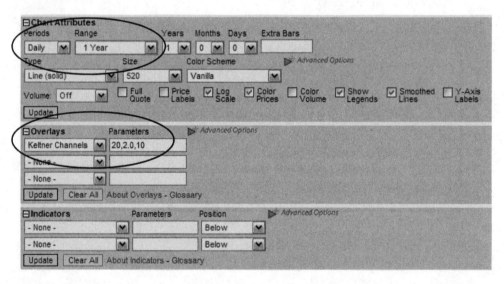

Click "Update" and the Apple price chart with the Keltner Channels will be displayed (see price chart on the following page).

This chart can be saved as a favorite for easy display going forward.

Apple Daily Price Chart with Keltner Channels

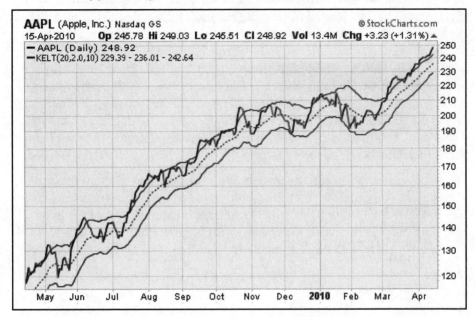

10-Month SMA Historical Studies

We would like to share with you some unique historical studies that were done using the 10-Month SMA. Professor Jeremy Siegel in his book *Stocks for the Long Run* tested the Dow Jones Industrial Average from 1886 to 2006 using a 200-Day SMA to time the market. The 200-Day SMA is very similar to the 10-Month SMA as there are 20 trading days in an average month. If the Dow Average closed 1% above its 200-Day SMA the Average was bought. When the Average closed at least 1% below the 200-Day SMA the Average was sold and proceeds were invested in T-Bills until the next buy signal. Professor Siegel also tested the Nasdaq Composite Index from 1972 to 2006.

He discovered that timing the market with the 200-Day SMA increased the returns compared to a buy and hold approach and also incurred significantly lower risk by exiting the market during bear markets and avoiding the painful losses associated with big down moves. Timing increases returns and decreases risk by avoiding the big down moves.

We previously discovered how *PowerTrend* will exit a market if the 1-Month price closes below the 10-Month SMA. This can reduce risk by avoiding the big down moves that occur during bear markets. The price graph below shows how the 1-Month SPY price closed below the 10-Month SMA in late 2007 generating a sell signal. Selling at the 1310 would have avoided painful loses when the S&P 500 Index declined further to the 670 level.

Avoiding Big Losses

Below is another example of how *PowerTrend* prevented big losses during the 2001 – 2003 bear market when the 1-Month SPY price closed below the 10-Month SMA in late 2000 generating a sell signal. Selling at the 1150 level avoided painful loses when the S&P 500 Index plunged to the 720 level.

PowerTrend is a valuable tool that can help prevent large losses during severe down turns. At one time or another the stock markets of all of the G-7 countries have experienced declines of 75% or more. When you experience a 75% decline it requires a 300% return to get back to even. It would take 15 years with a 10% compounding return to get back to even.

PowerTrend can prevent big losses such as:

- Emerging Markets in late 1990s
- Japanese stocks in late 1980s
- US stocks during the 1920s and 1930s
- All German asset classes in 1910s and 1940s

In Mebane Faber's book, *The Ivy Portfolio,* he presented a historical model for five asset classes using the 1-Month and 10-Month SMA to time entry and exit signals. During the historical test, investment funds were divided equally among the five asset classes which included US Stocks, Foreign Stocks, Real Estate, Commodities and 10-Year Treasury bonds.

When the 1-Month price closed above the 10-Month SMA an asset class was bought. When the 1-Month price closed below the 10-Month SMA an asset class was sold and the proceeds were invested in T-Bills until the next buy signal. Below are recent examples of asset class buy signals for US Stocks, Real Estate and Foreign Stocks.

1-Month Price 10-Month SMA 'Buy' Signal US Stocks

1-Month Price 10-Month SMA 'Buy' Signal Real Estate

1-Month Price 10-Month SMA 'Buy' Signal Foreign Stocks

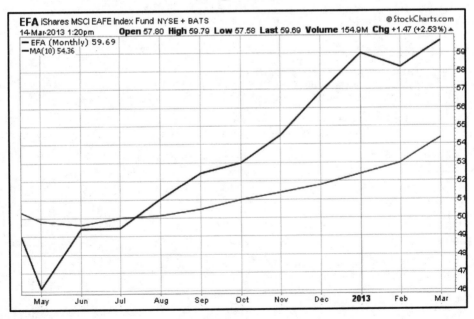

Investing equally in five different asset classes diversifies your portfolio and invests in asset classes that are generally strong and weak in different phases of the economic cycle. Investing in non-correlated asset classes can reduce portfolio risk and provide more consistent returns compared to investing in just one or two asset classes. The Monthly price graphs that follow show non-correlations between different asset classes over the same time period. For example, the price graphs below show a weak S&P 500 Index on a 1-Month Price 10-Month SMA sell signal compared to a strong Treasury Bond performance over the same time period.

S&P 500 Index Versus US Treasury Bonds

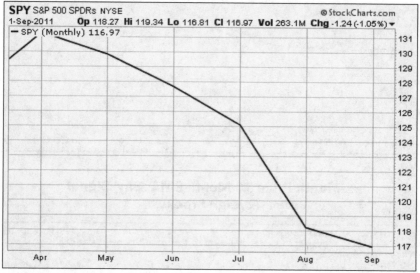

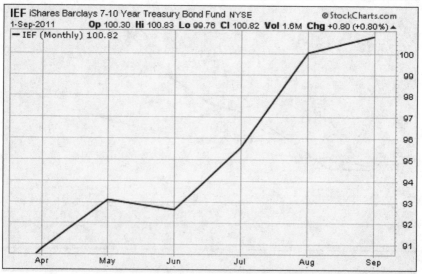

S&P 500 Index Versus Real Estate

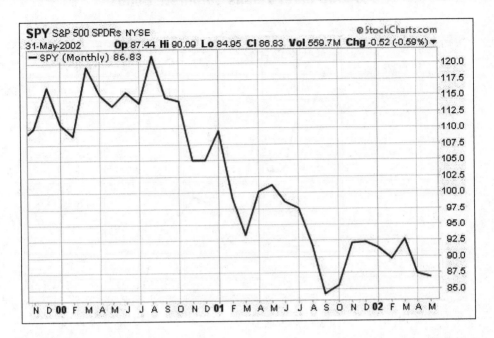

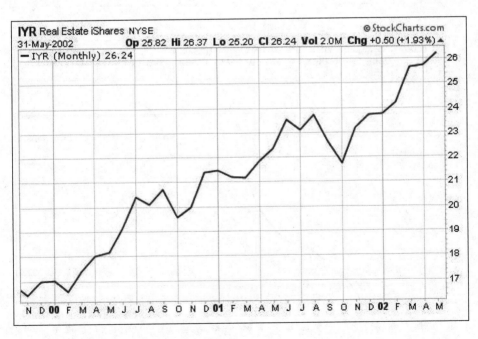

S&P 500 Index Versus Corporate Bonds

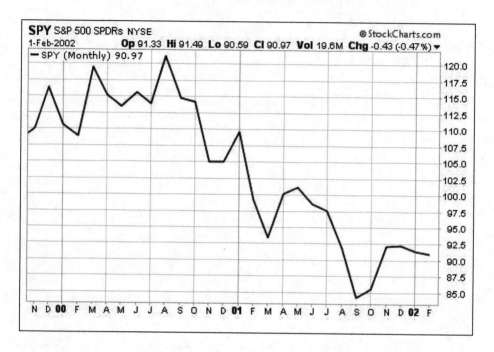

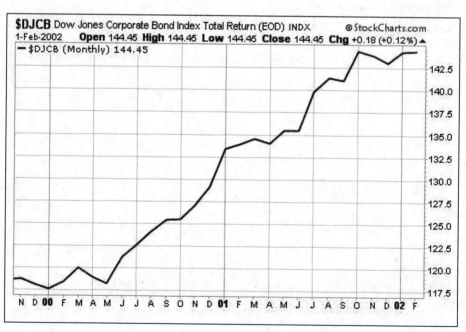

S&P 500 Index Versus Treasuries

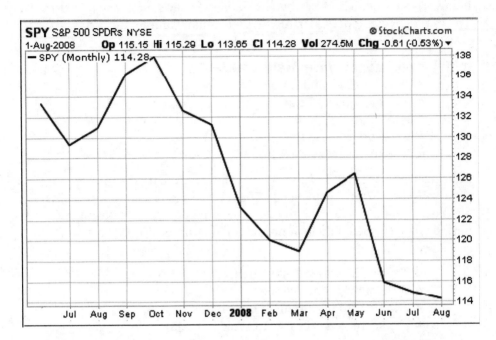

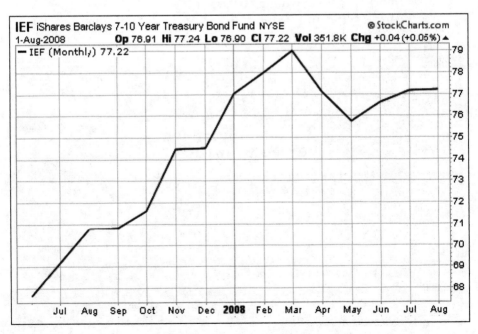

Let's take a look at the historical profit results for the 1-Month Price/10-Month SMA system to time buy and sell signals for the five asset classes below. This model was described in Mebane Faber's book *The Ivy Portfolio*. The initial investment is $10,000 divided equally among the 5 classes starting in 1973. Results are compounded yearly.

Initial Investment in Five Asset Classes
- US Stocks - $2,000
- Foreign Stocks - $2,000
- Real Estate - $2,000
- Commodities - $2,000
- 10-Year Treasury Bonds - $2,000

Historical results since 1973 show that the initial $10,000 investment grew to $618,747 producing a 6,087% return before commissions. There were no losing years despite the three severe bear markets during the test period when the S&P 500 lost more than 50% of its value. The historical results reveal:

- The Model was invested about 70% of the time
- 50% of trades are winners
- Winning trades are nine times larger than losing trades
- The secret to success is to avoid devastating losses during down markets and let winning trades run
- Model is the 'Holy Grail' of investing providing higher returns and lower volatility

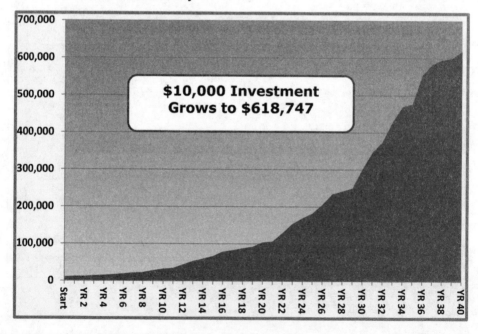

Shorter Term *PowerTrend* System

The 1-Month Price in relation to the 10-Month SMA has been very successful in identifying the major price trend for a stock. We are now going to look at a trend following system we use for shorter term trades when we have a one to three month time horizon for a trade.

We use a stock's 50-Day Exponential Moving Average (EMA) line in relation to its 100-Day Exponential Moving Average (EMA) line to identify the shorter term trend.

If the 50-Day EMA line is above the 100-Day EMA line it indicates the price momentum for the stock is to the upside.

If the 50-Day EMA line is below the 100-Day EMA line it indicates the price momentum for the stock is to the downside.

```
50-Day EMA Line Above 100-Day EMA = Price Up Trend = Buy

50-Day EMA Line Below 100-Day EMA = Price Down Trend = Sell
```

Buying and Selling Pressure

When the 50-Day EMA line is above the 100-Day EMA line it is an indication that the buying pressure for a stock is exceeding the selling pressure. And the most likely future price movement of the stock is up. The stock is on a 'buy' signal.

When the shorter term 50-Day EMA line is below the longer term 100-Day EMA line it is an indication that the selling pressure for a stock is exceeding the buying pressure. And the most likely future price movement of the stock is down. The stock is on a 'sell' signal.

```
50-Day EMA Line Above 100-Day EMA = Buying Pressure
                Exceeding Selling Pressure

50-Day EMA Line Below 100-Day EMA = Selling Pressure
                Exceeding Buying Pressure
```

'Buy' Signal Example

Let's look at an example of a 'buy' signal. The Apple stock daily price chart below displays the 50-Day EMA line and the 100-Day EMA line. The moving average lines indicate that Apple stock entered a price 'up' trend in April (circled) as the 50-Day EMA crossed above the 100-Day EMA line.

When the 50-Day EMA crossed above the 100-Day EMA it was a good indication that buying pressure was exceeding selling pressure and you want to buy Apple stock. As long as the 50-Day EMA line remains above the 100-Day EMA line Apple stock remains a 'buy'.

In this example, the Apple 50-Day EMA line crossed above the 100-Day EMA line in April. We have been purchasing Apple stock after the April buy signal as long as the 50-Day EMA line remains above the 100-Day EMA. Apple stock remains in a price 'up' trend as long as the 50-Day EMA line remains above the 100-Day EMA line indicating that buying pressure continues to exceed selling pressure. Monitoring the 50-Day and 100-Day EMA lines is an easy and effective way to determine the current shorter term price trend for Apple stock.

If the 50-Day EMA crosses below the 100-Day EMA it would indicate a reversal to a price 'down' trend as the selling pressure is now exceeding the buying pressure. And you should consider selling a stock if you have a shorter term time horizon. We will look at an example of a sell signal next.

50-Day EMA Line Above 100-Day EMA Line = Buy

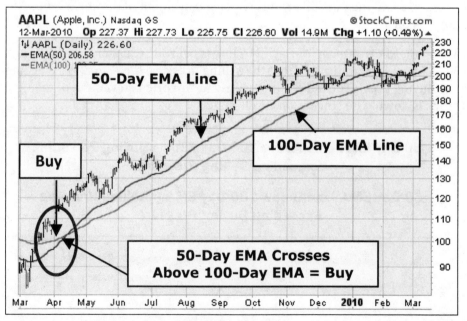

'Sell' Signal Example

Let's look at an example of a 'sell' signal. The daily price chart below shows the daily price movement and the 50-Day and 100-Day EMA lines for Merck stock. This chart reveals that in February the Merck 50-Day EMA line crossed below the 100-Day EMA line (circled) resulting in an EMA System 'sell' signal for Merck stock.

When the 50-Day EMA crossed below the 100-Day EMA it was a good indication that selling pressure was exceeding buying pressure. And you want to sell Merck stock if you have a shorter term time horizon. At this point the length and severity of the price decline is still unknown.

As long as the 50-Day EMA line remains below the 100-Day EMA line Merck stock remains a 'sell'. Merck does not qualify as a buy until the 50-Day EMA line crosses above the 100-Day EMA line.

Monitoring the 50-Day and 100-Day EMA lines is an easy and effective way to determine the current price trend which tells us if we should be buying or selling a stock.

50-Day EMA Line Below 100-Day EMA Line = Sell

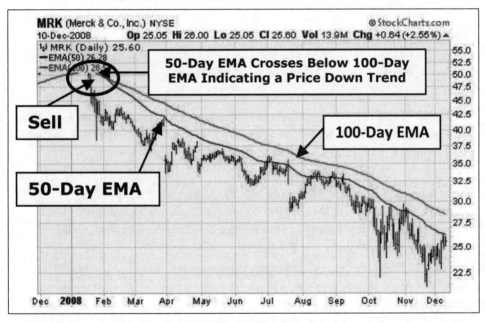

The *50/100-Day EMA System* is your road map to following trends and investing success. Trend following is a powerful, systematic approach that allows us to profit from the powerful profit opportunities available from trading options.

Historical Results of EMA System

The *50/100-Day EMA System* is a rule based system with clearly defined 'buy' and 'sell' rules which enables us to do historical testing. Historical profit results are based on buying a stock when its 50-Day EMA line crosses above the 100-Day EMA and selling a stock when its 50-Day EMA line crosses below the 100-Day EMA. The profit/loss for each trade is calculated and a cumulative total is maintained for each testing period.

The EMA System is universal in nature and has been profitable for shorter term investing across a wide range of markets including: stocks, options, indexes, closed-end funds, zero coupon bonds, mutual funds, index funds and sector funds. The fact that the system is profitable in virtually every type of market confirms its credibility as a viable, robust approach to trading the financial markets.

Included on the following page are profit results for a well-diversified sampling of both growth and value stocks that represent a broad cross section of 26 different industry groups. This sampling includes small, mid and large cap stocks. Historical profit results were generated over a recent twenty four year period.

Profitable with Low Risk

Keep in mind that four bear markets occurred during this period. Results are based on trading one hundred shares of stock for each 'buy' signal and do not include commissions.

Let's review the tests conducted using the first stock tested Aetna Health Care (AET). The first time Aetna's 50-Day EMA crossed above the 100-Day EMA during the test period one hundred shares of Aetna were purchased at 10.18.

The profit/loss for each AET trade was calculated and the profits totaled $5,376 over the test period based on trading 100 shares for each buy signal. This $5,376 profit represents a 528% return on the initial investment of $1,018.

The software divides the total profits by the total losses to calculate the Profit to Loss Ratio. Aetna had a Profit to Loss Ratio of 3.9 as there were 3.9 dollars of profit for each 1 dollar of loss. There were 10 losing trades over the 24-year period and the average losing trade incurred a -$120 loss.

24-Years of Historical Results

Stock	Profit on 100 Shares	Profit to Loss Ratio	Initial Cost 100 Shares	% Return Initial Cost	Avg Loss
Aetna	$5,376	3.9	$1018	528%	-120
Adobe Systems	$5,679	4.4	$5	126200%	-173
Altria	$4,602	3.2	$220	2092%	-180
Analog Devices	$3,559	2.0	$92	3868%	-251
Applied Materials	$2,419	3.0	$3	96760%	-70
Auto Data Process	$2,878	3.5	$182	1581%	-98
Bunge	$3,282	100.0	$1,585	207%	0
Centex	$3,810	4.3	$216	1764%	-143
Cisco Systems	$5,474	10.1	$8	68425%	-100
Corning	$6,153	12.4	$178	3457%	-54
CVS Drug	$4,237	2.7	$505	839%	-250
Eaton Vance	$1,682	6.7	$10	16820%	-27
eBay	$2,453	3.7	$120	2044%	-156
EMC Corp	$7,257	80.0	$5	145140%	-18
Franklin Resources	$5,264	3.2	$5	112000%	-18
General Electric	$3,675	5.2	$130	2827%	-97
Golden West Fin'l	$3,700	4.4	$40	9250%	-78
Home Depot	$4,092	4.0	$4	102300%	-174
Illinois Tool Works	$5,924	4.8	$176	3366%	-225
Intel	$2,845	3.5	$39	7295%	-71
Johnson & Johnson	$4,877	4.5	$227	2148%	-181
KB Homes	$6,654	3.4	$840	792%	-202
Legg Mason	$4,212	7.1	$187	2252%	-78
Microsoft	$2,651	2.8	$10	26510%	-108
M&T Bank	$6,445	5.5	$37	17419%	-95
NVR Inc	$50,070	5.0	$1,080	4636%	-1050
PMC Sierra	$15,603	41.5	$225	6935%	-48
Procter & Gamble	$3,096	3.1	$223	1388%	-108
Sun Microsystems	$3,342	7.5	$25	13368%	-26
Texas Instruments	$4,227	3.7	$184	2297%	-111
Taro Pharma	$4,551	4.7	$87	5231%	-113
Unitedhealth	$7,627	9.5	$32	23834%	-91
Water Corp	$4,898	4.5	$375	1306%	-471
Yahoo!	$7,964	63.0	$132	6033%	-129
Totals / Averages	**$210,578**	**12.7**	**$8,204**	**2,567%**	**-150**

Average Yearly Return of 107%

The total initial investment required to buy 100 shares of each of the 34 stocks over the test period was $8,204. This $8,204 initial investment produced a total of $210,578 in profits over the test period which equates to a 2,567% return. The average yearly return was 107% which would enable us to double our initial investment every year on average. This average 107% annual return was achieved without the use of leverage or margin.

The historical results demonstrate that the EMA System has the ability to produce handsome short term profits with very low risk. Of the trades that were losing trades, the average loss over the twenty four year period was $150 and when compared to the total profits of $210,578 demonstrates the ability of the system to keep losses to a minimum. The average Profit to Loss Ratio was a very healthy 12.7 with over 12 dollars of profit for each 1 dollar of loss again demonstrating a very favorable risk-adjusted return.

The preceding investing results demonstrate the importance of 'investing with the trend'. The *50/100-Day EMA System* allows us to know in advance the most likely future price movement of a stock and reduces the entry and exit timing risk associated with short term investing.

It is a versatile, effective method for profiting in any type of market and can quickly identify stocks on a 'buy' or 'sell' signal.

Equally important is the ability of the system to avoid large losses which can quickly ruin an investment plan. The system keeps losses to a minimum and almost always exits a trade before a big loss occurs. Following a discipline that keeps losses to a minimum is one of the most important characteristics of a successful trading program. Keep in mind several bear markets occurred during this test period.

The 50-Day and 100-Day EMA Lines Are the 'Key' to Developing a Profitable Strategy

The stock market is in a constant state of flux. The constant up and down price movement of a stock makes it difficult at times to see the real price trend of a stock. That is why it is important for a trader to become comfortable with the 50/100-Day EMA lines.

The position of the 50-Day EMA in relation to the 100-Day EMA gives us a quick and accurate indication of a stock's current price trend. If the stock is in a price up trend the stock should be bought. And if the stock is in a price down trend a stock should be sold if you have a shorter term time horizon.

In order to be a successful investor we do not have to know what an analyst's rating is for a stock or the current earnings projection. All of that information is already reflected in a stock's price movement which can be quantitatively measured by the 50/100-Day EMA lines.

This simple but effective trend following system is mechanical in nature and instantly tells you if you should be buying or selling a stock. We prefer mechanical systems as they take the emotion out of trading. There is no judgment or interpretation involved. You don't have to rely on trying to predict future price movement. The *50/100-Day EMA System* allows us to 'invest with the trend' instead of trying to predict the price direction of a stock. The historical studies presented demonstrate that price trends tend to continue in the same direction and can continue on longer than one may initially expect.

Our investing experience confirms that this allows us to know in advance the most likely future price movement of a stock and whether we should be buying or selling a stock.

Downloading the 50/100-Day EMA Lines

The 50/100-Day EMA Lines can be easily downloaded from
www.StockCharts.com. On the home page type in the stock symbol and
click "Go". In this example I typed in the symbol for Apple stock AAPL.

Once you click "Go" the default chart for Apple will appear. Below the
default chart for Apple select "Daily" under **Periods** and "1 Year" under
Range. Under **Overlays** select "Exp Mov. Avg" and under **Parameters**
select "50". On the second row, select "Exp Mov. Avg" under **Overlays** and
select "100" under **Parameters**.

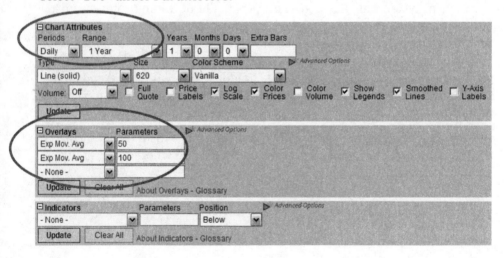

Click "Update" and the Apple price chart with the 50/100-Day EMA Lines
will be displayed (see price chart on the following page).

Apple One Year Price Chart with 50/100-Day EMA Lines

In the next chapter, we will look at the risk management guidelines we use that allow us to invest with limited risk and unlimited profit potential.

CHAPTER 2
The Most Important Investing Principle Is Not What You Think

Over the years, the *Legacy Publishing Team* has presented their trading strategies at many live seminars around the country and live webinars. At these live seminars we like to ask this question about the most important investing principle.

What is the most important investing principle vital to your success as a stock investor?

- Buying stocks that are under valued

- Using fundamental analysis to select stocks

- Using technical analysis to select stocks

- Risk management

- Invest in blue chip dividend paying stocks

- Buying low cost stocks

- Buying stock in companies with popular products or services

- Getting stock picks on TV

Most seminar and webinar attendees answer that fundamental or technical analysis are the most important investing principles. We agree that fundamental and technical analysis are important but in our experience risk management is the most important factor in investing success. As we will see, it is possible to be a successful investor even if only 10% of your trades are profitable!

Overall Goal is a 3 to 1 Profit to Loss Ratio

Let's look at the risk management principles that we use every day in managing our portfolio risk. The overall goal of the *Legacy Publishing Strategies* is to maintain at least a 3 to 1 profit to loss ratio. This ratio is calculated by dividing your total profits by your total losses and is a good overall measure of reward versus risk.

In our 60 years of combined investing experience we discovered that successful risk management can be achieved by following basic rules:

- Limit the size of your trading positions
- Close out your losing trades before they develop into large losses
- Don't limit your profits by selling winning trades with a small profit
- Invest using several different types of strategies for diversification

In order to achieve a 3 to 1 profit to loss ratio you must practice sound risk management by closing out your losing trades before they develop into large losses and by not limiting your profits by selling winning trades with a small profit.

This defies human nature as most investors want to do just the opposite and take a quick 10% or 15% profit as soon as possible. People like the euphoria associated with winning and will take a small profit even though they are giving up a potentially greater profit later by holding on to winning trades. Most traders tend to trade with limited upside and unlimited downside. They will sell a stock when they have a small profit but continue to hold losing stocks eventually winding up with a portfolio of losers.

A successful investor wants to achieve the highest profit to loss ratio possible. A high profit to loss ratio is a good indication that you are keeping trading losses to a minimum. Many investors with good trading systems fail because they don't pay enough attention to risk. Maintaining a trading discipline that forces you to think in terms of reward versus risk can help you become a successful investor.

When you establish an investing portfolio there is no way to predict which holdings are going to produce big profits over time. Typically, if you own a diversified portfolio of let's say eight stocks, usually there are one or two of the eight stocks that produce a big profit that accounts for most of the gain for the entire portfolio.

It's The Few Big Winners That Produce Profitable Portfolios

It's the big winners not the small winners that produce profitable portfolios. You can't tell in advance which of the eight stocks might produce a large profit. So you want to practice sound risk management and continue to hold on to the profitable trades and take small losses with losing positions before they develop into large losses.

If you are willing to risk 7% on a trade, then you should be expecting a 21% profit on your winning trades in order to achieve a 3 to 1 profit to loss ratio. If you are willing to risk 10% on a trade, then you should be expecting a 30% profit on your winning trades which can be difficult to achieve. We always think in terms of taking measured risks with every trade.

Also, if you have enough investing funds, don't risk more than 10% of your investing funds on any one trade. This is important as it spreads your risk between 10 trades and helps prevent a large portfolio loss if one of your trades experiences a big loss.

Practicing sound risk management is important for your trading success and is often overlooked in the search for finding profitable trading strategies. In our experience, risk management is just as important as trade selection. Risk management involves several steps.

When we purchase a stock we normally will sell a stock before we incur a 5% loss. As mentioned previously, if you are willing to risk 5% on a trade then you should be expecting a 15% profit on your profitable trades if you want to maintain a 3 to 1 profit to loss ratio.

Taking small losses is essential to your investing success as it may take years for you to recover from a large loss. For example, if your portfolio suffered a 50% loss it would take a subsequent gain of 100% for your portfolio just to break even!

Let's assume you had a $10,000 portfolio that incurred a 50% loss which resulted in the value of your portfolio declining to $5,000. You would then have to achieve a 100% return on your $5,000 portfolio in order break even with the value returning to $10,000.

Taking small losses before they develop into big losses has allowed us to maintain a better than 3 to 1 profit to loss ratio. Our online brokerage account allows us to download the past three years of closed trade results.

We listed all of our stock/ETF closed trades over the past three years on the next several pages. We analyzed all of our trades to calculate the total profits, total losses, profit to loss ratio, average return for winning and losing trades and percentage of winning trades. The three year results are summarized below.

We had a total of 204 trades over the past three years with 143 winning trades and 61 losing trades resulting in 70% accuracy. The 204 closed trades produced the following results:

Three Year Trade Results Summary

Total Profits $1,175,384.12

Total Losses $ 61,876.07

Profit to Loss Ratio 19 to 1

Average Winning Trade +52.5%

Average Losing Trade - 3.1%

143 Wining Trades and 61 Losing Trades

70% Winning Trades

The Profit to Loss Ratio was calculated by dividing the total profits of $1,175,384.12 by the total losses of $61,876.07 ($1,175,384.12/$61,876.07 = 19 to 1).

The average winning trade produced a 52.5% profit and the average losing trade incurred a 3.1% loss. These trade results demonstrate that we were able to exit losing trades quickly and not exit winning trades with a small profit. We would not average a 52.5% return for winning trades if we took a quick 10 or 15% profit on winning trades.

Profit With Just 10% Accuracy

On average, we could incur sixteen 3.1% losing trades and still profit with just one 52.5% winning trade. Our risk management principle of exiting losing trades quickly and not exiting winning trades with a small profit allows us to produce portfolio profits with less than 10% winning trades.

The 19 to 1 Profit to Loss Ratio also confirms this profit statistic. If your closed trades produce 19 dollars of profits for each 1 dollar of loss then you only need 10% or less winning trades to produce a profitable portfolio.

These profit results demonstrate that it is possible to profit with a small percentage of winning trades if you utilize simple risk management rules to exit losing trades before they develop into big losses and not exiting winning trades with small profits. As successful traders we always want to think in terms of trading with limited downside an unlimited upside.

In the next chapter we will learn a simple strategy for purchasing insurance on our profitable stock trades that helps protect profits if the stock declines in price. This stock insurance does not limit our profit potential if our stock continues to increase in price enabling us to invest with limited downside and unlimited upside.

3 Years of Closed Trade Results
Trade by Trade Listing

Stock	Qty	Buy Date	Buy Price	Cost	B/S	Sell Date	Sell Price	Sale Proceeds	Profit	Loss	% Profit	% Loss
AAPL	50.00	12/23/	418.27	20921.5	S	01/15	488.258	24408.36	3,486.87		0.167	
AAPL	50.00	01/10/	418.27	20921.5	S	01/15	488.258	24408.36	3,486.87		0.167	
AAPL	50.00	11/30/	374.7	18743	S	01/24	450.661	22530.55	3,787.56		0.203	
AAPL	30.00	10/12/	398.2	11948.4	S	01/24	450.661	13518.33	1,569.93		0.132	
AAPL	20.00	11/23/	366.7	7341.99	S	01/24	450.661	9012.22	1,670.23		0.229	
AAPL	100.00	11/22/	370.29	37037	S	01/24	450.661	45061.1	8,024.11		0.217	
AAPL	100.00	08/28/	493	49308	S	09/12	472.721	47267.28		-2,040.71		-0.041
AAPL	100.00	09/10/	495.32	49540	S	09/12	472.721	47267.28		-2,272.71		-0.046
AAPL	30.00	10/12/	400.35	12015.3	S	01/15	488.11	14638.18	2,622.88		0.219	
AAPL	20.00	10/24/	402.35	8050.2	S	01/15	488.11	9758.78	1,708.58		0.213	
AAPL	30.00	12/05/	388.35	11658.5	S	01/24	452.675	13578.35	1,919.86		0.166	
AAPL	20.00	10/12/	400.35	8010.2	S	01/24	452.675	9052.23	1,042.03		0.131	
AAPL	100.00	11/22/	373.33	37341	S	01/24	452.675	45261.15	7,920.16		0.213	
AAPL	1,900.00	07/17/	87.7998	166840	S	07/20	131	248887.43	82,047.80		0.492	
AGNC	7.42	12/20/	22.6575	168.19	S	05/03	30.755	228.24	60.05		0.357	
AGNC	192.58	10/27/	22.6575	4364.14	S	05/03	30.755	5922.62	1,558.48		0.357	
AGNC	0.26	04/27/	22.6575	5.92	S	05/03	30.75	8.03	2.11		0.357	
AGNC	0.75	07/27/	22.6575	16.95	S	05/03	30.75	23	6.05		0.357	
AGNC	0.41	10/26/	22.6575	9.34	S	05/03	30.75	12.67	3.33		0.357	
AGNC	178.63	01/28/	30.3798	5426.7	S	05/03	30.75	5492.4	65.70		0.012	
AGNC	179.37	04/26/	31.4851	5647.53	S	05/03	30.75	5515.24		-132.29		-0.023
AGNC	1,492.58	12/20/	22.6575	33826.1	S	05/03	30.75	45893.21	12,067.16		0.357	
AGNC	73.00	01/31/	22.6575	1654	S	05/03	30.75	2244.57	590.58		0.357	
AGNC	0.58	10/27/	22.6575	13.11	S	05/03	30.75	17.79	4.68		0.357	
AGNC	1,752.42	10/27/	22.6575	39712.7	S	05/03	30.75	53882.74	14,170.06		0.357	
AGNC	1,000.00	06/11/	22.6575	22665.5	S	05/03	30.75	30747.6	8,082.11		0.357	
AGNC	23.00	12/05/	22.4382	516.07	S	01/09	21.981	505.48		-10.60		-0.021
AGNC	1,600.00	10/29/	22.4382	35909.1	S	01/09	21.981	35163.76		-745.36		-0.021
AGNC	900.00	11/13/	22.6872	20426.5	S	01/09	21.981	19779.61		-646.86		-0.032
AGNC	25.05	01/09/	21.9554	549.87	S	01/14	21.52	531.25		-18.62		-0.034
AMJ	700.00	04/19/	45.7386	32025	S	06/20	44.24	30964.8		-1,060.21		-0.033
AMJ	700.00	04/22/	45.982	32195.4	S	06/20	44.24	30964.8		-1,230.59		-0.038
AMJ	700.00	05/03/	46.622	32643.4	S	06/20	44.24	30964.8		-1,678.59		-0.051
AMJ	700.00	10/29/	51	35708	S	12/01	46.2717	32384.39		-3,323.60		-0.093
AMJ	400.00	11/13/	49.979	19999.6	S	12/01	46.2717	18505.36		-1,494.23		-0.075
BA	320.00	07/05/	103.96	33275.2	S	08/27	103.471	33107.58		-167.61		-0.005
BA	320.00	07/09/	104.7	33512	S	08/27	103.471	33107.58		-404.41		-0.012
BA	320.00	07/25/	106.96	34235.2	S	08/27	103.471	33107.58		-1,127.61		-0.033
CI	200.00	07/05/	73.74	14751.6	S	10/18	74.61	14913.75	162.20		0.012	
CI	250.00	07/05/	73.74	18439.4	S	10/18	74.6	18649.67	210.24		0.012	
CI	450.00	07/09/	74.6	33578	S	10/18	74.6	33569.41		-8.58		0.000
CI	450.00	07/25/	77.76	35000	S	10/18	74.6	33569.41		-1,430.58		-0.041
CI	200.00	11/17/	73.6576	14751.5	S	11/18	84.106	16812.91	2,061.40		0.142	

3 Years of Closed Trade Results
Trade by Trade Listing

Stock	Qty	Buy Date	Buy Price	Cost	B/S	Sell Date	Sell Price	Sale Proceeds	Profit	Loss	% Profit	% Loss
CVS	800.00	04/11/	72.878	58308.8	S	04/30	72.771	58215.47		-93.32		-0.002
CVS	200.00	04/11/	72.878	14577.2	S	04/30	72.775	14546.68		-30.52		-0.002
DFE	16.00	04/11/	59.6	953.6	S	04/15	59.2713	948.32		-5.28		-0.006
DFE	56.00	04/11/	59.68	3342.08	S	04/15	59.2713	3319.12		-22.96		-0.007
DFE	1,128.00	04/11/	59.7	67341.6	S	04/15	59.2713	66856.54		-485.06		-0.007
EDC	100.00	12/20/	104.73	10477	S	03/04	97.4	9737.78		-739.21		-0.071
EDC	100.00	12/20/	104.73	10477	S	03/04	97.4	9737.78		-739.21		-0.071
EDC	200.00	12/20/	104.965	21001	S	03/04	97.4	19475.56		-1,525.43		-0.073
FAS	200.00	11/26/	106.38	21284	S	01/03	130.35	26067.42	4,783.43		0.225	
FAS	200.00	11/26/	106.5	21308	S	01/03	130.35	26067.42	4,759.43		0.224	
FAS	400.00	11/28/	105.16	42072	S	01/03	130.35	52134.83	10,062.84		0.240	
FAS	300.00	11/19/	34.0633	10223	S	02/11	79.5996	23874.44	13,651.47		1.337	
FAS	500.00	11/19/	34.0766	17045	S	02/11	79.5996	39790.74	22,745.78		1.336	
FAS	300.00	11/19/	34.0633	10223	S	02/11	79.5996	23874.44	13,651.47		1.337	
FAS	300.00	11/19/	34.1566	10249	S	02/12	79.5996	23864.9	13,615.93		1.330	
FAS	100.00	11/19/	34.0766	3408.99	S	02/12	79.5996	7954.97	4,545.98		1.336	
FAS	900.00	11/19/	34.1566	30746.9	S	02/27	86.0448	77427.44	46,680.53		1.519	
FAS	200.00	03/07/	53.6613	10732.3	S	02/27	86.0448	17206.1	6,473.84		0.603	
FAS	300.00	03/07/	53.6846	16113.4	S	02/27	86.0448	25809.15	9,695.77		0.603	
FAS	100.00	03/07/	53.6613	5366.13	S	04/01	95.685	9565.62	4,199.49		0.783	
FAS	200.00	02/12/	34.0677	6814.99	S	04/01	95.685	19131.25	12,316.25		1.809	
FAS	400.00	02/28/	43.2765	17312.9	S	04/01	95.68	38271.15	20,958.27		1.211	
FAS	900.00	02/12/	34.0677	30667.5	S	04/01	95.6801	86110.17	55,442.71		1.809	
FAS	400.00	02/13/	34.1566	13670.6	S	04/01	95.6801	38271.19	24,600.56		1.801	
FAS	1,000.00	02/28/	43.2765	43282.2	S	04/01	95.6801	95677.97	52,395.77		1.211	
FAS	93.00	11/23/	106.5	9908.22	S	01/03	128.99	11992.08	2,083.87		0.211	
FAS	107.00	11/23/	107	11453.3	S	01/03	128.99	13797.35	2,344.07		0.206	
FAS	300.00	11/23/	35.4964	10652.9	S	02/11	79.579	23853.71	13,200.78		1.242	
FAS	279.00	11/23/	35.6631	9953.72	S	02/27	86.0157	23979.79	14,026.07		1.412	
FAS	21.00	11/23/	35.4964	745.71	S	02/27	86.0157	1804.93	1,059.23		1.423	
FAS	300.00	02/12/	35.4964	10656.9	S	03/20	92.0357	27590.71	16,933.80		1.593	
FAS	300.00	02/28/	38.12	11444	S	04/14	83.6	25075.45	13,631.46		1.193	
FAS	300.00	03/21/	39.4906	11855.2	S	04/14	83.6	25075.45	13,220.28		1.117	
FDN	3,000.00	04/03/	62.0369	186131	S	04/03	58.9111	176721.4		-9,409.31		-0.051
FDN	1,600.00	04/03/	61.1101	97796.1	S	04/03	58.9115	94248.32		-3,547.79		-0.036
HAL	100.00	04/11/	57.795	5787.49	S	08/26	70.1933	7011.18	1,223.69		0.215	
HAL	1,200.00	04/11/	57.7999	69359.9	S	10/08	59.8901	71858.54	2,498.66		0.036	
HAL	50.00	04/14/	58.49	2925.17	S	08/26	70.26	3504.93	579.76		0.201	
HAL	550.00	04/14/	58.49	32176.8	S	10/08	59.9127	32943.27	766.44		0.024	

3 Years of Closed Trade Results
Trade by Trade Listing

Stock	Qty	Buy Date	Buy Price	Cost	B/S	Sell Date	Sell Price	Sale Proceeds	Profit	Loss	% Profit	% Loss
HD	400.00	08/22/	56.45	22585.3	S	03/04	83.02	33207.39	10,622.07		0.471	
HD	200.00	08/24/	56.69	11340.7	S	03/04	83.02	16603.7	5,263.03		0.464	
HD	100.00	08/24/	56.69	5670.33	S	03/04	83.021	8301.95	2,631.62		0.464	
HD	200.00	08/22/	56.45	11292.7	S	03/04	83.025	16596.71	5,304.05		0.471	
HD	300.00	08/24/	56.69	17011	S	04/10	115.463	34635.27	17,624.27		1.037	
HD	500.00	09/28/	60.22	30118	S	04/10	115.463	57725.44	27,607.45		0.917	
HD	100.00	01/12/	42.6984	4272.12	S	07/21	76.7924	7659.25	3,387.13		0.798	
HD	400.00	02/17/	46.145	18464.4	S	03/04	82.9814	33185.58	14,721.19		0.798	
HD	100.00	07/25/	79	7907.99	S	03/04	82.9814	8296.4	388.41		0.050	
HD	100.00	02/17/	46.145	4616.1	S	11/21	98.633	9855.09	5,238.99		1.137	
HD	250.00	01/12/	42.6984	10680.3	S	08/24	112.268	28061.39	17,381.08		1.629	
HD	150.00	01/17/	43.16	6477.42	S	08/24	112.268	16836.83	10,359.41		1.601	
KMI	2,100.00	11/28/	41.2	86526.7	S	01/13	40.784	85636.51		-890.20		-0.010
KMI	400.00	11/28/	41.2	16481.3	S	03/16	40.32	16126.04		-355.24		-0.022
KMI	1,000.00	12/01/	40.2	40208	S	03/16	40.32	40315.1	107.11		0.003	
KMI	500.00	01/16/	41.4396	20727.8	S	03/16	40.32	20157.55		-570.24		-0.028
KMI	1,000.00	11/28/	41.2	41208	S	01/13	40.7928	40783.9		-424.09		-0.010
LLL	403.00	04/11/	113.96	45930.8	S	05/02	113.46	45715.37		-215.46		-0.005
LLL	247.00	04/11/	113.96	28151.2	S	05/02	113.42	28006.15		-145.00		-0.005
LLL	100.00	04/14/	114.12	11414.7	S	05/02	113.45	11344.74		-69.92		-0.006
LLL	200.00	04/14/	114.12	22829.3	S	05/02	113.451	22681.69		-147.64		-0.006
MMM	300.00	04/11/	124.088	37230.4	S	08/01	140.38	42105.07	4,874.68		0.131	
MMM	300.00	04/11/	124.088	37230.4	S	08/01	140.34	42093.1	4,862.71		0.131	
MMM	300.00	04/21/	138.68	41612	S	05/27	141.49	42438.07	826.08		0.020	
O	400.00	10/31/	45.9782	18396.6	S	01/28	50.9789	20378.25	1,981.65		0.109	
O	200.00	10/31/	45.94	9195.99	S	01/28	50.9789	10189.13	993.14		0.110	
O	200.00	10/31/	45.9782	9198.3	S	03/27	50.9224	10183.28	984.97		0.108	
O	400.00	11/13/	46.15	18468	S	03/27	50.9224	20366.55	1,898.56		0.103	
O	360.00	01/09/	50.28	18108.8	S	03/27	50.9224	18329.9	221.11		0.013	
O	600.00	02/02/	45.965	27587	S	03/27	50.9224	30549.83	2,962.84		0.108	
RWX	730.00	04/22/	45.06	32901.8	S	04/23	45.09	32906.96	5.17		0.001	
SBUX	500.00	07/08/	68.3	34158	S	11/21	81.58	40781.29	6,623.30		0.194	
SHW	240.00	08/22/	138.3	33200	S	08/14	170.05	40804.15	7,604.16		0.230	
SHW	29.00	08/24/	142.72	4139.85	S	08/14	170.05	4930.5	790.66		0.191	
SHW	211.00	08/24/	142.72	30120.9	S	08/14	170.053	35880.56	5,759.61		0.192	
SHW	2.00	09/28/	148.195	296.39	S	08/14	170.053	340.1	43.71		0.147	
SHW	218.00	09/28/	148.2	32315.6	S	08/14	170.053	37070.91	4,755.32		0.147	
SSO	900.00	12/12/	61.25	55133	S	01/03	63.09	56772.53	1,639.54		0.030	
SSO	100.00	12/10/	59.75	5975.89	S	01/03	63.09	6308.06	332.17		0.056	
SSO	300.00	12/10/	59.75	17927.7	S	01/03	63.1	18929.57	1,001.91		0.056	
SSO	200.00	12/10/	59.75	11951.8	S	01/04	60.1097	12001.96	50.18		0.006	

3 Years of Closed Trade Results
Trade by Trade Listing

Stock	Qty	Buy Date	Buy Price	Cost	B/S	Sell Date	Sell Price	Sale Proceeds	Profit	Loss	% Profit	% Loss
SSO	600.00	11/30/	59.25	35556	S	02/14	94.3823	56614.41	21,058.42		0.593	
SSO	200.00	11/30/	59.25	11852	S	02/14	94.3823	18871.47	7,019.47		0.593	
SSO	300.00	12/10/	59.75	17927.7	S	04/03	104.757	31419.71	13,492.05		0.753	
SSO	500.00	12/13/	59.6	29808	S	04/03	104.757	52366.18	22,558.19		0.758	
SSO	800.00	02/18/	59.25	47408	S	04/11	99.013	79204.65	31,796.66		0.671	
SSO	800.00	12/13/	59.73	47792	S	04/11	99.013	79204.65	31,412.66		0.658	
TJX	500.00	11/30/	30.67	15339	S	02/26	60.48	30236.8	14,897.80		0.972	
TJX	850.00	12/07/	31.5	26781.8	S	02/26	60.48	51402.56	24,620.77		0.920	
TJX	150.00	06/12/	31.5	4732.99	S	02/26	60.48	9071.04	4,338.05		0.920	
TJX	500.00	11/30/	30.67	15339	S	07/16	52.7827	26388.1	11,049.11		0.721	
TJX	1,000.00	11/08/	30.3	30308	S	07/16	52.7827	52776.21	22,468.22		0.742	
TJX	400.00	12/07/	31.57	12633.3	S	01/30	57.65	23056.93	10,423.60		0.826	
TJX	400.00	12/21/	31.27	12516	S	01/30	57.65	23056.93	10,540.94		0.844	
TJX	400.00	12/30/	32.12	12856	S	01/30	57.65	23056.93	10,200.94		0.795	
TJX	400.00	11/30/	30.37	12154.4	S	02/28	61.2835	24507.65	12,353.26		1.018	
TJX	200.00	12/07/	31.57	6316.66	S	02/28	61.2835	12253.82	5,937.16		0.941	
TJX	100.00	11/30/	30.37	3038.6	S	07/17	52.2727	5225.82	2,187.22		0.721	
TJX	500.00	11/08/	30.05	15033	S	07/17	52.2727	26129.11	11,096.12		0.740	
TNA	100.00	11/28/	55.5	5552	S	01/03	69.93	6984.85	1,432.85		0.260	
TNA	300.00	11/28/	55.5	16656	S	01/04	62.089	18622.69	1,966.70		0.119	
TNA	200.00	11/28/	55.4	11088	S	01/04	62.089	12415.13	1,327.14		0.121	
TNA	400.00	11/26/	54.67	21876	S	01/04	62.089	24830.25	2,954.26		0.136	
TNA	200.00	11/28/	55.22	11052	S	01/04	62.089	12415.13	1,363.14		0.124	
TNA	400.00	11/23/	54.2885	21723.4	S	01/04	62.089	24830.25	3,106.86		0.144	
TNA	700.00	04/12/	25.61	17935	S	04/13	42.0503	29415.21	11,480.22		0.642	
TNA	200.00	11/19/	25.725	5146	S	04/17	38.1	7619.43	2,473.43		0.481	
TNA	100.00	11/19/	25.61	2562	S	04/17	38.1	3809.71	1,247.72		0.488	
TNA	800.00	11/19/	25.55	20448	S	04/17	38.1	30477.71	10,029.72		0.491	
TNA	1,400.00	11/19/	25.725	36022	S	04/17	38.1	53336	17,314.01		0.481	
TNA	700.00	11/19/	25.61	17934	S	04/17	38.1	26668	8,734.01		0.488	
TNA	800.00	03/07/	42.025	33628	S	04/17	38.1	30477.71		-3,150.28		-0.094
TNA	400.00	01/04/	70.2799	28120	S	01/04	62.1823	24862.92		-3,257.03		-0.116
TNA	200.00	11/21/	52.8385	10575.7	S	01/04	62.1823	12431.46	1,855.77		0.177	
TNA	200.00	11/21/	52.84	10576	S	01/04	62.1823	12431.46	1,855.47		0.177	
TNA	800.00	11/23/	26.4196	21143.7	S	04/13	42.0423	33613.85	12,470.16		0.591	
TNA	60.00	04/12/	26.4196	1593.17	S	11/16	65.4323	3924.44	2,331.27		1.477	
TNA	200.00	04/12/	26.4196	5291.91	S	11/16	65.4323	13081.47	7,789.56		1.477	
TNA	540.00	04/15/	26.4196	14274.6	S	11/16	65.4323	35319.96	21,045.39		1.477	
TNA	200.00	11/18/	26.4196	5285.92	S	12/26	71.5923	14298.48	9,012.56		1.710	
TNA	600.00	11/18/	26.4196	15857.8	S	04/14	66.4545	39865.82	24,008.07		1.515	
TNA	200.00	12/26/	26.4196	5291.91	S	04/14	66.4545	13288.61	7,996.70		1.515	
USB	200.00	06/10/	35.65	7137.99	S	10/07	36.1835	7228.58	90.59		0.015	
V	180.00	07/09/	187.5	33758	S	08/07	180.76	32532.24		-1,225.75		-0.036
V	180.00	07/25/	195	35108	S	08/07	180.76	32532.24		-2,575.75		-0.073

3 Years of Closed Trade Results
Trade by Trade Listing

Stock	Qty	Buy Date	Buy Price	Cost	B/S	Sell Date	Sell Price	Sale Proceeds	Profit	Loss	% Profit	% Loss
VGK	210.00	04/17/	48.3363	10158.6	S	04/17	48.35	10145.28		-13.33		-0.001
VNQ	100.00	04/17/	72.8999	7289.99	S	06/10	70.14	7013.29		-276.70		-0.038
VNQ	350.00	04/17/	72.9	25523	S	06/10	70.14	24546.5		-976.49		-0.038
VNQ	450.00	04/19/	73.46	33065	S	06/10	70.14	31559.79		-1,505.20		-0.046
VNQ	450.00	04/23/	74.16	33380	S	06/10	70.14	31559.79		-1,820.20		-0.055
VYM	600.00	05/30/	57.96	34784	S	07/09	57.9508	34765.88		-18.11		-0.001
VYM	200.00	06/10/	57.7199	11552	S	07/09	57.9508	11588.63	36.66		0.004	
VYM	200.00	06/10/	57.7399	11556	S	07/09	57.9508	11588.63	32.66		0.004	
VYM	200.00	06/10/	57.76	11560	S	07/09	57.9508	11588.63	28.64		0.003	
WFC	800.00	07/05/	41.9	33528	S	08/27	41.3517	33078.12		-449.87		-0.013
WFC	800.00	07/11/	41.5	33208	S	08/27	41.3517	33078.12		-129.87		-0.004
WFC	800.00	07/25/	43.5	34808	S	08/27	41.3517	33078.12		-1,729.87		-0.050
WFC	1,600.00	04/11/	48.56	77704	S	07/15	51.3601	82166.35	4,462.36		0.058	
WFC	700.00	04/14/	48.035	33632.5	S	07/17	50.7624	35524.9	1,892.41		0.057	
XLK	1,070.00	05/03/	31.24	33434.8	S	10/08	31.6	33808.74	373.95		0.012	
XLK	1,070.00	05/06/	31.36	33563.2	S	10/08	31.6	33808.74	245.55		0.008	
XLK	1,060.00	05/09/	31.6188	33523.9	S	10/08	31.6	33492.77		-31.15		-0.001
XLP	800.00	04/17/	40.52	32424	S	07/05	39.93	31940.78		-483.21		-0.015
XLP	800.00	04/19/	40.9	32728	S	07/05	39.93	31940.78		-787.21		-0.024
XLP	800.00	04/23/	41.3	33048	S	07/05	39.93	31940.78		-1,107.21		-0.034
XLP	800.00	10/29/	46.13	36912	S	03/26	48.4728	38773.48	1,861.48		0.051	
XLP	400.00	11/13/	48.0473	19226.9	S	03/26	48.4728	19386.74	159.83		0.009	
XLP	369.47	01/09/	49.3	18222.7	S	03/26	48.4728	17906.89		-315.80		-0.017
XLP	9.00	03/30/	48.9951	440.96	S	04/06	49.18	434.62		-6.34		-0.014
XLU	800.00	04/19/	40.48	32392	S	05/16	40.14	32108.62		-283.37		-0.009
XLU	800.00	04/22/	40.8	32648	S	05/16	40.14	32108.62		-539.37		-0.017
XLU	800.00	05/03/	41.06	32856	S	05/16	40.14	32108.62		-747.37		-0.023
XLU	600.00	10/29/	44.49	26700	S	12/18	46.679	27987.38	1,287.39		0.049	
XLU	200.00	10/29/	44.49	8900	S	03/06	43.35	8668.83		-231.17		-0.026
XLU	400.00	11/13/	45.0873	18042.9	S	03/06	43.35	17337.66		-705.25		-0.039
XLU	600.00	12/19/	44.49	26702	S	03/06	43.35	26006.5		-695.49		-0.026
XLU	379.87	01/09/	47.55	18070.6	S	03/06	43.35	16464.97		-1,605.64		-0.089
XLV	490.00	04/17/	47.5399	23302.5	S	11/22	55.2101	27050.7	3,748.16		0.161	
XLV	210.00	04/17/	47.46	9974.59	S	11/22	55.2101	11593.16	1,618.57		0.163	
XLV	700.00	04/19/	47.44	33216	S	11/22	55.2101	38643.85	5,427.86		0.164	
XLV	700.00	04/23/	48.2	33748	S	11/22	55.2101	38643.85	4,895.86		0.145	
XLV	100.00	06/10/	48.62	4869.99	S	11/22	55.2101	5520.55	650.56		0.150	
							Total/Averages	1,175,384.12	-61,876.07	0.525	-0.031

CHAPTER 3
Stress Less Investing

The profit results presented in Chapter 2 demonstrate that the *PowerTrend* System combined with our low risk entry points using the Keltner Channels has produced a lot of winning stock trades.

And we learned that it is better not to sell profitable trades with a small profit if you want to maintain a better than 3 to 1 Profit to Loss Ratio.

In this chapter, we are going to explore a strategy that allows us to purchase 'insurance' on our profitable stock trades whenever we have a modest 5 to 6% profit.

The best way to insure your house against a loss from a fire is to buy fire insurance and hope you never need the insurance. If there is no fire, the money you spend on the insurance premium is well spent. Similarly, the best way to protect your stock investment from loss is to buy 'stock insurance'.

Limited Risk and Unlimited Profit Potential Investing
This stock insurance provides protection for our stock trade in case the stock declines in price. At the same time the insurance allows us to hold the trade for further profits if the stock continues to rally. This results in limited risk and unlimited profit potential trading which gives you your best chance to succeed as an investor.

As we will discover shortly, the insurance we purchase can even guarantee our trade will be profitable no matter how far the stock declines in price even in the unlikely event the stock declines to zero!

Let's take a look at one of our stock trades so you can understand the important concept of stock insurance.

Amazon stock symbol AMZN is in a strong price uptrend with the AMZN monthly price above its 10-Month Simple Moving Average indicating a *PowerTrend* 'buy' signal. The daily price chart for Amazon that follows shows that AMZN is also on a shorter term buy signal with its 50-Day EMA above the 100-Day EMA.

AMZN 50-Day EMA Above Its 100-Day EMA = 'Buy' Signal

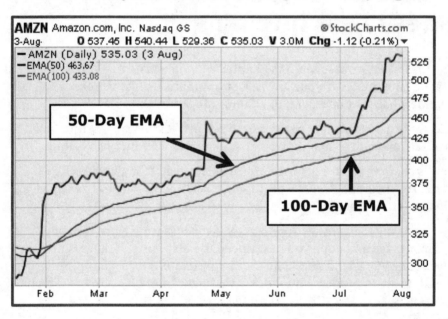

We wanted to participate in the profit potential for the strong AMZN price uptrend so we waited for AMZN to pull back to the Middle Keltner Channel before purchasing so we could get a low risk entry.

The AMZN price chart below displays the daily price movement for AMZN stock and the 3 Keltner Channels. We like to purchase stocks in increments and started purchasing AMZN stock in July when AMZN stock was trading near the Middle Keltner Channel.

Bought AMZN When Stock Was Trading
Near Middle Keltner Channel

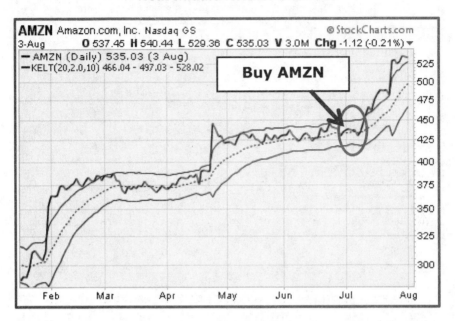

Our brokerage account Portfolio Report below shows that we purchased 300 shares of Amazon at an average price of 499.01 points.

Bought 300 Shares AMZN at 449.01

Symbol		Last Trade	Change $	Change %	Day's Gain	Qty	Price Paid	Total Gain $	Total Gain %	Market Val	Edit
⊞ AMZN	Buy / Sell	518.37	17.60	3.51%	$5,280.00	300	$449.01	$20,800.01	15.44%	$155,511.00	Edit

Purchasing AMZN stock when it retraced to the Middle Keltner Channel allowed us to get a low risk entry point for our stock purchase. The AMZN stock price chart below shows that AMZN did not retrace much from our entry point and rallied after our purchase.

Low Risk Entry for AMZN Stock Purchase

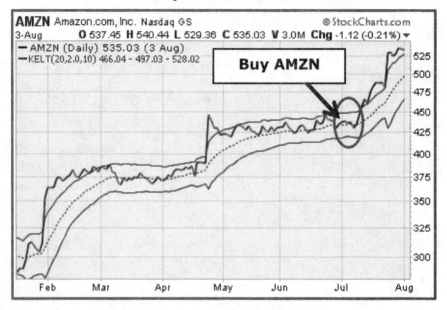

We had a modest profit with our AMZN stock purchase and then purchased 'insurance' to protect our profit in the event AMZN stock declined in price.

Our brokerage account Portfolio Report below shows that our insurance policy was implemented by purchasing an AMZN January 515-Strike put option. Purchasing the 515-Strike put option allows us to sell our AMZN stock at 515 but does not obligate us to sell our stock.

The right to sell AMZN stock at 515 establishes a minimum value for our stock of 515 points. The AMZN 515-Strike put was purchased for 53.13 points. We purchased 1 put option for each 100 shares of stock we owned (1 option covers 100 shares of stock).

Note: In this example smaller accounts could buy 10 shares of AMZN stock and the AMZN January mini option (which covers 10 shares of stock) at a cost of $531.30 in this example.

Buy AMZN 515-Strike Put Option at 53.13 Points

Portfolios										Portfolios | Orders | Balances | Transaction History | ⑦ Help		
Portfolios	Performance & Value	Margin	Gains & Losses	Risk Analyzer	Portfolio Analyzer	Income Estimator						
REFRESH 🔄	STREAMING QUOTES	EXPORT TO EXCEL' ⬇							Results per Page: 200 ▼			
⊞ Symbol ⊟		Last Trade	Change		Day's Gain	Qty	Price Paid	Total Gain		Market Val	Edit
			$	%				$	%		
⊞ AMZN	Buy / Sell	518.37	17.60	3.51%	$5,280.00	300	$449.01	$20,800.01	15.44%	$155,511.00	Edit
⊞ AMZN Jan $515 Put	Opn/Cls	47.94	-10.16	-17.49%	-$2,715.00*	3	$53.13	-$2,554.33*	-16.02%*	$13,395.00*	Edit

The total cost for our stock purchase at 449.01 and our 515-Strike put option at 53.13 was 502.14 points.

Total Cost = 502.14 Points

Buy AMZN stock at   449.01
Buy AMZN 515-Strike put at   53.13
                              Total Cost 502.14 points

The AMZN 515-Strike put option gives us the right but not the obligation to sell our AMZN stock at 515 points at any time prior to January option expiration in 6 months. This results in a minimum value for this stock/put option spread of 515 points. If AMZN stock trades above 515 we are not obligated to sell our shares at 515.

With a minimum value of 515 and a cost of 502.14 we are guaranteed a profit of 12.86 points for our spread regardless of the price movement of AMZN stock even in the unlikely event AMZN stock declines to zero!

Guaranteed Profit = 12.86 Points

Minimum value of stock/option spread   515.00
Cost of spread   - 502.14
                              Guaranteed Profit   12.86 points

No Risk and Unlimited Profit Potential

The stock/put option spread not only guarantees a profit for our trade, it also does not limit the profit potential of our AMZN stock purchase. If AMZN stock continues to increase in price our profits continue to increase with no limit on the profit potential. This combination gives us no risk and unlimited profit potential resulting in *stress less investing*.

As you can imagine, no risk and unlimited profit potential is a great way to invest! Once you buy the put option protection for your stock investment, you can forget about your stock trade! No need to monitor the markets or world events. Bad earnings reports don't matter. A severe selloff in your stock is of no concern and you don't have to worry about placing protective stops. You can place the trade and take a vacation!

Transforms Stock Investing To a Low Risk Investment

Once you have your put option insurance in place you can ride out unexpected selloffs or volatile price moves in the stock that might normally require you to sell your stock using risk management rules. This strategy is often called a *married put* as your put option protection is married to your stock position.

You can also purchase stock and put option insurance simultaneously. The simultaneous purchase of stock and a put option can typically limit your total risk to 5 or 6% or less. There is no need to place a protective stop or worry about unexpected adverse news for your stock. With a married put, the worst case scenario is you take a 5 or 6% loss if the trade does not work out and move on to another profit opportunity.

The prevailing wisdom characterizes option trading as 'high risk'. But purchasing put option insurance transforms stock investing from a high risk investment to one of the lowest risk investments in the investment universe.

Not Familiar With Option Investing?

We have found that just about anybody can learn how to trade options as long as they understand the basics of options investing. And if you don't understand options, then no problem . . . We have the resources to teach you what you need to know.

We wrote a Report titled *"Option Basics"* which is designed as a "refresher" course for options veterans . . . and an essential guide if you are new to options investing. For your convenience, we have included this Report in the Appendix.

This guidebook is short and simple ... teaching you only what you need to know about options and none of the complicated theories you don't need. It gives you the practical, real-world knowledge required in order to successfully invest using options.

You don't need to know complicated math or formulas like you have probably been led to believe. You just need to know the simple mechanics of buying and selling options. And this guide breaks options trading down to the bare essentials you need. It even includes quizzes to make sure you understand each topic.

Trading Options Online

Trading options online has made options trading quick and easy with low costs. The *Legacy Publishing Team* trades at three of the major online brokerage houses and pay commissions ranging from $5 to $8 to trade options.

These three brokerage houses have provided us with excellent telephone support over the years if we have a question about our option trade or if we want to give a broker an option order over the phone. Option specialists are available to help with option orders.

Options can be traded in most standard brokerage accounts and is similar to trading stocks like Apple or Microsoft. When you trade stocks, you only make money when the stock price goes up. One of the great advantages of option trading is that you can profit if the price of the underlying stock goes up, down, or even sideways.

Follow Up On Our Amazon Married Put

Shortly after purchasing the previously mentioned AMZN 515-Strike put option insurance there was a very sharp correction in US stocks due to global financial concerns. There was no change in the strong earnings growth outlook for Amazon as most of its revenue is generated in the US. But growth stocks in general were hit hard by this correction. The daily price chart below shows that AMZN stock declined 16% over a one week period during this period.

We already had a guaranteed profit for our AMZN married put and were able to ride out the unexpected sharp correction with no stress. Shortly after this correction Amazon stock rallied to a new all time high which produced nice profits for our married put trade.

Sharp Price Correction for Amazon Stock

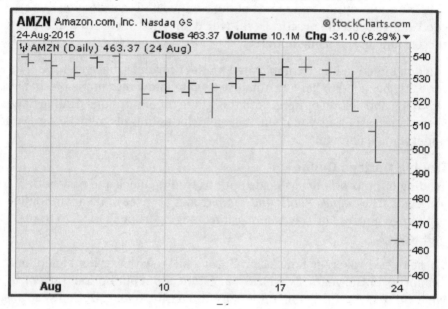

Trading Married Puts In Retirement Accounts

Due to the low risk nature of married puts they can be traded in most
retirement accounts just as we do here at *Legacy Publishing* in our
retirement accounts. Our brokerage account Profit/Loss Reports
for two of our retirement accounts that follow show that we have
$109,442.47 in open trade profits for our married put trades.

These Married Put Portfolios can't lose money regardless of the price
movement of the stocks. At the same time there is no limit on the
profit potential of these portfolios if the stocks continue to increase in
price. A total market meltdown or severe price declines in these stocks
would still result in profitable portfolios.

$73,140.62 Profit For Retirement Account #1

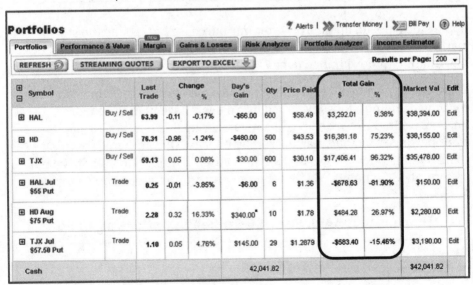

Portfolios   Alerts | Transfer Money | Bill Pay | Help

Portfolios | Performance & Value | Margin | Gains & Losses | Risk Analyzer | Portfolio Analyzer | Income Estimator

REFRESH | STREAMING QUOTES | EXPORT TO EXCEL   Results per Page: 200

Symbol		Last Trade	Change $	Change %	Day's Gain	Qty	Price Paid	Total Gain $	Total Gain %	Market Val	Edit
HAL	Buy / Sell	63.99	-0.11	-0.17%	-$143.00	1,300	$57.80	$8,039.63	10.70%	$83,187.00	Edit
HD	Buy / Sell	76.31	-0.96	-1.24%	-$768.00	800	$58.90	$13,919.02	29.53%	$61,048.00	Edit
MMM	Buy / Sell	141.60	-0.83	-0.58%	-$498.00	600	$124.09	$10,499.21	14.10%	$84,960.00	Edit
TJX	Buy / Sell	59.13	0.05	0.08%	$75.00	1,500	$30.42	$43,048.02	94.31%	$88,695.00	Edit
HAL Jul $55 Put	Trade	0.25	-0.01	-3.85%	-$13.00	13	$1.79	-$2,020.04	-86.14%	$325.00	Edit
HD Aug $75 Put	Trade	2.28	0.32	16.33%	$884.00	26	$1.78	$1,271.91	27.32%	$5,928.00	Edit
MMM Jul $130 Put	Trade	0.6899	0.06	9.51%	$35.94	6	$2.695	-$1,223.68	-74.72%	$413.94	Edit
TJX Jul $57.50 Put	Trade	1.10	0.05	4.76%	$100.00	20	$1.285	-$393.45	-15.17%	$2,200.00	Edit
Cash							199,685.94			$199,685.94	

$36,301.85 Profit For Retirement Account #2

Portfolios   Alerts | Transfer Money | Bill Pay | Help

Portfolios | Performance & Value | Margin | Gains & Losses | Risk Analyzer | Portfolio Analyzer | Income Estimator

REFRESH | STREAMING QUOTES | EXPORT TO EXCEL   Results per Page: 200

Symbol		Last Trade	Change $	Change %	Day's Gain	Qty	Price Paid	Total Gain $	Total Gain %	Market Val	Edit
HAL	Buy / Sell	63.99	-0.11	-0.17%	-$66.00	600	$58.49	$3,292.01	9.38%	$38,394.00	Edit
HD	Buy / Sell	76.31	-0.96	-1.24%	-$480.00	500	$43.53	$16,381.18	75.23%	$38,155.00	Edit
TJX	Buy / Sell	59.13	0.05	0.08%	$30.00	600	$30.10	$17,406.41	96.32%	$35,478.00	Edit
HAL Jul $55 Put	Trade	0.25	-0.01	-3.85%	-$6.00	6	$1.36	-$678.63	-81.90%	$150.00	Edit
HD Aug $75 Put	Trade	2.28	0.32	16.33%	$340.00	10	$1.78	$484.28	26.97%	$2,280.00	Edit
TJX Jul $57.50 Put	Trade	1.10	0.05	4.76%	$145.00	29	$1.2879	-$583.40	-15.46%	$3,190.00	Edit
Cash							42,041.82			$42,041.82	

The 'insurance' put options in the retirement accounts guarantee that these portfolios will be very profitable regardless of the price movement of the stocks. These profits demonstrate the ability of the married put strategy to deliver substantial returns with low risk.

Actual Trade Examples

We like to present examples of real time married put trades over different time periods and different market conditions to demonstrate the ability of the strategy to deliver substantial profits in any type of market condition.

At option expiration, if our stock is still on a *PowerTrend* 'buy' signal we normally will 'roll over' the expiring option by selling the expiring put and purchasing a put that expires in 3 to 6 months or longer.

Let's take a look at several examples of married put trades. Our brokerage account confirmations below show that we purchased 200 shares of Apple Inc at an average price of 339.05.

Buy 200 Shares AAPL At 339.05

Transaction History   Alerts | Transfer Money | Bill Pay | Help

Transactions | Check Summary | Deposit Summary | Categories | Reports

Date	Type	View	Description	Categories (hide)	Amount ($)
02/01/11	Bought		50 of AAPL @ $345.00 (Order #1998)		-17,257.99
02/03/11	Bought		50 of AAPL @ $344.00 (Order #2000)		-17,207.99
03/17/11	Bought		50 of AAPL @ $334.90 (Order #2094)		-16,752.99
03/18/11	Bought		50 of AAPL @ $332.31 (Order #2467)		-16,623.49

Apple stock moved up in price after our purchase but in May the stock market entered a correction and price volatility started to increase. The VIX Volatility Index jumped over 74% from 15.00 in March to 26.20 in May.

We wanted to protect our profits in Apple stock in case the correction continued and possibly developed into a bear market. At the same time we wanted to participate in any further upside potential if Apple stock bottomed out and started to rally in price. Our brokerage account confirmation below shows that we purchased 2 Apple Sep 560-Strike put options at 43.50 points which provided protection for our 200 shares of Apple stock.

Purchased 2 AAPL Sep 560-Strike Put Options at 43.50

Transaction History   Alerts | Transfer Money | Bill Pay | Help

Transactions | Check Summary | Deposit Summary | Categories | Reports

Date	Type	View	Description (show categories)	Amount ($)
05/22/12	Bought To Open		2 AAPL Sep 22 '12 $560 Put(AAPL) @ $43.50	-8,709.51

Locking In a $35,490 Profit

Purchasing the put options allowed us to 'lock in' a profit of $35,490 regardless of how much Apple stock may decline. The *Legacy Publishing Team* designed a series of calculators to calculate the profit potential for six different types of trading strategies.

The calculators allow us to know in advance the profit/loss potential for a trade before we take the trade.

The Married Put Calculator will calculate the profit/loss potential for a married put trade assuming various price changes in the underlying stock at option expiration. The Married Put Calculator below displays the profit/loss potential for our Apple married put trade.

The first row labeled 'Stock % Change' in the table below assumes various price changes for AAPL stock at option expiration from an 80% increase in price to a 100% decline in price in this example. The calculator will calculate the profit/loss potential and percent return based on these price changes in AAPL stock at option expiration.

The row labeled 'Profit(Loss)' lists the net profit or loss for the combination of purchasing AAPL stock @ 339.05 and AAPL put option @ 43.50 for the various assumed stock prices at option expiration listed on the second row labeled 'Stock Price' . The first column assumes that AAPL stock increases 80% to 610.29 at option expiration (circled). This would produce a $22,774 profit and a 59.5% return for the married put.

Wealth Creation Alliance

Married Put Calculator

Stock Symbol	Stock Price	Entry Date	Exit Date	Put Strike	Put Premium	Quarterly Dividend
AAPL	339.05	05/22/12	09/22/12	560	43.5	0

Calculate   New Analysis   Print

Stock % Change	80%	40%	0%	-40%	-60%	-80%	-100%
Stock Price	$610.29	$474.67	$339.05	$203.43	$135.62	$67.81	$0.00
Stock Value	$61,029	$47,467	$33,905	$20,343	$13,562	$6,781	$0
Option Value	$0	$8,533	$22,095	$35,657	$42,438	$49,219	$56,000
Sub Total	$61,029	$56,000	$56,000	$56,000	$56,000	$56,000	$56,000
Dividends	$0	$0	$0	$0	$0	$0	$0
Total Value	$61,029	$56,000	$56,000	$56,000	$56,000	$56,000	$56,000
Cost	$38,255	$38,255	$38,255	$38,255	$38,255	$38,255	$38,255
Profit(Loss)	$22,774	$17,745	$17,745	$17,745	$17,745	$17,745	$17,745
% Return	59.5%	46.4%	46.4%	46.4%	46.4%	46.4%	46.4%

Note: The prices in this trade example are not adjusted for the subsequent 7 for 1 stock split for Apple stock.

The last column assumes Apple stock closes at zero at option expiration (circled) which is highly unlikely for such a high quality stock. Nevertheless, if AAPL stock closes at zero then the value of 100 shares of AAPL stock would be zero but the value of the 560-Strike put option would be $56,000.

The value of the put option is calculated by subtracting the stock price of 0 from the strike price of 560 and multiplying by 100 (560 - 0 x 100 = 56,000). Regardless of how much AAPL stock drops in price, the combination of 100 shares of stock and the 560-Strike put option will always be worth at least $56,000. Subtracting the cost of the spread of $38,255 from the minimum worth of $56,000 would result in a $17,745 profit and 46.4% return (before commissions).

> *"In investing, the return you want should depend on whether you want to eat well or sleep well."*–J. Kenfield Morley

Eat Well and Sleep Well

Locking in a 46.4% return for this married put trade regardless of the price movement of Apple stock demonstrates the low risk nature of the married put strategy and the ability of the strategy to produce profits despite severe corrections or wild price swings in the underlying stock. We owned 200 shares of Apple and 2 puts which resulted in locking in total profits of $35,490 for this married put trade.

With the put protection we do not have to worry about a disappointing earnings report for Apple or the slowing world economies and potential bear markets. There is no need to worry about 'flash crashes' or placing a protective stop for our stock purchase or exiting our position with a 20 or 40% decline in the stock price enabling us to eat well and sleep well!

After purchasing the 2 AAPL put options, Apple stock did bottom out and resumed its upward price trend and was trading at 618.22. We had a $47,132 profit and a 61.5% return for our married put trade.

Return Potential for Apple Married Put Trade

If AAPL Stock Increases 80% = 59.5% Return
If AAPL Stock Remains Flat = 46.6% Return
If AAPL Stock Decreases 40% = 46.6% Return
If AAPL Stock Decreases 80% = 46.6% Return
If AAPL Stock Decreases 100% = 46.6% Return

Note: In smaller accounts a married put trade can be initiated by purchasing 10 shares of Apple stock and purchasing an AAPL mini put option which costs 1/10 of the cost of a regular option.

ETF Married Put Trade Example

Let's now look at an example of an ETF married put trade. Our brokerage account confirmations below show that we purchased 400 shares of the leveraged financial ETF symbol FAS at an average price of 106.75. After this purchase FAS had a 3 for 1 stock split. We then owned 1,200 shares at a split adjusted price of 35.58.

Bought 1,200 Shares FAS at 35.58 (split adjusted)

Transaction History				Alerts | Transfer Money | Bill Pay | Help
Transactions	Check Summary	Deposit Summary	Categories	Reports
Date	Type	View	Description (show categories)	Amount ($)
11/23/12	Bought		200 of FAS @ $107.00 (Order #3656)	-21,407.99
11/23/12	Bought		200 of FAS @ $106.50	-21,307.99

After our purchase, the FAS ETF moved up in price but then the stock market entered a correction phase with increased price volatility. There is no way to predict in advance how long a correction will last or how deep the price correction will be.

We did not want to give up our profits in the FAS ETF and purchased protective put options to lock in our profits. On the other hand, if the correction ended we wanted to participate in further upside potential for FAS.

Our brokerage account confirmation below shows that we purchased FAS Oct 70-Strike put options at 2.85 points which provided protection for our FAS ETF shares.

Purchased FAS Oct 70-Strike Put Options at 2.85

Transaction History				Alerts | Transfer Money | Bill Pay | Help
Transactions	Check Summary	Deposit Summary	Categories	Reports
Date	Type	View	Description (show categories)	Amount ($)
09/23/13	Bought To Open		11 FAS Oct 19 '13 $70 Put(FAS) @ $2.85	-3,151.41

As we learned in the previous example, the Married Put Calculator will calculate the profit/loss potential for a married put trade assuming various price changes in the underlying stock at option expiration.

In the example that follows, the first column assumes various price changes in FAS from a 100% increase in price to a 100% decrease in price at option expiration (circled). A 100% increase in price would produce a $3,273 profit and a 85.2% return for the FAS married put.

In this example, the last column assumes FAS closes at zero at option expiration (circled) which is highly unlikely. Nevertheless, if FAS closes at zero then the value of 100 shares of FAS would be zero but the value of the 70-Strike put option would be $7,000.

Wealth Creation Alliance

Married Put Calculator

Stock Symbol	Stock Price	Entry Date	Exit Date	Put Strike	Put Premium	Quarterly Dividend
FAS	35.58	11/23/12	10/18/13	70	2.85	

Calculate   New Analysis   Print

	100%	60%	40%	0%	-40%	-60%	-100%
Stock % Change	100%	60%	40%	0%	-40%	-60%	-100%
Stock Price	$71.16	$56.93	$49.81	$35.58	$21.35	$14.23	$0.00
Stock Value	$7,116	$5,693	$4,981	$3,558	$2,135	$1,423	$0
Option Value	$0	$1,307	$2,019	$3,442	$4,865	$5,577	$7,000
Sub Total	$7,116	$7,000	$7,000	$7,000	$7,000	$7,000	$7,000
Dividends	$0	$0	$0	$0	$0	$0	$0
Total Value	$7,116	$7,000	$7,000	$7,000	$7,000	$7,000	$7,000
Cost	$3,843	$3,843	$3,843	$3,843	$3,843	$3,843	$3,843
Profit(Loss)	$3,273	$3,157	$3,157	$3,157	$3,157	$3,157	$3,157
% Return	85.2%	82.1%	82.1%	82.1%	82.1%	82.1%	82.1%

Locking in a 82.1% Profit

Purchasing the put options allowed us to lock in an 82.1% profit regardless of how much the FAS ETF may decline. The cost of purchasing one hundred shares of FAS and one Oct 70-Strike put option was $3,843. With the 70-Strike put option, the value of this married put spread cannot go below $7,000.

Subtracting the $3,843 cost of the spread from the minimum value of $7,000 would result in a minimum profit of $3,273 and a 82.1% return (before commissions).

Locking in an 82.1% return for this married put trade regardless of the price movement in the FAS once again demonstrates the low risk nature of the married put strategy and the ability of the strategy to produce profits despite severe corrections in the underlying stock.

With the put protection we do not have to be concerned about placing a protective stop or exiting our stock position if the FAS price declines sharply.

Note: The prices in this trade example are not adjusted for the subsequent 4 for 1 stock split for the FAS ETF.

TJX Trade Example

Let's now take a look at another example of a married put trade for a lower priced stock. Our brokerage account confirmations below show that we purchased 1,000 shares of T.J. Maxx at an average price of 60.97. After this purchase TJX had a 2 for 1stock split. We then owned 2,000 shares at a split adjusted price of 30.48.

Bought 2,000 Shares TJX at 30.48 (split adjusted)

Transaction History   Alerts | ⟫ Transfer Money | ⟫ Bill Pay | ⓘ Help

Transactions	Check Summary	Deposit Summary	Categories	Reports	
Date	Type	View	Description (show categories)		Amount ($)
11/08/11	Bought		500 of TJX @ $60.60 (Order #2544)		-30,307.99
11/30/11	Bought		500 of TJX @ $61.34 (Order #2572)		-30,677.99

After our purchase, TJX stock moved up in price and we purchased put insurance. We then rolled over these puts. Our brokerage account confirmation below shows that we purchased 20 TJX Oct 40-Strike put options at 2.49 points which provided 5 months of insurance protection for our 2,000 shares of TJX stock.

The stock market then entered a correction phase with increased price volatility. The protective put options allowed us to lock in our profits and at the same time, if the correction ended, we would be able to participate in further upside potential for TJX stock.

Purchased 20 TJX Oct 40-Strike Put Options at 2.49

Transaction History   Alerts | ⟫ Transfer Money | ⟫ Bill Pay | ⓘ Help

Transactions	Check Summary	Deposit Summary	Categories	Reports	
Date	Type	View	Description (show categories)		Amount ($)
05/22/12	Bought To Open		20 TJX Oct 20 '12 $40 Put(TJX) @ $2.49		-5,003.23

As we learned in the previous AAPL example, the Married Put Calculator will calculate the profit/loss potential for a married put trade assuming various price changes in the underlying stock at option expiration.

In the example that follows, the first column assumes that TJX stock increases 60% to 48.77 at option expiration (circled). This would produce a $1,580 profit and a 47.9% return for the TJX married put.

And in this example, the last column assumes TJX stock closes at zero at option expiration (circled) which is highly unlikely for such a successful retailer. Nevertheless, if TJX stock closes at zero then the value of 100 shares of TJX stock would be zero but the value of the 40-Strike put option would be $4,000.

Wealth Creation Alliance

Married Put Calculator

Stock Symbol	Stock Price	Entry Date	Exit Date	Put Strike	Put Premium	Quarterly Dividend
TJX	30.48	05/22/12	10/20/12	40	2.49	0

Calculate   New Analysis   Print

Stock % Change	60%	40%	0%	-40%	-60%	-80%	-100%
Stock Price	$48.77	$42.67	$30.48	$18.29	$12.19	$6.10	$0.00
Stock Value	$4,877	$4,267	$3,048	$1,829	$1,219	$610	$0
Option Value	$0	$0	$952	$2,171	$2,781	$3,390	$4,000
Sub Total	$4,877	$4,267	$4,000	$4,000	$4,000	$4,000	$4,000
Dividends	$0	$0	$0	$0	$0	$0	$0
Total Value	$4,877	$4,267	$4,000	$4,000	$4,000	$4,000	$4,000
Cost	$3,297	$3,297	$3,297	$3,297	$3,297	$3,297	$3,297
Profit(Loss)	$1,580	$970	$703	$703	$703	$703	$703
% Return	47.9%	29.4%	29.4%	21.3%	21.3%	21.3%	21.3%

Locking In a $14,060 Profit

Purchasing the put options allowed us to lock in a profit of $14,060 regardless of how much TJX stock may decline. The cost of purchasing one hundred shares of TJX stock and one Oct 40-Strike put option was $3,297. With the 40-Strike put option, the value of this married put spread cannot go below $4,000.

Subtracting the $3,297 cost of the spread from the minimum value of $4,000 would result in a minimum profit of $703 and a 21.3% return (after commissions). We own 2,000 shares of TJX and 20 put options so purchasing the put options allowed us to lock in a total profit of $14,060 ($703 x 20).

Locking in a 21.3% return for this married put trade regardless of the price movement of TJX stock once again demonstrates the low risk nature of the married put strategy and the ability of the strategy to produce profits despite severe corrections in the underlying stock.

With the put protection we do not have to be concerned about placing a protective stop or exiting our stock position if TJX stock price declines sharply.

After purchasing the TJX put options, TJX stock continued to decline but then it did reverse course and resume its upward price trend. TJX stock was trading at 45.17 and we had a $24,400 profit and a 37% return for our married put trade.

Married Put Current Profit Results

We utilized the Married Put Calculator to calculate the average profit potential for our current married put trades. The table below shows that we currently have $157,573.52 in open trade profits and an average return of 167.0% for our advisory service Married Put Portfolio. These profit results reflect the profits after rolling over some of the put option trades at option expiration.

The guaranteed profit for the portfolio is $125,250.22 and the guaranteed return is 160.4% regardless of the price movement in the stocks. The US stock market is currently experiencing a very sharp price correction but our married put *stress less* strategy will deliver substantial profits regardless of the severity of the current correction.

Stock	Current Profit	Percent Return	Guaranteed Profit	Percent Return
ADP	$5,374.00	48.4%	$5,097.00	44.1%
Dupont	$7,143.00	65.1%	$7,130.00	64.7%
Amazon	$31,116.00	23.6%	$7,053.00	4.8%
Netflix	$10,270.00	9.0%	$7,120.00	6.3%
Magellan Midstream LP	$20,620.00	248.2%	$18,988.00	217.9%
Johnson & Johnson	$2,285.00	30.2%	$2,004.00	26.7%
Enterprise Products	$12,752.00	107.1%	$12,400.00	106.9%
Two Harbors	$4,830.00	89.6%	$4,830.00	88.7%
Utilities ETF	$1,330.00	17.8%	$816.00	11.1%
Kinder Morgan Inc	$14,303.52	943.9%	$14,266.22	938.4%
MarkWest Energy	$6,216.00	55.0%	$4,734.00	43.0%
American Capital	$8,590.00	440.5%	$8,562.00	439.6%
Plains Pipeline	$16,194.00	144.3%	$16,190.00	144.1%
3 M Company	$16,550.00	116.4%	$16,060.00	109.7%
Total Profit / Avg Gain	**$157,573.52**	**167.0%**	**$125,250.22**	**160.4%**

Let's face it. It's a crazy world out there. Isn't nice to know that having financial security is one thing you will not have to worry about? The married put strategy along with the income strategy presented in the next chapter have allowed us the privilege to lead a stress free retirement.

These strategies have allowed us the time and freedom to concentrate on the things that really matter; family, their wellbeing, and of course our tennis game! You've got to love it! This is the ultimate way to enjoy retirement or generate income!

In the next chapter, we will look at an income strategy for our stocks that can pay for the entire cost of the put option insurance for our stocks. The income generated reduces the cost basis of our stocks and increases our guaranteed return.

CHAPTER 4
Income Strategy

Let's explore our next strategy which is an income strategy that allows you to generate cash income from your stocks. This income strategy has generated consistent returns during every type of market condition.

The income strategy is a 'covered call' strategy that generates cash income from selling call option premium on your stocks. The strategy produced consistent returns during the last financial crisis and the severe 2008 - 2009 bear market by investing in covered calls on bearish ETFs. And it has produced consistent returns since the last bear market including bullish, volatile and non-trending types of markets.

Most investors are not familiar with the concept of selling call option premium to generate cash income. Selling option premium is a very simple but lucrative income strategy. The option income strategy is known as a 'covered call' or 'buy write'.

When you sell a call option, cash equal to the option price or premium is immediately credited to your brokerage account. Unlike a traditional stock dividend you don't have to own the stock on the dividend date to receive the quarterly dividend and you don't have to wait a year to receive a 3% or 4% annual dividend yield.

When you sell option premium on longer term options, you can get paid up to a 20% to 30% cash payment up front when the option is sold. You get to keep this cash payment regardless of the price movement of the underlying stock.

Ideal Strategy for Any Type of Market

Selling option premium on your stocks to generate immediate cash income is the ideal strategy for today's volatile markets and uncertain global economies. We will look at an actual trade example shortly that allowed us to purchase Morgan Stanley stock at a 30% discount to its current price.

When you buy stock at a 30% discount you can profit if the stock price increases, remains flat or even declines 20% to 25% resulting in a much higher probability that the stock trade will be profitable. This gives the option income strategy a huge advantage over a stock purchase strategy and allows you to profit in any type of market condition.

Added Dimension

The option income strategy works just as well with bearish trades which allow you to profit in bear markets when stocks and ETFs are declining in price. Bearish income trades not only reduce portfolio risk but can dramatically increase profit opportunities and provide a whole new dimension to income investing.

$4 Million in Cash Income Over the Past 5 Years

We have been trading the option income strategy for many years. Due to the versatility of the option income strategy and its ability to profit in up, down or flat markets, we were very active generating option premium income during the last severe bear market and during the strong bull market that followed.

Our brokerage account Transaction Reports included in the Appendix show that we collected $4,068,824.22 in option premium income over the past 5 years which resulted in over $67,000 in cash income per month. Brokerage confirmations list the options we sold and the amount of cash that was credited to our brokerage account for each option sale.

The key to selling option premium to generate cash income is to make sure the option you sell is 'covered'. There are both bullish and bearish covered call trades:

Bullish Covered Call Trades

- **Buy 100 shares of a stock or ETF and sell 1 call option or**
- **Buy 10 shares of stock and sell 1 mini call option (if available)**

Bearish Covered Call Trades

- **Buy 100 shares of a bearish ETF and sell 1 call option or**
- **Buy 10 shares of a bearish ETF and sell 1 mini call option (if available)**

Note: Mini options cover 10 shares of stock and cost 1/10th the cost of regular options. Not all stocks and ETFs trade mini call options.

For bullish trades the short option is 'covered' by owning a stock or ETF. And for bearish trades the short option is 'covered' by owning a bearish ETF.

Because the short option is 'covered' this is a limited risk strategy. **Selling 'covered' option premium incurs considerably less risk than investing in stocks.**

Selling option premium enables us to profit if the market goes up, down or remains flat and has given us the edge in producing consistent returns during any type of market condition.

Let's look at an example of an option sale and the resulting amount of cash that was credited to our brokerage account. The brokerage confirmation below shows that we 'sold to open' 10 of the National Oilwell Jan 25-strike call options at 12.72 points.

Options cover one hundred shares of stock so a 12.72 point option is worth $1,272 ($12.72 x 100 = $1,272). Selling 10 options at 12.72 points resulted in $12,720 cash being credited to our brokerage account ($1,272 x 10 = $12,720).

We get to keep this $12,720 cash payment ($12,708 after commission) regardless of the price movement of National Oilwell stock.

Sale of 10 Options at 12.72 Points Results in
$12,720 Cash Dividend Credited to Brokerage Account
$1,272 x 10 Contracts = $12,720

TRADE CONFIRMATION

TRADE DATE	SETL DATE	MKT/ CPT	SYMBOL/ CUSIP	BUY/ SELL	QUANTITY	PRICE	ACCT TYPE		
03/26/09	03/27/09	5 1	YMPA25	SELL	10	$12.72	Margin	PRINCIPAL	$12,720.00
CALL NATL OILWELL JAN 025								COMMISSION	$11.49
01/16/2010 EXPIRATION DATE								FEE	$0.08
OPEN CONTRACT								NET AMOUNT	$12,708.43

Let's look at an example of a covered call trade that is initiated by purchasing stock and selling a related call option. This is also known as a 'buy write' trade. Our brokerage confirmation below shows that we bought 600 shares of Morgan Stanley stock at 24.22 and sold to open 6 Morgan Stanley July 20-Strike call options at 7.27. These options had 4 months until option expiration.

Buy Morgan Stanley Stock at 24.22 and Sell 20-Strike Call at 7.27

TRADE CONFIRMATION

TRADE DATE	SETL DATE	MKT/ CPT	SYMBOL/ CUSIP	BUY/ SELL	QUANTITY	PRICE	ACCT TYPE		
03/18/09 MORGAN STANLEY	03/23/09	1 3	MS	BUY	600	$24.22	Margin	PRINCIPAL COMMISSION NET AMOUNT	$14,532.00 $7.99 $14,539.99
03/18/09 CALL MORGAN STANL JUL 020 07/18/2009 EXPIRATION DATE OPEN CONTRACT	03/19/09	6 1	MSG20 ****	SELL	6	$7.27	Margin	PRINCIPAL COMMISSION FEE NET AMOUNT	$4,362.00 $12.49 $0.03 $4,349.48

Selling to open the 20-strike call option at 7.27 points resulted in $727 in cash per contract being credited to our brokerage account or a total of $4,362 ($4,349 after commission) for 6 contracts.

Purchasing the stock at 24.22 points and receiving 7.27 points in cash resulted in a 30% cash payment we received up front on the day we initiated the trade. We get to keep this 30% cash payment regardless of the price movement of Morgan Stanley stock.

> ### Buy Stock at 24.22 Points and Sell Option at 7.27 Points
> ### Equals 30% Cash Dividend Over a Four Month Period

When this option expires in 4 months we can sell another option and collect another cash payment. This is called a 'rollover'. If we rollover this option a second time we would receive a total of 3 cash payment over the course of one year. This has the potential of producing up to a 90% cash payment over the course of one year which could almost pay for the initial cost of the stock and dramatically lower risk.

> ### Up to 90% Cash Dividend Potential
> ### Over the Course of One Year
> ### By 'Rolling Over' Option

Buying Morgan Stanley stock at a 30% discount reduces risk considerably. This trade will profit if Morgan Stanley stock increases, remains flat or even declines 20% to 25% resulting in a much higher probability that the trade will be profitable.

This can result in a high percentage of winning trades even if your market timing is not very accurate. This gives the covered call strategy a big advantage over a stock purchase strategy which requires correct timing and a stock price increase to be profitable.

The brokerage account Profit/Loss Report that follows shows covered call trades for one of my trading accounts. This account was my International Trading Championship contest account. I started the trading contest with a $311,800 starting balance when I initiated the covered call trades. There are $118,546.86 in net profits after commissions for this portfolio.

49% Cash Income by Rolling Over Trades

We normally reinvest the cash income we receive from covered call trades in additional covered call trades allowing us to compound our trading results. I received a total of $152,900 in cash income from selling call option premiums for his stocks resulting in an average cash payment of 49% for the portfolio.

This portfolio is widely diversified across different industry groups. All of the trades in this portfolio were showing a net profit for the stock/call option spread demonstrating the ability of the covered call strategy to produce a high percentage of winning trades. Even if the underlying stocks in this portfolio decline moderately I can still realize a good return for the portfolio.

We normally take profits when a covered call trade reaches 90% of its profit potential. This enables us to take profits on trades well before option expiration and initiate new covered call trades allowing us to compound the cash income we receive.

Note: I traded a large number of option contracts in this account. Trading one option contract would require a smaller trading account.

Covered Call Portfolio with $118,546.86 in Profits

Realized P&L on Closed Positions

Symbol	Date Bought	Date Sold	Shares	Cost Basis	Sales Price	Gain-loss
+FCXEG	3/26/2009 11:59:59 PM	3/17/2009 12:46:27 PM	10	$0.00	$5,164.89	$5,164.89
+FCXEG	3/26/2009 11:59:59 PM	3/18/2009 3:18:38 PM	5	$0.00	$3,022.44	$3,022.44
+FPAEG	4/30/2009 10:18:36 AM	3/26/2009 11:59:59 PM	15	$11,697.59	$0.00	-$11,697.59
+GSGM	3/25/2009 3:40:27 PM	5/6/2009 10:00:37 AM	15	$72,027.59	$109,244.57	$37,216.98
+GSGS	5/6/2009 10:00:37 AM	3/25/2009 3:40:27 PM	15	$65,832.59	$38,492.16	-$27,340.43
+NOVEF	5/4/2009 11:59:59 PM	3/17/2009 12:49:34 PM	10	$3,218.39	$3,564.89	$346.50
+NOVEF	5/4/2009 11:59:59 PM	3/18/2009 3:36:31 PM	5	$1,609.20	$1,722.45	$113.25
+YCPAU	5/8/2009 11:59:59 PM	5/1/2009 12:36:20 PM	15	$0.00	$9,422.13	$9,422.13
+YFQAW	5/8/2009 11:59:59 PM	5/6/2009 3:17:12 PM	15	$0.00	$10,307.11	$10,307.11
+YHBAE	5/8/2009 11:59:59 PM	5/1/2009 1:41:20 PM	15	$0.00	$7,322.19	$7,322.19
FCX	3/17/2009 12:45:32 PM	4/30/2009 10:20:38 AM	800	$29,052.72	$33,960.39	$4,907.67
FCX	3/17/2009 12:45:32 PM	4/30/2009 10:20:38 AM	200	$7,282.20	$8,490.10	$1,207.90
FCX	3/18/2009 3:17:41 PM	4/30/2009 10:20:38 AM	300	$11,353.77	$12,735.15	$1,381.38
FCX	3/18/2009 3:17:41 PM	4/30/2009 10:20:38 AM	100	$3,784.60	$4,245.05	$460.45
FCX	3/18/2009 3:17:41 PM	4/30/2009 10:20:38 AM	100	$3,804.58	$4,245.05	$440.47
NOV	3/17/2009 12:48:27 PM	5/4/2009 10:13:50 AM	100	$2,987.60	$3,271.87	$284.27
NOV	3/17/2009 12:48:27 PM	5/4/2009 10:13:50 AM	200	$5,995.20	$6,543.75	$548.55
NOV	3/17/2009 12:48:27 PM	5/4/2009 10:13:50 AM	500	$14,938.00	$16,359.37	$1,421.37
NOV	3/17/2009 12:48:27 PM	5/4/2009 10:13:50 AM	200	$5,975.20	$6,543.75	$568.55
NOV	3/18/2009 3:35:49 PM	5/4/2009 10:13:50 AM	500	$14,898.00	$16,359.37	$1,461.37

Total Realized Gain-Loss: $46,559.45

Unrealized P&L on Open Positions

Symbol	Description	Position	Avg Price	Cost Basis	Market Value	Type	Unrealized Val.
+AASAH	Allegheny Technologies Inc Jan 2010 40.00 Call	-15	$0.0000	$0.00	$0.00	Stock Option	$0.00
+CLFAA	Cliffs Natural Resources Inc Jan 2010 20.00 Call	-15	$0.0000	$0.00	$0.00	Stock Option	$0.00
+CLFGD	Cliffs Natural Resources Inc Jul 2009 20.00 Call	-15	-$3.5715	$5,357.31	-$17,550.00	Stock Option	-$12,192.69
+CXJHD	Caterpillar Inc Del Aug 2009 30.00 Call	-15	-$3.3516	$5,027.35	-$16,200.00	Stock Option	-$11,172.65
+HBUAE	Bucyrus Intl Inc New Jan 2010 25.00 Call	-15	$0.0000	$0.00	$0.00	Stock Option	$0.00
+HBUGD	Bucyrus Intl Inc New Jul 2009 20.00 Call	-15	-$2.5615	$3,842.28	-$11,700.00	Stock Option	-$7,857.72
+MDRHC	Mcdermott Intl Inc Aug 2009 15.00 Call	-15	-$2.6249	$3,937.35	-$6,600.00	Stock Option	-$2,662.65
+MOSFH	Mosaic Co Jun 2009 40.00 Call	-15	-$7.8582	$11,787.30	-$10,500.00	Stock Option	$1,287.30
+MSGD	Morgan Stanley New Jul 2009 20.00 Call	-15	-$6.4249	$9,637.30	-$12,750.00	Stock Option	-$3,112.70
+PBRGY	Petroleo Brasileiro Sa Petrobr Sponsored Adr Jul 2009 27.50 Call	-15	-$5.7915	$8,687.31	-$18,900.00	Stock Option	-$10,212.69
+SIIGY	Smith Intl Inc Jul 2009 27.50 Call	-10	-$3.3649	$3,364.88	-$5,600.00	Stock Option	-$2,235.12
+STTHF	State Str Corp Aug 2009 32.00 Call	-15	-$7.8915	$11,837.31	-$20,550.00	Stock Option	-$8,712.69
+UNEAR	United States Natl Gas Fund Lp Unit Jan 2010 18.00 Call	-30	-$2.1715	$6,514.58	-$8,550.00	Stock Option	-$2,035.42
+WFCGT	Wells Fargo & Co New Jul 2009 17.50 Call	-15	-$3.5716	$5,357.34	-$16,200.00	Stock Option	-$10,842.66
+YNMAE	Foster Wheeler Ag Jan 2010 25.00 Call	-15	-$4.5715	$6,857.20	-$7,800.00	Stock Option	-$942.80
ATI	Allegheny Technologies Inc	1500	$38.0293	$57,044.00	$57,390.00	Equities	$346.00
BUCY	Bucyrus Intl Inc New	3000	$21.3533	$64,060.00	$83,430.00	Equities	$19,370.00
CAT	Caterpillar Inc Del	1500	$28.7083	$43,062.50	$59,460.00	Equities	$16,397.50
CLF	Cliffs Natural Resources Inc	3000	$21.9788	$65,936.50	$93,060.00	Equities	$27,123.50
FWLT	Foster Wheeler Ag	1500	$23.5293	$35,294.00	$37,470.00	Equities	$2,176.00
MDR	Mcdermott Intl Inc	1500	$14.4960	$21,744.00	$27,615.00	Equities	$5,871.00
MOS	Mosaic Co	1500	$42.0493	$63,073.90	$68,175.00	Equities	$5,101.10
MS	Morgan Stanley New	1500	$23.1305	$34,695.80	$42,300.00	Equities	$7,604.20
PBR	Petroleo Brasileiro Sa Petrobr Sponsored Adr	1500	$30.2159	$45,323.90	$60,000.00	Equities	$14,676.10
SII	Smith Intl Inc	1000	$25.7360	$25,736.00	$31,720.00	Equities	$5,984.00
STT	State Str Corp	1500	$32.7483	$49,122.50	$65,625.00	Equities	$16,502.50
UNG	United States Natl Gas Fund Lp Unit	3000	$15.3793	$46,138.00	$50,790.00	Equities	$4,652.00
WFC	Wells Fargo & Co New	1500	$16.9293	$25,394.00	$42,270.00	Equities	$16,876.00

Total Unrealized Gain-Loss: $71,987.41

Calculating the Profit Potential for Covered Call Trades

The goal of the covered call or buy write strategy is to have the underlying stock close at or above the strike price of the short call option at option expiration. This results in the stock being called and the maximum profit potential being realized for the trade. Covered call trades can be rolled over prior to option expiration by buying to close the expiring call and selling to open a call with a later expiration date. This prevents the stock from being called and allows you to keep your stock in your brokerage account.

There are both bullish and bearish covered call trades. Let's first take a look at calculating the profit potential for bearish covered calls.

Bearish Covered Call Trade Example

Bearish covered call trades can be established by purchasing a bearish ETF and selling the related call option. Let's look at an actual trade example of a bearish covered call. Our brokerage confirmation below shows that on August 26th we purchased 300 shares of the bearish Emerging Market ETF symbol EEV at 96.80. About 2 weeks later we sold to open 3 of the EEV December 120-Strike call options at 20.00 points which created a covered call trade. The bearish Emerging Market ETF increases in value as the price of the Emerging Market ETF declines. These options had 3 months until expiration.

Selling to open the 120-strike call option at 20.00 points resulted in $2,000 in cash per contract being credited to our brokerage account or a total of $6,000 (before commission) for 3 contracts.

Buy EEV at 96.80, Sell 120-Strike call at 20.00

USD - US DOLLAR

Trades

Trade Date	Settlement Date	Trade Time	Action	Quantity	Symbol	Price
08/26/2008	08/29/2008	2:32:13 pm	Buy	300	EFU	107.790000
08/26/2008	08/29/2008	2:39:36 pm	Buy	100	EEV	96.800000
08/26/2008	08/29/2008	2:39:36 pm	Buy	100	EEV	96.800000
08/26/2008	08/29/2008	2:39:36 pm	Buy	100	EEV	96.800000
08/26/2008	08/27/2008	3:51:00 pm	Buy to Open	5	+RSXWX	13.000000

USD - US DOLLAR

Trades

Trade Date	Settlement Date	Trade Time	Action	Quantity	Symbol	Price
09/11/2008	09/12/2008	9:59:01 am	Sell to Open	-3	+EEVLD	20.000000

Profiting in Down Markets

The Buy Write Analysis below displays the profit/loss potential for buying the bearish Emerging Market ETF symbol EEV at 96.80 and selling the EEV December 120-Strike call for 20.0 points. The Analysis displays potential profit results for various price changes for the EEV ETF at option expiration from a 25% increase to a 10% decrease in price. The cost of this buy write 76.80 points and is calculated by subtracting the 20.0 points we received from the sale of the 120-Strike call from the 96.80 cost of the EEV purchase.

Wealth Creation Alliance

Buy Write Analysis

Stock Symbol	Current Stock Price	Call Strike	Call Price
EEV	96.80	120	20.00

Break Even
76.80   Calculate | New Analysis | Print

% Change	25.0%	20.0%	15.0%	10.0%	0.0%	-5.0%	-10.0%
Stock Price	$121.00	$116.16	$111.32	$106.48	$96.80	$91.96	$87.12
Stock Prof/Loss	$2,420.00	$1,936.00	$1,452.00	$968.00	$0.00	$-484.00	$-968.00
Call Value	$1.00	$0.00	$0.00	$0.00	$0.00	$0.00	$0.00
Call Profit/Loss	$1,900.00	$2,000.00	$2,000.00	$2,000.00	$2,000.00	$2,000.00	$2,000.00
Net Profit/Loss	$4,320.00	$3,936.00	$3,452.00	$2,968.00	$2,000.00	$1,516.00	$1,032.00
% Return	56.3%	51.3%	44.9%	38.6%	26.0%	19.7%	13.4%

The Buy Write Analysis reveals that if the EEV ETF price remains flat at 96.80 at option expiration a 26% return will be realized (circled). A 25% increase in price for the EEV ETF to 121.00 results in a 56.3% return and a 10% decrease in price to 87.12 results in a positive 13.4% return (circled). The return calculations for this buy write trade demonstrate the ability of the buy write strategy to provide excellent profit opportunities during down markets.

Profit Potential for EEV Covered Call Trade

If EEV ETF Increases 25% = 56.3% Return

If EEV ETF Increases 10% = 38.6% Return

If EEV ETF Remains Flat = 26.0% Return

If EEV ETF Decreases 10% = 13.4% Return

$1,633 Stock Loss = $3,553 Covered Call Profit

Let's take a look at an example of how a buy write trade can be profitable even if the underlying stock declines in price. Our brokerage confirmation below shows that we purchased 1,500 shares of Mosaic stock at an average price of 42.0 and sold to open 15 of the Mosaic 40-strike call options at an average price of 7.90 points. We received $11,850 in cash income for this option sale which provides substantial downside protection if Mosaic stock declines in price.

Buy MOS at 42.00, Sell 40-Strike call at 7.90

USD - US DOLLAR

Trades

Trade Date	Settlement Date	Trade Time	Action	Quantity	Symbol	Price
03/17/2009	03/20/2009	12:50:25 pm	Buy	1,000	MOS	42.059900
03/18/2009	03/23/2009	3:30:49 pm	Buy	500	MOS	41.900000
03/17/2009	03/18/2009	1:04:43 pm	Sell to Open	-10	+MOSFH	8.000000
03/18/2009	03/19/2009	3:33:00 pm	Sell to Open	-5	+MOSFH	7.700000

Mosaic stock price declined after we initiated this trade. Below is a snapshot of our Mosaic buy write trade in our online brokerage account. Even though we have a $1,633 loss in Mosaic stock we have a $5,187 gain in the short Mosaic options giving us an overall net profit of $3,553 for this covered call trade.

$3,553 Net Profit Even Though Stock Declined in Price

Positions	Open Orders	Activity	Summary	Trade Journal	Balances	
Type	Sy...	Last	Change	Qty	Avg Price	Profit/Loss
2	MOS	$40.96	$2.75	1500	42.0493	$-1633.95
2	+MOSFH	$4.20	$1.10	-15	7.8582	$5187.30

Covered Call Strategy Incurs
Less Risk than Owning Stock

Bullish Covered Call Trade Example

Bullish covered call trades can be established by purchasing a stock or ETF and selling the related call option. Let's look at an actual trade example of a bullish covered call trade.

Buying PBR Stock at a 29% Discount

Our brokerage confirmation below shows that we purchased 300 shares of Petrobras (PBR) energy at 23.08 and simultaneously sold the PBR January 25-Strike call option for 6.58 points. The sale of the 25-Strike call option at 6.58 points provided substantial downside protection and reduced the cost basis of PBR stock from 23.08 to 16.50 resulting in a 29% discount.

Buy PBR at 23.08, Sell 25-Strike call at 6.58

Daily Account Activity						
Trade Date	Settlement Date	Activity	Quantity	Trade #	Currency	Price
		PURCHASES AND SALES				
PBR: 10/23/2008	10/28/2008	Petroleo Brasileiro Sa Petrobr Sponsored Adr Buy	300.0000	72181748	USD	23.080000
+YMOAE: 10/23/2008	10/24/2008	Petroleo Brasileiro Sa Petrobr Sponsored Adr Jan 2010 25.0 Sell to Open	-3.0000	72182508	USD	6.580000

The Buy Write Analysis that follows displays the profit/loss potential for buying PBR stock at 23.08 and selling the January 25-Strike call for 6.58 points. The Analysis displays the profit potential for this buy write trade assuming various price changes for PBR stock at option expiration.

The Break Even price (circled) is the cost of the buy write trade and is calculated by subtracting the 6.58 points received from the sale of the 25-Strike call option from the 23.08 cost of the stock.

If PBR stock closes above the 16.50 breakeven at option expiration a profit will be realized. If PBR stock closes below the 16.50 breakeven at option expiration a loss will be realized.

The sale of the 25-Strike call option allowed us to buy PBR stock at a 29% discounted price of 16.50.

Wealth Creation Alliance						

Buy Write Analysis

Stock Symbol	Current Stock Price	Call Strike	Call Price
PBR	23.08	25	6.58

Break Even
16.50

[Calculate] [New Analysis] [Print]

% Change	15.0%	10.0%	5.0%	0.0%	-5.0%	-10.0%	-15.0%
Stock Price	$26.54	$25.39	$24.23	$23.08	$21.93	$20.77	$19.62
Stock Prof/Loss	$346.20	$230.80	$115.40	$0.00	$-115.40	$-230.80	$-346.20
Call Value	$1.54	$0.39	$0.00	$0.00	$0.00	$0.00	$0.00
Call Profit/Loss	$503.80	$619.20	$658.00	$658.00	$658.00	$658.00	$658.00
Net Profit/Loss	$850.00	$850.00	$773.40	$658.00	$542.60	$427.20	$311.80
% Return	51.5%	51.5%	46.9%	39.9%	32.9%	25.9%	18.9%

The first row of the table is labeled '% Change' and assumes various percent changes in PBR stock at option expiration from a 15% increase to a 15% decrease in price. The second row is labeled 'Stock Price' and is the PBR stock price that corresponds to the percentage change listed on the row above.

The 'Stock Prof/Loss' row displays the dollar profit/loss for PBR stock assuming various price changes for PBR stock at option expiration. The 'Call Value' row displays the value of the short 25-Strike call option and the 'Call Profit/Loss' displays the profit/loss for the short call assuming various changes of PBR stock at option expiration.

The 'Net Profit/Loss' row lists the net dollar profit for the trade and is calculated by adding the Stock Profit/Loss to the Call Profit/Loss. The '% Return' displays the % profit or loss and is calculated by dividing the Net Profit/Loss by the cost or Break Even.

The Analysis below reveals that if PBR stock increases 10% to 25.39 at option expiration a 51.5% return would be realized (circled). If PBR stock price remains flat at 23.08 a 39.9% return will be realized (circled) and a 15% decrease in PBR stock to 19.62 results in an 18.9% return.

Let's think about this for a minute. There are not many investments that will produce a 39.9% return if the stock is flat or an 18.9% return if the stock declines 15% in price.

Wealth Creation Alliance

Buy Write Analysis

Stock Symbol	Current Stock Price	Call Strike	Call Price
PBR	23.08	25	6.58

Break Even					Calculate	New Analysis	Print
16.50							

% Change	15.0%	10.0%	5.0%	0.0%	-5.0%	-10.0%	-15.0%
Stock Price	$26.54	$25.39	$24.23	$23.08	$21.93	$20.77	$19.62
Stock Prof/Loss	$346.20	$230.80	$115.40	$0.00	$-115.40	$-230.80	$-346.20
Call Value	$1.54	$0.39	$0.00	$0.00	$0.00	$0.00	$0.00
Call Profit/Loss	$503.80	$619.20	$658.00	$658.00	$658.00	$658.00	$658.00
Net Profit/Loss	$850.00	$850.00	$773.40	$658.00	$542.60	$427.20	$311.80
% Return	51.5%	51.5%	46.9%	39.9%	32.9%	25.9%	18.9%

At option expiration there are two possible outcomes for a buy write trade:

1) The stock closes above the strike price of the short call option

2) The stock closes at or below the strike price of the short call option

If the underlying stock closes above the strike price of the short call option then the stock will be 'called'. The shares in your account will be sold at the strike price of the call option. This transaction is handled automatically by your broker on the Saturday following option expiration.

Prior to option expiration you can always close out the expiring call option and sell to open a new call option with expiration further out in time. This will prevent your stock from being called.

If the underlying stock closes at or below the strike price of the short call then the call option expires worthless and your stock remains in your account allowing you to write another buy write trade.

This Buy Write Analysis reveals:

- The sale of the call option allowed us to purchase PBR stock at a substantial 29% discount

- The call option sold profits if the price of PBR stock decreases in price and from the time decay of the short option

- Buy write trades normally profit if the price of the underlying stock increases, remains flat or decreases depending on the strike price

- Buy writes can provide substantial downside protection if the underlying stock declines in price

- A small increase in stock price can result in large buy write profit

- A flat stock price can result in a large buy write profit

- Profit potential is limited

Profit Potential for PBR Covered Call Trade

If PBR Stock Increases 10% = 51.5% Return

If PBR Stock Increases 5% = 46.9% Return

If PBR Stock Remains Flat = 39.9% Return

If PBR Stock Decreases 15% = 18.9% Return

Note: Covered call trades can be closed out any time prior to option expiration. We normally will close out a covered call trade and take profits if the covered call reaches about 90% of its maximum profit potential. Covered calls can be closed prior to expiration by 'buying to close' the short call and selling the stock.

Covered call trades can also be rolled over by 'buying to close' the expiring call and 'selling to open' a call with a later expiration. Rolling over a covered call trade allows you to keep your stock and collect another option premium. We normally roll over our covered call trades and keep our stock in our brokerage account.

In the next chapter, we will look at trading covered calls using weekly options which is even more profitable than using monthly options as you get to sell 52 option premiums over the course of a year.

Selling Option Premium to Pay For Put Option Insurance

Establishing covered calls and the resulting cash income received for selling call option premium can help pay for put option insurance discussed in Chapter 3.

In Chapter 3 we discussed a current married put trade that we have in our Married Put Portfolio. We purchased AMZN stock for 449.01 points and the AMZN 515-Strike put option for 53.13 points. This put option expires in six months. The total cost for this married put was 502.14 points.

Total Cost = 502.14 Points

Buy AMZN stock at	449.01
Buy AMZN 515-Strike put at	53.13
Total Cost	502.14 points

The AMZN 515-Strike put option gives us the right but not the obligation to sell our AMZN stock at 515 points at any time prior to January option expiration. This results in a minimum value for this stock/put option spread of 515 points.

With a minimum value of 515 and a cost of 502.14 we are guaranteed a profit of 12.86 points for our spread regardless of the price movement of AMZN stock.

Guaranteed Profit = 12.86 Points

Minimum value of stock/option spread	515.00
Cost of spread	- 502.14
Guaranteed Profit	12.86 points

We then established a covered call trade by selling AMZN call options. These call options were 'covered' by the shares of AMZN stock we owned in our trading account. Our brokerage account Gain/Loss Report below shows that we sold the AMZN 550-Strike call at 12.65 points on September 18th. Twelve days later we closed out the calls at 2.00 points. This resulted in a 10.65 point profit for the call option trade (sell call at 12.65 and buy to close at 2.00 points = 10.65 point profit).

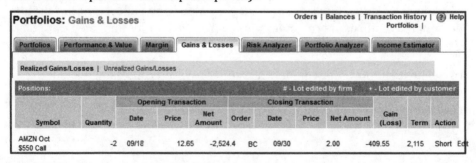

Portfolios: Gains & Losses   Orders | Balances | Transaction History | (?) Help
                                                                    Portfolios |

| Portfolios | Performance & Value | Margin | Gains & Losses | Risk Analyzer | Portfolio Analyzer | Income Estimator |

Realized Gains/Losses | Unrealized Gains/Losses

Positions: # - Lot edited by firm   + - Lot edited by customer

Symbol	Quantity	Opening Transaction			Closing Transaction				Gain (Loss)	Term	Action
		Date	Price	Net Amount	Order	Date	Price	Net Amount			
AMZN Oct $550 Call	-2	09/18	12.65	-2,524.4	BC	09/30	2.00		-409.55	2,115	Short Edit

Closing the 550-Strike call allowed us to keep our AMZN stock and sell another call option. The 10.65 point call option profit helped pay for the cost of the put option insurance and further reduced the cost of our married put trade. The cost basis for our married put trade was reduced to 491.49 points.

New Cost Basis = 491.49 Points

Cost of married put trade	502.14
Minus 10.65 point profit for call	- 10.65
New Cost Basis	491.49 points

The 10.65 point profit for the call option sale increased our guaranteed profit for the married put from 12.86 points to 23.51 points. The six month 515-Strike put option protection gives us the opportunity to sell six monthly call option premiums further reducing the cost basis and increasing the guaranteed profit for our married put.

In the next chapter, we will explore trading covered calls using weekly options.

CHAPTER 5
I'm Retired But I Still Collect a Weekly Paycheck

Our next strategy is the *weekly paycheck* program which generates cash income from selling weekly call options. We have been very active selling option premium with weekly covered calls. Today we collected $11,836 in cash income sitting on the beach in Hanalei Kauai.

Weekly options started trading in 2010. Weeklys start trading on Thursday and expire the following Friday giving weekly options a six trading day life. Weekly covered calls are initiated by buying 100 shares of stock and selling 1 weekly call option.

As noted previously, when you sell an option, cash equal to the option premium sold is immediately credited to your brokerage account. For example, if you sell a weekly option with a 1.5 point premium, $150 in cash is credited to your brokerage account. This cash credit reduces the cost basis of the stock and reduces the overall risk of the trade.

As we will discover later in this chapter, weekly options can provide up to 6 times more premium compared to monthly options over the same period of time. These rich premiums make selling weekly option premium a very lucrative strategy that can deliver a 100% 'cash on cash' return over the course of a year.

Let's look at a weekly covered call trade we took so that you can understand this important concept. We own 1,800 shares of the small cap ETF symbol TNA. We have been selling weekly covered calls against our shares of the TNA ETF.

We like to rollover the expiring option and sell to open the new option each week which allows us to keep our TNA shares. We use option spread orders to rollover options to save on transaction costs.

Our brokerage account option spread order below shows that we closed out 18 of the May 25 weekly calls and sold to open 18 of the TNA Jun 1st 49-Strike calls. The TNA ETF was trading at 48.43.

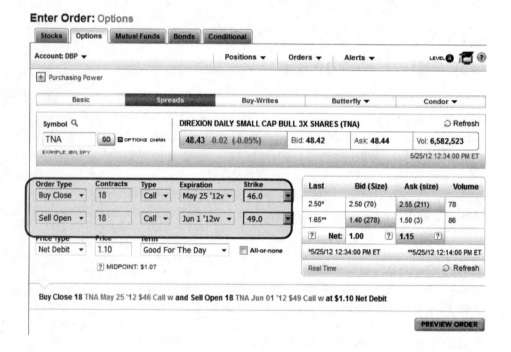

Enter Order: Options

| Stocks | Options | Mutual Funds | Bonds | Conditional |

Account: DBP ▼   Positions ▼   Orders ▼   Alerts ▼   LEVEL ❹

+ Purchasing Power

| Basic | Spreads | Buy-Writes | Butterfly ▼ | Condor ▼ |

Symbol 🔍   DIREXION DAILY SMALL CAP BULL 3X SHARES (TNA)   ↻ Refresh

| TNA | **GO** | ▣ OPTIONS CHAIN | **48.43** -0.02 (-0.05%) | Bid: 48.42 | Ask: 48.44 | Vol: 6,582,523 |

EXAMPLE: IBM, SPY   5/25/12 12:34:00 PM ET

Order Type	Contracts	Type	Expiration	Strike		Last	Bid (Size)	Ask (size)	Volume
Buy Close ▼	18	Call ▼	May 25 '12v ▼	46.0 ▼		2.50*	2.50 (70)	2.55 (211)	78
Sell Open ▼	18	Call ▼	Jun 1 '12w ▼	49.0 ▼		1.65**	1.40 (278)	1.50 (3)	86

Price Type	Price	Term			? Net: 1.00 ? 1.15 ?
Net Debit ▼	1.10	Good For The Day ▼	☐ All-or-none		*5/25/12 12:34:00 PM ET **5/25/12 12:14:00 PM ET

? MIDPOINT: $1.07   Real Time   ↻ Refresh

Buy Close 18 TNA May 25 '12 $46 Call w **and Sell Open 18** TNA Jun 01 '12 $49 Call w **at $1.10 Net Debit**

PREVIEW ORDER

Our brokerage account confirmation below shows that we were filled on this order and sold the 18 TNA Jun 01 49-Strike weekly calls at 1.47 points. After the commission, $2,628.31 in cash was credited to our brokerage account for the sale of the 18 options.

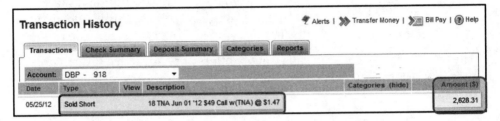

162% 'Cash on Cash' Return

Purchasing 100 shares of the TNA ETF at the current price of 48.43 and selling the 49-Strike call at 1.47 would cost $4,696 to initiate this covered call trade (48.43-1.47 = 46.96 x 100 = $4,696 cost basis).

If you were to rollover this trade weekly and receive a similar premium you have the potential to collect $7,644 in cash over the next year. Receiving $7,644 in cash over the next year would result in a 162% 'cash on cash' return ($7,644 cash income / by original $4,696 investment cost = 162%).

If you receive a 162% cash on cash return a lot can go wrong and you could still profit from the trade. The underlying stock/ETF could decline substantially and you could still profit. If you had bad timing on entering the trade you could still profit. And there could be volatile price swings in the underlying stock/ETF and you could still profit.

This gives the weekly covered call strategy a huge advantage over stock trades that require the stock to increase in price to profit. Also, many times directional trades can get 'stopped' out during volatile price swings if you employ a portfolio risk management system.

162% Cash on Cash Return Can Profit . . .

- If you have bad timing when entering a trade

- During volatile price swings

- Even if the underlying stock/ETF price declines substantially

162% Return Potential Increases When We Rollover Options

We normally rollover our weekly options using an option spread order similar to the spread order just displayed for the TNA ETF. If you receive a cash income of $147 each week and a total income of $7,644 over the course of a year, this income will allow you to purchase additional shares of the TNA ETF and make additional covered call trades. This would allow you to compound your returns and increase the 162% cash on cash return.

The weekly option covered call strategy offers very attractive returns and very low risk making this one of the best overall strategies for the average investor.

Selling Weekly Option Premium

Our brokerage account Transaction History below shows profits from selling weekly option premium. We sold $16,053.53 in option premium over a one week period. The right hand column of the report shows the amount of cash that was credited to our account for each option sale. These covered call trades were in our retirement accounts.

$16,053.53 Weekly Paycheck

Transaction History

Transactions	Check Summary	Deposit Summary	Categories	Reports

Date	Type	Description	Amount ($)
04/13/12	Sold Short	10 HD Apr 21 '12 $50 Call(HD) @ $1.00	984.38
04/12/12	Sold Short	10 SSO Apr 21 '12 $57 Call(SSO) @ $0.70	684.41
04/12/12	Sold Short	1 MA Apr 21 '12 $435 Call(MA) @ $5.10	501.23
04/12/12	Sold Short	2 AAPL Apr 21 '12 $630 Call(AAPL) @ $9.00	1,790.44
04/12/12	Sold Short	1 PCLN Apr 21 '12 $740 Call(PCLN) @ $14.40	1,431.21
04/12/12	Sold Short	8 QQQ Apr 21 '12 $67 Call(QQQ) @ $0.70	545.93
04/12/12	Sold Short	15 WFC Apr 21 '12 $34 Call(WFC) @ $0.61	899.56
04/12/12	Sold Short	1 CMG Apr 21 '12 $435 Call(CMG) @ $8.37	832.23
04/12/12	Sold Short	12 JPM Apr 21 '12 $45 Call(JPM) @ $0.75	886.88
04/12/12	Sold Short	8 AIG Apr 21 '12 $34 Call(AIG) @ $0.45	345.94
04/12/12	Sold Short	8 AIG Apr 21 '12 $33 Call(AIG) @ $0.72	561.93
04/11/12	Sold Short	1 ISRG Apr 21 '12 $550 Call(ISRG) @ $12.43	1,234.22
04/12/12	Sold Short	1 MA Apr 21 '12 $435 Call(MA) @ $4.90	481.23
04/12/12	Sold Short	1 AAPL Apr 21 '12 $630 Call(AAPL) @ $9.00	891.22
04/12/12	Sold Short	1 PCLN Apr 21 '12 $740 Call(PCLN) @ $14.38	1,433.21
04/12/12	Sold Short	4 QQQ Apr 21 '12 $67 Call(QQQ) @ $0.71	272.97
04/12/12	Sold Short	8 WFC Apr 21 '12 $34 Call(WFC) @ $0.55	429.94
04/12/12	Sold Short	1 CMG Apr 21 '12 $435 Call(CMG) @ $9.56	951.22
04/12/12	Sold Short	6 JPM Apr 21 '12 $45 Call(JPM) @ $0.77	453.44
04/12/12	Sold Short	4 AIG Apr 21 '12 $34 Call(AIG) @ $0.44	164.97
04/12/12	Sold Short	4 AIG Apr 21 '12 $33 Call(AIG) @ $0.72	276.97

And the brokerage account Transaction History below shows that we have been increasing our weekly covered call trades. We sold $28,454.92 in weekly option premium over this one week period. The right hand column of the report shows the amount of cash that was credited to our account for each option sale. These covered call trades were in our retirement accounts.

$28,454.92 Weekly Paycheck

Transaction History: Reports   🔔 Alerts | ≫ Transfer Money | ≫ Bill Pay | ⑦ Help

Transactions	Check Summary	Deposit Summary	Categories	Reports

Type	Date	Category	Subcategory	Description	Amount
Sold Short					
	05/16/12	Unassigned		1 MA May 19 '12 $410 Call(MA) MASTERCARD INC CL A SHORT...	$482.23
	05/16/12	Unassigned		2 AAPL May 19 '12 $550 Call(AAPL) APPLE INC COM SHORT...	$1,172.46
	05/16/12	Unassigned		50 USO May 19 '12 $35 Call(USO) UNITED STATES OIL FUND,...	$2,304.05
	05/16/12	Unassigned		38 EEM May 19 '12 $38 Call(EEM) ISHARES MSCI EMERGING M...	$1,977.16
	05/16/12	Unassigned		51 FXI May 19 '12 $34 Call(FXI) ISHARES FTSE CHINA 25 I...	$2,299.29
	05/16/12	Unassigned		18 EWZ May 19 '12 $53 Call(EWZ) ISHARES MSCI BRAZIL IND...	$1,130.28
	05/16/12	Unassigned		13 HD May 19 '12 $49 Call(HD) HOME DEPOT INC COM SHORT...	$502.14
	05/15/12	Unassigned		18 XLE May 19 '12 $66 Call(XLE) ENERGY SELECT SECTOR SP...	$878.34
	05/15/12	Unassigned		10 EFA May 19 '12 $50 Call(EFA) ISHARES MSCI EAFE INDEX...	$524.37
	05/15/12	Unassigned		23 FXI May 19 '12 $35 Call(FXI) ISHARES FTSE CHINA 25 I...	$802.56
	05/15/12	Unassigned		15 EWZ May 19 '12 $54 Call(EWZ) ISHARES MSCI BRAZIL IND...	$1,090.61
	05/14/12	Unassigned		14 EFA May 19 '12 $50 Call(EFA) ISHARES MSCI EAFE INDEX...	$1,105.31
	05/14/12	Unassigned		21 FXI May 19 '12 $35 Call(FXI) ISHARES FTSE CHINA 25 I...	$757.07
	05/14/12	Unassigned		21 EWZ May 19 '12 $55 Call(EWZ) ISHARES MSCI BRAZIL IND...	$1,261.06
	05/11/12	Unassigned		15 WFC May 19 '12 $33 Call(WFC) WELLS FARGO & CO NEW CO...	$944.61
	05/11/12	Unassigned		2 AAPL May 19 '12 $570 Call(AAPL) APPLE INC COM SHORT...	$1,330.46
	05/11/12	Unassigned		12 USO May 19 '12 $36 Call(USO) UNITED STATES OIL FUND,...	$798.89
	05/11/12	Unassigned		9 EFA May 19 '12 $51 Call(EFA) ISHARES MSCI EAFE INDEX ...	$759.15
	05/11/12	Unassigned		12 FXI May 19 '12 $35 Call(FXI) ISHARES FTSE CHINA 25 I...	$882.88
	05/11/12	Unassigned		8 EWZ May 19 '12 $57 Call(EWZ) ISHARES MSCI BRAZIL INDE...	$561.89
	05/10/12	Unassigned		1 MA May 19 '12 $425 Call(MA) MASTERCARD INC CL A SHORT...	$801.23
	05/10/12	Unassigned		20 USO May 19 '12 $37 Call(USO) UNITED STATES OIL FUND,...	$796.83
	05/10/12	Unassigned		13 HD May 19 '12 $50 Call(HD) HOME DEPOT INC COM SHORT...	$1,607.10
	05/10/12	Unassigned		14 EFA May 19 '12 $52 Call(EFA) ISHARES MSCI EAFE INDEX...	$751.36
	05/10/12	Unassigned		21 FXI May 19 '12 $36 Call(FXI) ISHARES FTSE CHINA 25 I...	$900.06
	05/10/12	Unassigned		13 EWZ May 19 '12 $57 Call(EWZ) ISHARES MSCI BRAZIL IND...	$1,347.12
	05/10/12	Unassigned		1 CMG May 19 '12 $410 Call(CMG) CHIPOTLE MEXICAN GRILL ...	$496.23
	05/10/12	Unassigned		9 WMB May 19 '12 $33 Call(WMB) WILLIAMS COS INC DEL COM...	$390.18
				Total Sold Short	**$28,454.92**

Double Dipping

When trading covered calls, if the underlying stock/ETF declines in price we like to close the short call if the value of the short call declines 75% to 85% from the sale price. For example, if we sell a weekly call option at 1.00 points we will enter a GTC (Good Until Cancelled) limit order to buy to close the call at .25 or .15. If the call declines to .25 or .15 it will be closed out. We can then sell another call option and collect two premiums in one week.

The first brokerage account Transaction History Report below shows short calls that we closed out when the value of the call declined 75% to 85% from the sale price. The second brokerage account Transaction History Report shows additional calls we sold that allowed us to collect an additional $6,618.22 in premium within a one week period.

Bought Back Short Calls

Transaction History   Alerts | Transfer Money | Bill Pay | Help

Date	Type	View	Description	Categories (hide)	Amount ($)
04/16/12	Bought To Cover		2 AAPL Apr 21 '12 $630 Call(AAPL) @ $0.76		-161.51
04/16/12	Bought To Cover		1 PCLN Apr 21 '12 $740 Call(PCLN) @ $2.90		-298.75
04/16/12	Bought To Cover		8 QQQ Apr 21 '12 $67 Call(QQQ) @ $0.12		-110.05
04/16/12	Bought To Cover		1 AAPL Apr 21 '12 $630 Call(AAPL) @ $0.78		-86.75
04/16/12	Bought To Cover		1 PCLN Apr 21 '12 $740 Call(PCLN) @ $3.30		-338.75
04/16/12	Bought To Cover		4 QQQ Apr 21 '12 $67 Call(QQQ) @ $0.12		-59.03

And Sold an Additional $6,618.22 in Premium

Transaction History   Alerts | Transfer Money | Bill Pay | Help

Date	Type	View	Description	Categories (hide)	Amount ($)
04/17/12	Sold Short		1 PCLN Apr 21 '12 $720 Call(PCLN) @ $9.60		951.22
04/17/12	Sold Short		2 AAPL Apr 21 '12 $600 Call(AAPL) @ $10.00		1,990.44
04/17/12	Sold Short		8 QQQ Apr 21 '12 $66 Call(QQQ) @ $0.60		465.93
04/17/12	Sold Short		1 PCLN Apr 21 '12 $720 Call(PCLN) @ $10.00		991.22
04/17/12	Sold Short		2 AAPL Apr 21 '12 $600 Call(AAPL) @ $10.00		1,990.44
04/17/12	Sold Short		4 QQQ Apr 21 '12 $66 Call(QQQ) @ $0.60		228.97

Covered Call Trade Examples

The weekly covered call trade examples that follow include our brokerage confirmations that show the purchase price of the stock and the strike price and option premium for the call option sold. The Covered Call Calculator shows the annualized profit potential for the covered call trade.

Buy ISRG at 541.225, Sell Apr 21 550 call @ 12.43

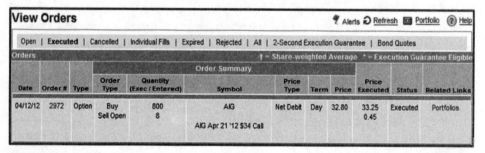

Stock	Entry Date	Option Expiration	Stock Price	Call Strike	Call Price	Cost	Net Profit Potential	Percent Return	Annualized Return
ISRG	4/11/2012	4/21/2012	541.22	550.0	12.43	528.79	$2,121	4.0%	146.4%

Buy AIG at 33.25, Sell Apr 21 34 call @ .45

Stock	Entry Date	Option Expiration	Stock Price	Call Strike	Call Price	Cost	Net Profit Potential	Percent Return	Annualized Return
AIG	4/12/2012	4/21/2012	33.25	34.0	0.45	32.80	$120	3.7%	148.4%

Rolling Over Expiring Options

We like to rollover our weekly covered call trades using option spread orders. Option spread orders help reduce commission costs and can help you to save on the 'bid/ask' spread costs associated with buying and selling options if you use a limit spread order that is mid-way between the bid/ask prices. We normally can get filled on spread orders at a limit price that is mid-way between the bid/ask prices.

Examples of option spread orders used to rollover our expiring weekly covered call trades follow.

Spread Orders Used to Rollover Weekly Covered Calls - Example 1

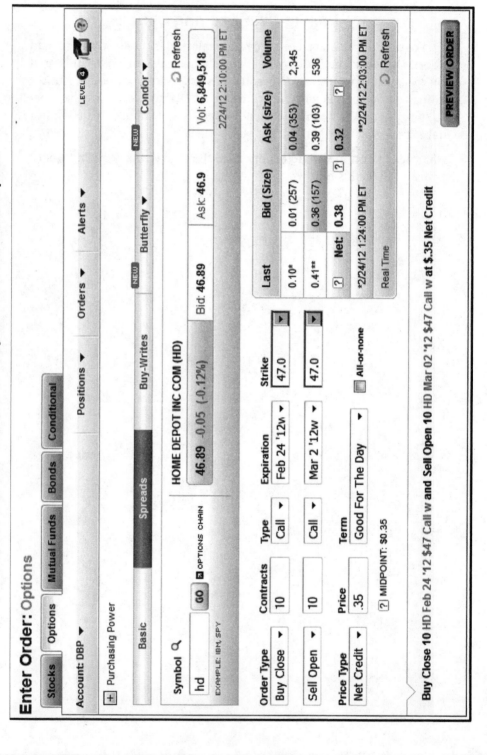

Spread Orders Used to Rollover Weekly Covered Calls - Example 2

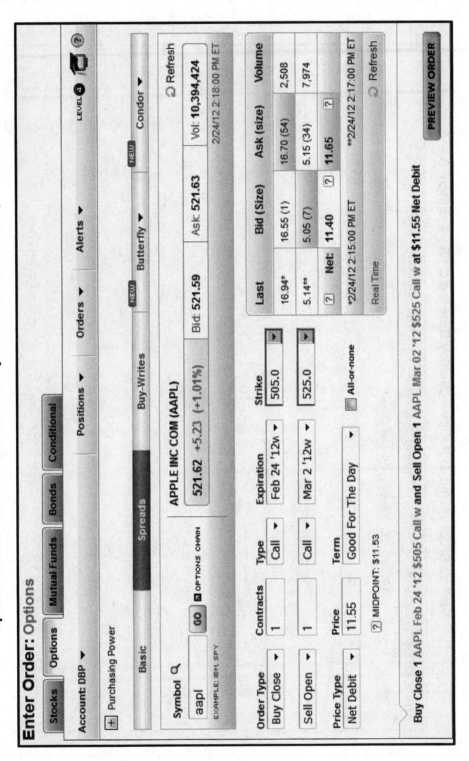

Enter Order: Options

Stocks | Options | Mutual Funds | Bonds | Conditional

Account: DBP ▼ | Positions ▼ | Orders ▼ | Alerts ▼ | LEVEL ❹ 🖥 ⑦

⊞ Purchasing Power

Basic | Spreads | Buy-Writes | [NEW] Butterfly ▼ | [NEW] Condor ▼

Symbol 🔍

aapl GO 🅰 OPTIONS CHAIN

EXAMPLE: IBM,SPY

APPLE INC COM (AAPL)

521.62 +5.23 (+1.01%)   Bid: 521.59   Ask: 521.63   Vol: **10,394,424**

🔄 Refresh   2/24/12 2:18:00 PM ET

	Last	Bid (Size)	Ask (size)	Volume
	16.94*	16.55 (1)	16.70 (54)	2,508
	5.14**	5.05 (7)	5.15 (34)	7,974
⑦ Net:	**11.40**	⑦ 11.40	11.65 ⑦	

*2/24/12 2:15:00 PM ET   **2/24/12 2:17:00 PM ET

Real Time   🔄 Refresh

Order Type	Contracts	Type	Expiration	Strike
Buy Close ▶	1	Call ▶	Feb 24 '12w ▶	505.0 ▶
Sell Open ▶	1	Call ▶	Mar 2 '12w ▶	525.0 ▶

Price Type   **Price**   **Term**

Net Debit ▶   11.55   Good For The Day ▶   ☐ All-or-none

⑦ MIDPOINT: $11.53

PREVIEW ORDER

Buy Close 1 AAPL Feb 24 '12 $505 Call w and Sell Open 1 AAPL Mar 02 '12 $525 Call w at **$11.55 Net Debit**

Spread Orders Used to Rollover Weekly Covered Calls - Example 3

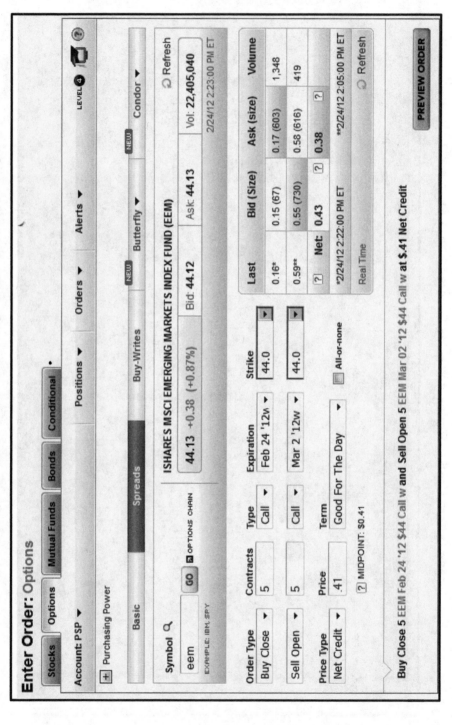

Enter Order: Options

Stocks | Options | Mutual Funds | Bonds | Conditional

Account PSP ▼ Positions ▼ Orders ▼ NEW Alerts ▼ LEVEL ④ 🖥️❓

+ Purchasing Power

Basic | Spreads | Buy-Writes | Butterfly ▼ NEW | Condor ▼

Symbol Q ISHARES MSCI EMERGING MARKETS INDEX FUND (EEM) 🔄 Refresh

eem GO 🔲 OPTIONS CHAIN
EXAMPLE: IBM, SPY

44.13 +0.38 (+0.87%) | Bid: 44.12 | Ask: 44.13 | Vol: 22,405,040
2/24/12 2:23:00 PM ET

		Last	Bid (Size)	Ask (size)	Volume
	Strike	0.16*	0.15 (67)	0.17 (603)	1,348
	44.0 ▶	0.59**	0.55 (730)	0.58 (616)	419
	44.0 ▶	❓ Net: 0.43	❓	❓ 0.38	❓
	☐ All-or-none	*2/24/12 2:22:00 PM ET		**2/24/12 2:05:00 PM ET	
		Real Time		🔄 Refresh	

Order Type	Contracts	Type	Expiration
Buy Close ▶	5	Call ▶	Feb 24 '12w ▶
Sell Open ▶	5	Call ▶	Mar 2 '12w ▶

Price Type	Price	Term
Net Credit ▶	.41	Good For The Day ▶

❓ MIDPOINT: $0.41

PREVIEW ORDER

Buy Close 5 EEM Feb 24 '12 $44 Call w and Sell Open 5 EEM Mar 02 '12 $44 Call w at $.41 Net Credit

Weekly Options Provide Up to Six Times More Premium Than Monthly Options

The option chain below displays option prices for the Mastercard May 04 weekly options and the MA July monthly options. Mastercard stock is trading at 457.58 and the at-the-money 460-Strike weekly call is trading at 11.90. The July 460-Strike monthly option is trading at 23.50 and expires in about 12 weeks.

Selling 12 of the MA weekly calls at 11.90 can provide up to 142 points ($14,280) of premium versus the 23.50 points of premium available for the July option over the same period of time. This demonstrates the substantial additional premium available from selling weekly options versus monthly options.

12 Weeklys Provide 142.8 Points of Premium versus 23.5 Points of Premium for Monthly

MASTERCARD INC CL A | S&P Capital IQ Options Report What's

Symbol	Bid	Ask	Last	Change	Change %	B/A Size	High
MA	458.00	458.10	457.58	3.60	0.79	700X100	462.3399

Calls and Puts | Learn more

MA Apr 27 2012 — -1 Days to Expiration (Weeklys)

MA May 4 2012 — 4 Days to Expiration (Weeklys)

Calls	Bid	Ask	Last	Change	Vol	Op Int	Strike
445.0 Call	19.75	21.50	20.50	1.99	0	88	445.00
450.0 Call	17.25	18.30	17.96	2.36	0	198	450.00
455.0 Call	14.15	15.50	15.09	2.13	0	143	455.00
460.0 Call	11.90	12.75	12.00	1.38	0	130	460.00
465.0 Call	9.65	10.65	10.15	1.58	0	82	465.00
470.0 Call	7.95	8.80	8.63	1.83	0	107	470.00

Color Indicates options that are in-the-money Indicates non-standard option

MA May 19 2012 — 19 Days to Expiration

MA Jun 16 2012 — 47 Days to Expiration

MA Jul 21 2012 — 82 Days to Expiration

Calls	Bid	Ask	Last	Change	Vol	Op Int	Strike
445.0 Call	31.75	32.30	30.40	1.03	0	126	445.00
450.0 Call	28.85	29.40	29.65	3.05	0	364	450.00
455.0 Call	26.15	26.55	26.60	2.76	0	361	455.00
460.0 Call	23.50	23.90	24.06	2.83	0	339	460.00
465.0 Call	21.05	21.55	22.03	2.97	0	282	465.00

Below is another example of the substantial option premium available from selling weekly options. The option chain below displays option prices for the AIG May 04 weekly options and the AIG Aug monthly options. AIG stock is trading at 34.46 and the 35-Strike weekly call is trading at .71. The Aug 35-Strike monthly option is trading at 2.39 and expires in about 16 weeks.

If you sold 16 weekly calls at .71 you would collect about 11.36 points of premium versus the 2.39 points of premium available for the Aug option over the same period of time. This again demonstrates the additional premium available from selling weekly options versus monthly options.

16 Weeklys Provide 11.36 Points of Premium versus 2.39 Points of Premium for Monthly

AMERICAN INTL GROUP INC COM NEW | S&P Capital IQ Options

Symbol	Bid	Ask	Last	Change	Change %	B/A Size	High	Low
AIG	34.48	34.50	34.46	0.75	2.18	100X1500	34.91	33.41

Calls and Puts | Learn more

AIG Apr 27 2012 — -1 Days to Expiration (Weeklys)

AIG May 4 2012 — 4 Days to Expiration (Weeklys)

Calls	Bid	Ask	Last	Change	Vol	Op Int	Strike
32.0 Call	2.53	2.77	2.83	0.80	0	101	32.00
33.0 Call	1.81	1.85	1.85	0.51	0	997	33.00
34.0 Call	1.17	1.22	1.25	0.42	0	842	34.00
35.0 Call	0.71	0.72	0.74	0.27	0	1,686	35.00
36.0 Call	0.39	0.43	0.40	0.15	0	233	36.00
37.0 Call	0.20	0.23	0.21	0.08	0	29	37.00

Color Indicates options that are in-the-money [NS] Indicates non-standard option

AIG May 19 2012 — 19 Days to Expiration

AIG Jun 16 2012 — 47 Days to Expiration

AIG Aug 18 2012 — 110 Days to Expiration

Calls	Bid	Ask	Last	Change	Vol	Op Int	Strike
32.0 Call	4.05	4.20	4.16	0.56	0	12,755	32.00
33.0 Call	3.45	3.55	3.50	0.47	0	6,762	33.00
34.0 Call	2.89	2.95	2.93	0.42	0	2,873	34.00
35.0 Call	2.39	2.45	2.54	0.48	0	43,121	35.00
36.0 Call	1.95	2.00	2.03	0.37	0	5,646	36.00

Overall Goal of Income Strategy

The overall goal of the income strategy is to:

- Profit regardless of market direction

- Produce consistent returns with the sale of option premium

- Generate a 100% 'cash on cash' return through the sale of weekly option premium

- Increase the profit potential of an existing stock or option trade

- Provide downside protection and reduce the risk for a stock

- Help you maintain a stock position during volatile markets and wide price swings and avoid being 'stopped out' of your position

Real Time Covered Call Results $332,597.96 in Profits and 36.9% Average Return

Copies of our two brokerage account Profit/Loss statements that follow show we have $332,597.96 in profits and an average return of 36.9%. Most of the trades in these two portfolios are weekly covered calls. Both of these accounts are retirement accounts.

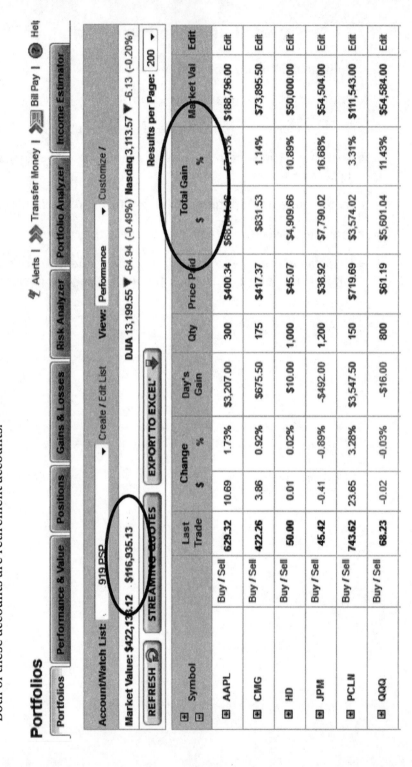

Portfolios

Alerts | Transfer Money | Bill Pay | ? Help

| Portfolios | Performance & Value | Positions | Gains & Losses | Risk Analyzer | Portfolio Analyzer | Income Estimator |

Account/Watch List: 919 PSP ▼ Create / Edit List   **View:** Performance ▼ Customize /

Market Value: $422,138.12 · $116,935.13

DJIA 13,199.55 ▼ -64.94 (-0.49%) **Nasdaq** 3,113.57 ▼ -6.13 (-0.20%)

REFRESH | STREAMING QUOTES   EXPORT TO EXCEL ►

Results per Page: 200 ▼

Symbol	Buy / Sell	Last Trade	Change $	Change %	Day's Gain	Qty	Price Paid	Total Gain $	Total Gain %	Market Val	Edit
AAPL	Buy / Sell	629.32	10.69	1.73%	$3,207.00	300	$400.34	$68,...	...%	$188,796.00	Edit
CMG	Buy / Sell	422.26	3.86	0.92%	$675.50	175	$417.37	$831.53	1.14%	$73,895.50	Edit
HD	Buy / Sell	50.00	0.01	0.02%	$10.00	1,000	$45.07	$4,909.66	10.89%	$50,000.00	Edit
JPM	Buy / Sell	45.42	-0.41	-0.89%	-$492.00	1,200	$38.92	$7,790.02	16.68%	$54,504.00	Edit
PCLN	Buy / Sell	743.62	23.65	3.28%	$3,547.50	150	$719.69	$3,574.02	3.31%	$111,543.00	Edit
QQQ	Buy / Sell	68.23	-0.02	-0.03%	-$16.00	800	$61.19	$5,601.04	11.43%	$54,584.00	Edit

Symbol	Buy / Sell	Last Trade	Change $	Change %	Day's Gain	Qty	Price Paid	Total Gain $	Total Gain %	Market Val	Edit
SSO	Buy / Sell	58.80	-0.41	-0.69%	-$410.00	1,000	$54.94	$3,844.02	6.99%	$58,800.00	Edit
TJX	Buy / Sell	39.61	-0.26	-0.65%	-$624.00	2,400	$31.28	$19,964.05	26.58%	$95,064.00	Edit
WFC	Buy / Sell	34.48	-0.03	-0.09%	-$48.00	1,600	$31.43	$4,864.02	9.67%	$55,168.00	Edit
AAPL Apr 05 '12 $615 Call w	Trade	15.45	7.05	83.93%	-$705.00	-1	$6.10	-$939.77	-152.87%	-$1,545.00	Edit
CMG Apr 05 '12 $420 Call w	Trade	4.00	1.50	60.00%	-$150.00	-1	$3.10	-$94.76	-30.10%	-$400.00	Edit
HD Apr 05 '12 $50 Call w	Trade	0.22	-0.08	-26.67%	$40.00	-5	$0.31	$37.20	22.85%	-$110.00	Edit
JPM Apr 05 '12 $46 Call w	Trade	0.16	-0.14	-46.67%	$84.00	-6	$0.32	$87.44	43.60%	-$96.00	Edit
PCLN Apr 05 '12 $715 Call w	Trade	28.90	18.90	189.00%	-$1,890.00	-1	$12.04	-$1,690.77	-139.88%	-$2,890.00	Edit
QQQ Apr 05 '12 $68 Call w	Trade	0.50	0.02	4.17%	-$4.00	-4	$0.30	-$83.04	-65.36%	-$196.00	Edit
SSO Apr 05 '12 $58 Call w	Trade	0.95	-0.39	-29.10%	$205.00	-5	$0.53	-$217.80	-79.84%	-$475.00	Edit
WFC Apr 05 '12 $34 Call w	Trade	0.55	-0.06	-9.84%	$48.00	-8	$0.33	-$186.09	-67.89%	-$440.00	Edit
Totals					$3,478.00			$116,935.13		$422,133.12	

Portfolios | Performance & Value | Positions | Gains & Losses | Risk Analyzer | Portfolio Analyzer | Income Estimator

Account/Watch List: 918 DBP ▸ Create / Edit List   View: Performance ▸ Customize /

Market Value: $820,939.__ | $215,662.83   DJIA 13,199.55 ▼ -64.94 (-0.49%) Nasdaq 3,113.57 ▼ -6.13 (-0.20%)

REFRESH | STREAMING QUOTES | EXPORT TO EXCEL*   Results per Page: 200 ▸

Symbol		Last Trade	Change $	Change %	Day's Gain	Qty	Price Paid	Total Gain $	Total Gain %	Market Val	Edit
⊞ AAPL	Buy / Sell	629.32	10.69	1.73%	$4,276.00	400	$400.36	$91,527.17	57.13%	$251,728.00	Edit
⊞ AGNC	Buy / Sell	30.06	0.15	0.50%	$1,003.65	6,691	$26.37	$24,684.60	13.99%	$201,131.46	Edit
⊞ CMG	Buy / Sell	422.26	3.86	0.92%	$579.00	150	$417.05	$765.52	1.22%	$63,339.00	Edit
⊞ HD	Buy / Sell	50.00	0.01	0.02%	$20.00	2,000	$46.17	$7,636.11	8.27%	$100,000.00	Edit
⊞ JPM	Buy / Sell	45.42	-0.41	-0.89%	-$984.00	2,400	$39.65	$13,811.04	14.51%	$109,008.00	Edit
⊞ MLPL	Buy / Sell	42.07	0.49	1.18%	$2,505.97	5,114.22958	$36.30	$29,445.19	15.86%	$215,155.64	Edit
⊞ PCLN	Buy / Sell	743.62	23.65	3.28%	$3,547.50	150	$719.98	$3,529.52	3.27%	$111,543.00	Edit
⊞ QQQ	Buy / Sell	68.23	-0.02	-0.03%	-$30.00	1,500	$60.99	$10,831.53	11.84%	$102,345.00	Edit
⊞ SSO	Buy / Sell	58.80	-0.41	-0.69%	-$820.00	2,000	$55.67	$6,229.53	5.59%	$117,600.00	Edit
⊞ TJX	Buy / Sell	39.61	-0.26	-0.65%	-$780.00	3,000	$30.82	$26,336.03	28.47%	$118,830.00	Edit

Symbol	Buy / Sell	Last Trade	Change $	Change %	Day's Gain	Qty	Price Paid	Total Gain $	Total Gain %	Market Val	Edit
WFC	Trade	34.48	-0.03	-0.09%	-$90.00	3,000	$31.35	$9,376.27	9.97%	$103,440.00	Edit
AAPL Apr 05 '12 $615 Call w	Trade	15.45	7.05	83.93%	-$1,410.00	-2	$6.53	-$1,789.54	-136.45%	-$3,090.00	Edit
CMG Apr 05 '12 $420 Call w	Trade	4.00	1.50	60.00%	-$150.00	-1	$3.46	-$58.76	-16.75%	-$400.00	Edit
HD Apr 05 '12 $50 Call w	Trade	0.22	-0.08	-26.67%	$80.00	-10	$0.33	$98.39	28.80%	-$220.00	Edit
JPM Apr 05 '12 $46 Call w	Trade	0.16	-0.14	-46.67%	$168.00	-12	$0.34	$202.86	48.17%	-$192.00	Edit
PCLN Apr 05 '12 $715 Call w	Trade	28.90	18.90	189.00%	-$1,890.00	-1	$11.97	-$1,697.78	-141.27%	-$2,890.00	Edit
QQQ Apr 05 '12 $68 Call w	Trade	0.50	0.02	4.17%	-$8.00*	-8	$0.32	-$146.09*	-54.90%*	-$392.00*	Edit
SSO Apr 05 '12 $58 Call w	Trade	0.95	-0.39	-29.10%	$410.00*	-10	$0.54	-$421.61	-76.43%	-$950.00	Edit
TJX Jan 19 '13 $28.75 Call	Trade	11.30	11.30	—	$70.00*	-7	$5.05	-$4,381.73	-123.72%	-$7,910.00	Edit
WFC Apr 05 '12 $34 Call w	Trade	0.55	-0.06	-9.84%	$90.00	-15	$0.35	-$315.42	-58.37%	-$825.00	Edit

Weekly Covered Calls Profits $323,069.44 Avg Return 54.8%

Our brokerage account Profit/Loss Report below shows $323,069.44 in profits and an average return of 54.8% from weekly covered call trades that we took in our retirement account.

Portfolios | Performance & Value | Positions | Gains & Losses | Risk Analyzer | Portfolio Analyzer | Income Estimator

Portfolios

Account/Watch List: QQQ

Market Value: $912,396.29   STREAMING QUOTES $323,069.44

Create / Edit List   View: | Performance   Customize /

DJIA 12,391.25 ▲ +73.11 (+0.59%)   Nasdaq 2,833.95 ▲ +2.37 (+0.08%)

REFRESH   EXPORT TO EXCEL   Results per Page: 200

Symbol		Last Trade	Change $	Change %	Day's Gain	Qty	Price Paid	Total Gain $	Total Gain %	Market Val	Edit
AAPL	Buy/Sell	350.56	-7.74	-2.16%	-$3,870.00	500	$273.82	$38,431.65	28.06%	$175,280.00	Edit
BIDU	Buy/Sell	126.80	-1.74	-1.35%	-$2,436.00	1,400	$84.47	$59,216.38	50.06%	$177,520.00	Edit
DIG	Buy/Sell	58.68	0.58	1.00%	$1,740.00	3,000	$49.36	$27,890.02	18.83%	$176,040.00	X
FAS	Buy/Sell	34.26	0.18	0.53%	$1,080.00	6,000	$29.56	$28,182.17	15.89%	$205,560.00	X
NOV	Buy/Sell	80.18	-1.22	-1.50%	-$2,440.00	2,000	$63.05	$34,208.41	27.12%	$160,360.00	Edit
QLD	Buy/Sell	94.44	-0.39	-0.41%	-$1,404.00	3,600	$70.28	$87,003.57	34.39%	$339,984.00	Edit
SSO	Buy/Sell	54.78	0.22	0.40%	$660.00	3,000	$50.61	$12,462.02	8.22%	$164,340.00	X
UWM	Buy/Sell	48.34	0.12	0.25%	$456.00	3,800	$44.19	$15,748.05	9.38%	$183,692.00	X

Symbol	Buy/Sel	Last Trade	Change $	Change %	Day's Gain	Qty	Price Paid	Total Gain $	%	Market Val	Edit
UYM		54.75	-1.32	-2.35%	-$4,208.00	3,200	$48.69	$19,336.13	12.41%	$175,200.00	Edit
BIDU Mar 19 '11 $130 Call	Trade	2.96	-0.89	-23.12%	$890.00	-10	$4.737	$1,781.28	37.06%	-$2,950.00	Edit
DIG Mar 19 '11 $58 Call	Trade	2.55	0.00	0.00%	$-0.00	-12	$1.72	-$1,009.19	-48.58%	-$3,060.00	Edit
DIG Mar 19 '11 $59 Call	Trade	2.05	0.05	2.50%	-$45.00	-9	$1.37	-$822.89	-50.08%	-$1,845.00	Edit
FAS Mar 19 '11 $36 Call	Trade	0.97	-0.05	-4.90%	$210.00	-42	$1.00	$89.86	2.12%	-$4,074.00	Edit
NOV Mar 19 '11 $85 Call	Trade	1.18	-0.47	-28.48%	$658.00	-14	$1.47	$391.28	18.88%	-$1,652.00	Edit
QLD Mar 19 '11 $96 Call	Trade	2.15	-0.51	-19.17%	$735.00	-15	$2.49	$464.49	12.38%	-$3,255.00	Edit
QLD Mar 19 '11 $97 Call	Trade	1.80	-0.35	-16.67%	$395.00	-11	$2.1827	$404.57	16.74%	-$1,980.00	Edit
SSO Mar 19 '11 $55 Call	Trade	1.38	0.02	1.47%	-$63.00	-21	$1.24	-$335.07	-12.77%	-$2,919.00	Edit
UYM Mar 19 '11 $49 Call	Trade	1.65	-0.08	-4.62%	$224.00	-28	$1.25	-$1,117.44	-31.45%	-$4,620.00	Edit
UYM Mar 19 '11 $57 Call	Trade	1.45	-0.63	-30.29%	$1,197.00	-19	$1.68	$418.44	13.03%	-$2,755.00	Edit
Totals					-$6,070.00			$323,069.44		$912,396.29	

Snapshot of Trading Contest Account

These brokerage account Profit/Loss Reports are from one of my International Trading Championship's real money contest account. I traded monthly covered calls in this contest account. I placed first in the competition with an annual return of 122%. The contest results are audited before being posted on the sponsor's website so the results are an accurate representation of your performance.

I traded monthly covered calls and rolled over the options which allowed me to compound my returns. Covered calls produced a great annual return in this account with low risk.

Realized P&L on Closed Positions

Symbol	Date Bought	Date Sold	Shares	Cost Basis	Sales Price	Gain-loss
+FCKEG	3/26/2009 11:59:59 PM	3/17/2009 12:46:27 PM	10	$0.00	$5,164.89	$5,164.89
+FCKEG	3/26/2009 11:59:59 PM	3/18/2009 3:18:38 PM	5	$0.00	$3,022.44	$3,022.44
+PAEG	4/30/2009 10:18:36 AM	3/26/2009 11:59:59 PM	15	$11,697.59	$0.00	-$11,697.59
+GSGM	3/25/2009 3:40:27 PM	5/6/2009 10:00:37 AM	15	$72,027.99	$109,244.57	$37,216.98
+GSGS	5/6/2009 10:00:37 AM	3/25/2009 3:40:27 PM	15	$65,832.59	$38,492.16	-$27,340.43
+NOVEF	5/4/2009 11:59:59 PM	3/17/2009 12:49:34 PM	10	$3,218.39	$3,564.89	$346.50
+NOVEF	5/4/2009 11:59:59 PM	3/18/2009 3:36:31 PM	5	$1,609.20	$1,722.45	$113.25
+YCPAU	5/8/2009 11:59:59 PM	5/1/2009 12:36:20 PM	15	$0.00	$9,422.13	$9,422.13
+YFQAW	5/8/2009 11:59:59 PM	5/6/2009 3:17:12 PM	15	$0.00	$10,307.11	$10,307.11
+YH6AE	5/8/2009 11:59:59 PM	5/1/2009 1:41:20 PM	15	$0.00	$7,322.19	$7,322.19
FCX	3/17/2009 12:45:32 PM	4/30/2009 10:20:38 AM	800	$29,052.72	$33,960.39	$4,907.67
FCX	3/17/2009 12:45:32 PM	4/30/2009 10:20:38 AM	200	$7,282.20	$8,490.10	$1,207.90
FCX	3/18/2009 3:17:41 PM	4/30/2009 10:20:38 AM	300	$11,353.77	$12,735.15	$1,381.38
FCX	3/18/2009 3:17:41 PM	4/30/2009 10:20:38 AM	100	$3,784.60	$4,245.05	$460.45
FCX	3/18/2009 3:17:41 PM	4/30/2009 10:20:38 AM	100	$3,804.58	$4,245.05	$440.47
NOV	3/17/2009 12:48:27 PM	5/4/2009 10:13:50 AM	100	$2,987.60	$3,271.87	$284.27
NOV	3/17/2009 12:48:27 PM	5/4/2009 10:13:50 AM	200	$5,995.20	$6,543.75	$548.55
NOV	3/17/2009 12:48:27 PM	5/4/2009 10:13:50 AM	500	$14,933.00	$16,359.37	$1,421.37
NOV	3/17/2009 12:48:27 PM	5/4/2009 10:13:50 AM	200	$5,975.20	$6,543.75	$568.55
NOV	3/18/2009 3:35:49 PM	5/4/2009 10:13:50 AM	500	$14,898.00	$16,359.37	$1,461.37

Total Realized Gain-Loss: **$46,559.45**

Realized P&L on Open Positions

Symbol	Description	Position	Avg Price	Cost Basis	Market Value	Type	Unrealized Val
+AASAH	Allegheny Technologies Inc Jan 2010 40.00 Call	-15	$0.0000	$0.00	$0.00	Stock Option	$0.00
+CLFAA	Cliffs Natural Resources Inc Jan 2010 20.00 Call	-15	$0.0000	$0.00	$0.00	Stock Option	$0.00
+CLFGD	Cliffs Natural Resources Inc Jul 2009 20.00 Call	-15	-$3.5715	$5,357.31	-$17,550.00	Stock Option	-$12,192.69
+CUHO	Caterpillar Inc Del Aug 2009 30.00 Call	-15	-$3.3516	$5,027.35	-$16,200.00	Stock Option	-$11,172.65
+BUAE	Bucyrus Intl Inc New Jan 2010 25.00 Call	-15	$0.0000	$0.00	$0.00	Stock Option	$0.00
+BUGD	Bucyrus Intl Inc New Jul 2009 20.00 Call	-15	-$2.5615	$3,842.28	-$11,700.00	Stock Option	-$7,857.72
+MDRHC	Mcdermott Intl Inc Aug 2009 15.00 Call	-15	-$2.6249	$3,937.35	-$6,600.00	Stock Option	-$2,662.65
+MOSFH	Mosaic Co Jun 2009 40.00 Call	-15	-$7.8582	$11,787.30	-$10,500.00	Stock Option	$1,287.30
+MSGD	Morgan Stanley New Jul 2009 20.00 Call	-15	-$6.4249	$9,637.30	-$12,750.00	Stock Option	-$3,112.70
+PBRGY	Petroleo Brasileiro Sa Petrobr Sponsored Adr Jul 2009 27.50 Call	-15	-$5.7915	$8,687.31	-$18,900.00	Stock Option	-$10,212.69
+SIIGY	Smith Intl Inc Jul 2009 27.50 Call	-15	-$3.3649	$3,364.88	-$5,600.00	Stock Option	-$2,235.12
+STTHF	State Str Corp Aug 2009 32.00 Call	-10	-$7.8915	$11,837.31	-$20,550.00	Stock Option	-$8,712.69
+UNEAR	United States Natl Gas Fund Lp Unit Jan 2010 18.00 Call	-30	-$2.1715	$6,514.58	-$8,550.00	Stock Option	-$2,035.42
+WFCGT	Wells Fargo & Co New Jul 2009 17.50 Call	-15	-$3.5716	$5,357.34	-$16,200.00	Stock Option	-$10,842.66
+WMAE	Foster Wheeler Ag Jan 2010 25.00 Call	-15	-$4.5715	$6,857.20	-$7,800.00	Stock Option	-$942.80
ATI	Allegheny Technologies Inc	1500	$38.0293	$57,044.00	$57,390.00	Equities	$346.00
BUCY	Bucyrus Intl Inc New	3000	$21.3533	$64,060.00	$83,430.00	Equities	$19,370.00
CAT	Caterpillar Inc Del	1500	$28.7083	$43,062.50	$59,460.00	Equities	$16,397.50
CLF	Cliffs Natural Resources Inc	3000	$21.9788	$65,936.50	$93,060.00	Equities	$27,123.50
FWLT	Foster Wheeler Ag	1500	$23.5293	$35,294.00	$37,470.00	Equities	$2,176.00
MDR	Mcdermott Intl Inc	1500	$14.4960	$21,744.00	$27,615.00	Equities	$5,871.00
MOS	Mosaic Co	1500	$42.0493	$63,073.90	$68,175.00	Equities	$5,101.10
MS	Morgan Stanley New	1500	$23.1305	$34,695.80	$42,300.00	Equities	$7,604.20
PBR	Petroleo Brasileiro Sa Petrobr Sponsored Adr	1500	$30.2159	$45,323.90	$60,000.00	Equities	$14,676.10
SII	Smith Intl Inc	1000	$25.7360	$25,736.00	$31,720.00	Equities	$5,984.00
STT	State Str Corp	1500	$32.7483	$49,122.50	$65,625.00	Equities	$16,502.50
UNG	United States Natl Gas Fund Lp Unit	3000	$15.3793	$46,138.00	$50,790.00	Equities	$4,652.00
WFC	Wells Fargo & Co New	1500	$16.9293	$25,394.00	$42,270.00	Equities	$16,876.00

Total Unrealized Gain-Loss: $71,987.41

Investment Required to Generate
$50,000 of Yearly Income
$6,756,756 versus $150,000 Investment

Let's now compare income returns for bank CDs versus weekly covered calls. Let's also assume you want to generate $50,000 a year in income.

According to the Bank Rate Monitor the average annual yield for 1 Year CDs is .34% and the average annual yield for a 5 Year CD is 1.14%. If you split your funds evenly between 1 and 5 Year CDs it would take an investment of $6,756,756 to generate a yearly income of $50,000! Of course your return is guaranteed but who has $6.7 million to invest?

The trading contest account had an annual return of 122% trading monthly covered calls. We also had a weekly covered call trading account with a 54.8% average return and one with an average return of 36.9%.

Based on these real time results, we think it is reasonable to assume a 33.3% annual return for weekly covered calls. A 33.3% annual return would require a $150,000 investment to generate a $50,000 yearly income.

And a 50% yearly return requires a $100,000 investment to generate a $50,000 yearly income demonstrating the ability of the covered call strategy to deliver excellent income returns compared to other fixed income investments.

Comparing Income Returns

- It would take an investment of $6,756,756 in 1 and 5 Year CDs to generate a yearly income of $50,000

- A 33.3% yearly return for selling weekly options would require a $150,000 investment to generate a $50,000 yearly income

- And a 50% yearly return for selling weekly options requires a $100,000 investment to generate a $50,000 yearly income

APPENDIX

Option Basics

The focus of Option Basics is to provide you with the practical knowledge you need to understand in order to trade options. Learning the mechanics of option investing can be a bit overwhelming particularly if you have never invested in options before.

To be a successful options investor you don't need to know complicated mathematical formulas or Greek letters. You only need to know the basic mechanics of buying and selling options. In our 60 years of combined trading experience, we have found option trading to be a versatile and rewarding approach to profitable trading.

Option trading enables many different types of traders to achieve their specific investment goals. We have traded many types of option strategies with different investment goals. We favor the three option strategies listed below as we have had good success trading these strategies.

- Purchasing put options to protect our stock positions
- Trading option spreads that can profit during an up or down market
- Selling option premium to produce cash income

Successful Option Trading

The overall goal of our option investing is to achieve at least a 3 to 1 profit to loss ratio. To achieve this goal we must be ready to close out our losing trades before they develop into large losses and not close out profitable trade with a small profit. Many option traders with good trading systems fail because they don't pay enough attention to risk. Maintaining a trading discipline that forces you to think in terms of reward versus risk can help you become a successful option trader.

If you are willing to risk 15% on an option trade, then you should be expecting a 45% profit on your winning trades in order to achieve a 3 to 1 profit to loss ratio. If you are willing to risk 30% on an option trade, then you should be expecting a 90% profit on your winning trades which is very difficult to achieve. We always think in terms of taking measured risks with every trade.

Also, if you have enough trading funds, don't risk more than 5 to 10% of your trading funds on any one trade. This helps prevent a large portfolio loss if one of your option trades experiences a big loss. This is especially important with options because they employ leverage.

Successful trade management can be summarized with three basics rules:
- Limit the size of your positions
- Close out your losing trades before they develop into large losses
- Don't limit your profits by selling winning trades with a small profit

There is no need to memorize all of the material presented. This section can be used as a future reference when implementing an option strategy.

Option Basics

Options are also known as derivatives because the option contract derives its price and value from the underlying asset on which it is based. The value of an option fluctuates as the price of the underlying asset rises or falls in price. Option values are also affected by other market conditions. These conditions could be a change in volatility due to sudden fluctuations of price in the underlying asset, interest rates, dividends or stock splits.

An option is the right, but not the obligation, to buy or sell a stock or index for a specified price on or before a specific date. A call option is the right to buy a stock/index, while a put option is the right to sell a stock/index. The investor who purchases an option, whether it is a put or call, is the option "buyer". Conversely, the investor who sells the put or call "to open" is the option "seller" or "writer".

Options are contracts in which the terms of the contract are standardized and give the buyer the right, but not the obligation, to buy or sell a particular stock/index at a fixed price (the strike price) for a specific period of time (until expiration). All option contracts traded on U.S. securities exchanges are issued, guaranteed and cleared by the Options Clearing Corporation (OCC). OCC is a registered clearing corporation with the Securities and Exchange Commission (SEC) and has received 'AAA' credit rating from Standard & Poor's Corporation. The 'AAA' credit rating corresponds to OCC's ability to fulfill its obligations as counter-party for options trades.

The options markets provide a mechanism where many different types of investors can achieve their specific investment goals. An options investor may be looking for long term or short term profits, or they may be looking to hedge an existing stock or index position. Whatever your objectives may be, you need a thorough understanding of the markets you will be trading.

Options Share the Following General Characteristics:
- Options give you the right to buy or sell an underlying security or index.
- If you buy an option, you are not obligated to buy the underlying security. You simply have the right to exercise the option.
- If you sell an option, you are obligated to deliver the underlying security at the strike price at which the option was sold if the buyer

exercises his/her right to take delivery.

- Options are good for a specified period of time after which they expire and you lose the right to buy or sell the underlying security.

- When options are purchased the buyer incurs a debit.

- When options are sold the seller receives a cash credit.

- Options are available in various strike prices representing the price of the underlying security.

- The cost of an option is referred to as the option premium. The premium is comprised of time value and intrinsic value.

- There are two kinds of options: calls and puts. Calls give you the right to buy the underlying security and puts give you the right to sell the underlying security.

- Options (put or call) which have the same underlying security are called a class of options. For example, all the calls for General Electric constitute an option class.

- All options which are in one class and have the same strike price are called an option series. For example, all the General Electric options with a strike price of 25 constitute an option series.

- Most options are never exercised and are closed out before option expiration.

Buying Options

Any investor can buy options if they have the required account established with their broker. Buying options limits the investor's risk to the amount of capital invested in the option purchase. Therefore the only requirement is that the investor has enough funds in their account to purchase the options. Since the purchase of an option contract results in a long position, a cash debit is subtracted from the buyer's account.

Selling Options

For every option buyer there is a seller or writer. If an option is exercised, the option writer is obligated by the option contract to deliver the specified number of shares of the underlying security at the specific strike price. Anyone can write options if they have the required account established with their broker.

Selling "naked" options can involve large capital loss risk and is not a suitable investment for all investors. Writing an option results in cash being credited to the seller's brokerage account. Since the writing of an option results in a short position, it requires that funds be held in margin to guarantee the writer's obligation. Margin requirements for writing naked options vary for different markets, and sometimes even for different stocks.

Underlying Security

The underlying security in options trading is defined as the financial instrument on which an option contract is based or derived. It is a stock or Exchange Traded Fund (ETF) that you have the right to purchase or sell. The symbol used for the underlying security in options trading is usually the symbol used by the exchange on which the underlying security is traded. For example, GE is used for General Electric and SPY is used for the S&P 500 Index ETF.

Strike Price

The strike price is the actual price at which the option holder may buy or sell the underlying security as defined in the option contract. For example, a GE Mar 20-Strike call gives the buyer of the option the right to buy 100 shares of General Electric at $20 per share between now and the monthly option expiration which is usually the third Friday of the month.

Expiration Date

The expiration date is the actual date that an option contract becomes void. Monthly options normally expire on the third Friday of each month. Be aware that at expiration options that are not closed prior to expiration and are in-the-money will be exercised automatically.

Option Types

There are two types of options - call options and put options.

A call option *purchase* profits when the price of the underlying security moves higher.

A call option *short sale* profits when the price of the underlying security moves lower.

A put option *purchase* profits when the price of the underlying security moves lower.

A put option *short sale* profits when the price of the underlying security moves higher.

How to Read Option Symbols

An option symbol is comprised of several components that define the underlying stock or ETF and information about the specific option contract. A weekly option symbol consists of the stock or ETF trading symbol, year of expiration, month of expiration, expiration date, option type (call or put) and strike-price.

There are many financial websites available today that will give you option quotes. We like to use Yahoo Finance or the Chicago Board Options Exchange website at www.cboe.com to obtain option quotes.

The symbol for the General Electric Jan 2017 25-Strike call option is GE170120C00025000. Let's look at the components of this option symbol.

GE, 17, 01, 20, C, 00025000

GE is the trading symbol for General Electric
17 is the expiration year 2017
01 is the expiration month of January
20 is the expiration date which is Friday January 20th in this example
C designates a call option (put options are designated with a "P")
00025000 designates a 25-Strike price

Stock Option Point Values

Normally, 1 stock option contract covers 100 hundred shares of the underlying stock. Therefore, an option with a 3.5 point premium would cost $350 (100 shares x $3.5). Mini options cover 10 shares of stock. A mini option with a 3.5 point premium would cost $35 (10 shares x $3.5)

Exercise and Assignment

Exercise is the term used when the buyer of an option uses his/her right to purchase or sell the underlying security at the terms of the option contract. Assignment is the term used when the seller of an option is obligated to deliver the underlying security at the contract specification.

When the option buyer exercises his/her option contract, the seller of that option contract receives a notice of assignment from their broker. The seller of the option contract must then deliver the underlying security at the specified price. Your broker handles the entire option exercise/assignment transaction, and the resulting cash profit/loss or stock position is transferred into or out of your account.

Section 1 Quiz

1. If you buy a Microsoft call option you are obligated to buy Microsoft stock.
   > A. True
   > B. False

2. If you sell an option, you are obligated to deliver the underlying security at the strike price at which the option was sold if the buyer exercises his/her right to take delivery.
   > A. True
   > B. False

3. When options are sold the seller receives a cash credit.
   > A. True
   > B. False

4. Call options give you the right to sell the underlying security and put options give you the right to buy the underlying security.
   > A. True
   > B. False

5. Monthly options normally expire on the third Friday of the month.
   > A. True
   > C. False

6. AAPL is the root symbol for Apple stock options. The symbol for the Apple Dec 2013 560-strike put option is _____.
   > A. AAPL131220C00560000
   > B. AAPL141220P00560000
   > C. AAPL131220P00560000
   > D. AAPL120405P00560000

7. The IBM Jan 2015 200-strike weekly call option is quoted at 4.25 points. It would cost _____ to purchase one option contract at the current quote.
   > A. $4.25
   > B. $425
   > C. $42.50
   > D. $4,250

8. All listed stocks trade weekly options
   > A. True
   > B. False

9. Exercise is the term used when the buyer of an option uses his/her right to purchase or sell the underlying security at the terms of the option contract.
>   A. True
>   B. False

10. Most option contracts are never exercised.
>   A. True
>   B. False

11. Each stock option contract normally represents 100 shares of the underlying stock.
>   A. True
>   B. False

Section 1 Quiz Key

1. B, False
2. A, True
3. A, True
4. B, False
5. A, True
6. C, AAPL131220P00560000
7. B, $425
8. B, False
9. A, True
10. A, True
11. A, True

Option Characteristics

There are three major factors that determine the price of an option:
- Strike Price in Relation to the Stock Price
- Time Until Expiration
- Volatility

Strike Price in Relation to the Stock Price

The most important factor that determines the price of an option is the price of the underlying stock or ETF relative to the strike price. This determines whether an option is in-the-money or out-of-the-money and quantifies an option's intrinsic and time value. In-the-money options have more intrinsic value and are more expensive than out-of-the-money options. The deeper an option is in-the-money the more intrinsic value it will have and the more expensive it will be. In-the-money options are more expensive than at-the-money and out-of-the-money options.

Time Until Expiration

An option is considered a wasting asset, and as the option's expiration date gets closer, the value of the option decreases. The more time remaining until expiration, the more time value the option contract has. If the underlying security price falls far below or far above the strike price of the option, the underlying security becomes more dominant in determining the price of the option. On the day the option expires, the only value the option has is its intrinsic value, which is determined by the amount by which the option contract is in-the-money. If an option has no intrinsic value at expiration, it expires worthless.

The passage of time works against the options buyer, as the price of out-of-the-money options decreases at an accelerating rate as the expiration date approaches. This is called "time decay". The opposite is true for the option seller. The passage of time works for the option seller as time decay results in profits.

The longer an option has before expiration, the more expensive it will be. More time until expiration means more time value and a higher price.

Volatility

Volatility is the amount in annual percent terms that the underlying security has moved or is expected to move on an annual basis. This number can help predict short-term price ranges and also helps determine the relative value for an option price.

There are two types of volatility used in option analysis: The first is statistical volatility, which is volatility based on the historical price movement of the underlying security. This is sometimes referred to as historical volatility. This volatility number tells us what has happened in the past.

The second type of volatility is implied volatility, which is an implied value based on the current option prices for an underlying security. This kind of volatility can give insight into potential price movement.

When option prices rise because of increased trading volume or nervousness in the market this can signal a significant market event. When option prices rise, implied volatility rises as well. Therefore, implied volatility can be seen as a measurement of risk. Higher volatility means higher risk for the option seller and increased prices for option premiums.

The more volatile the stock, the more expensive the option will be. Because volatile stocks have larger price moves, there is a higher probability that an out-of-the-money option will become an in-the-money option with intrinsic value.

Option Pricing

Option premiums consist of intrinsic value and time value. At option expiration options lose all time value and consist of only intrinsic value. Intrinsic value is the difference between the option strike price and the current price of the underlying stock or ETF. The intrinsic value of a call option is calculated by subtracting the strike price of the option from the current stock price. For example, let's assume IBM stock is currently trading at 75.00 and the May 70-Strike call option is priced at 7.00 points. The intrinsic value of this option would be 5.00 points.

Current Stock Price of 75.00 Minus Strike Price of 70.00 = 5.00 Intrinsic Value

The time value of an option is calculated by subtracting the intrinsic value from the total value of the option. In this example the 70-Strike option priced at 7.00 would have 2.00 points of time value.

Option Price of 7.00 Minus Intrinsic Value of 5.00 = Time Value of 2.00

In this example, if the IBM May 80-Strike call option is priced at 3.00 then this call option would have no intrinsic value and would only contain time value.

Current Stock Price of 75.00 Minus Strike Price of 80.00 = 0.00 Intrinsic Value

Option Price of 3.00 Minus Intrinsic Value of 0.00 = Time Value of 3.00

The intrinsic value of a put option is calculated by subtracting the current price of the stock from the strike price of the put. Let's assume again that IBM stock is trading at 75.00 and the IBM May 80-Strike put option is priced at 8.00 points. The intrinsic value of this option would be 5.00 points and the time value would be 3.00 points.

Strike Price of 80.00 Minus Current Stock Price of 75.00 = 5.00 Intrinsic Value

Option Price of 8.00 Minus Intrinsic Value of 5.00 = Time Value of 3.00

In the above example, if the IBM May 70-Strike put option is priced at 2.00 then this put option would have no intrinsic value and would only contain time value.

Strike Price of 70.00 Minus Stock Price of 75.00 = 0.00 Intrinsic Value

Option Price of 2.00 Minus Intrinsic Value of 0.00 = Time Value of 2.00

When the price of a stock or ETF is below the strike price of a call option, that option is said to be out-of-the-money. An option with a strike price that is closest to the price of the underlying security is at-the-money. A call option is in-the-money when the stock price is greater than the strike price. An in-the-money call option has intrinsic value equal to the amount the stock price exceeds the strike price.

A put option is just the opposite of a call option. A put option is out-of-the-money when the stock price is greater than the strike price. A put option is in-the-money when the stock is below the strike price. The intrinsic value of a put equals the amount by which the strike price exceeds the stock price. As with a call, a put will have value at expiration if the option is in-the-money. To clarify this concept, take a closer look at these terms:

	Call	Put
In-the-money	strike price<stock price	strike price>stock price
At-the-money	strike price=stock price	strike price=stock price
Out-of-the-money	strike price>stock price	strike price<stock price

Time (or days remaining until expiration) and volatility are the main components of time value. Interest rates and stock dividends are smaller factors in the pricing of option premiums. The more time remaining until expiration, or the higher the stock volatility, the greater the risk to the option seller, and therefore the higher the option premium will be.

Dividends

Dividends reduce the value of call options and increase the value of put options. This is due to the fact that paying out a dividend normally reduces the stock price by the amount of the dividend. Dividends increase the attractiveness of holding stock compared to buying call options and holding cash. Conversely, short-sellers must pay out dividends so buying puts is more desirable than shorting stock.

Interest Rates

Rising interest rates increase the value of call premiums and decrease the value of put premiums. Higher rates increase the underlying security's forward price, which is the stock price plus the risk-free interest rate over the life of the option.

Advantages of Options Versus Stocks/Mutual Funds

When you purchase options you commit a limited amount of capital and thus have less total dollars at risk in the market compared to stocks and mutual funds. The surplus dollars can be placed in safe investments like a money market fund. Instead of buying stocks consider "leasing" them with options especially when your market expectations are likely to change more frequently with today's volatile markets. Set aside a small portion of your portfolio for options to benefit from the frequent market swings that can create big profit opportunities for traders positioned to capitalize on market swings.

Options offer profit potential not only when the market rallies, but also when it declines. With stocks and most mutual funds you can only benefit from bullish markets. If you are bearish on the stock market cash is usually your only alternative. With options you can profit from both bullish and bearish markets.

A Lower Risk Alternative to 'Going Short'

Put options are normally a better choice than selling short a stock or ETF. Option purchases normally do not require a margin account, whereas short selling a stock does require a margin account. In addition, a short stock position has virtually unlimited loss potential if a stock continues to rally in price. Conversely, the maximum loss for a put option purchase is limited to the purchase price of the option.

Options offer greater leverage than stocks or mutual funds. A 10% move in a stock can easily translate into a 30 to 60% move in the related option. Purchasing options offers profit leverage if you are correct in your market view but also offers limited risk if your market view is incorrect.

Options can allow for stock or mutual fund portfolios to be hedged without losing long-term capital gain status. This results in a more favorable tax treatment. This can improve the after-tax returns on stock holdings while allowing you to protect those stocks during market volatility.

Risk Management

The first step toward intelligent risk management is to trade options only with that portion of your capital that can be comfortably devoted to speculation. This will permit you to trade rationally and to sleep soundly which is not possible if your 'Safe Money' is at risk. Never trade options with money needed to pay living expenses. Restrict your options trading to funds that can be lost without undue financial hardship.

Once you determine the amount of your available trading capital, allocate no more than 10% to any one trade. This should help mitigate losses when losing trades occur. This rule holds regardless of how successful you have been in the past and regardless of how attractive the next trade appears. There will always be losing trades. By compounding your capital after a few profitable trades, you are exposing yourself to potentially painful losses once that losing trade comes along.

Risk and Diversification

There are generally two types of portfolio risk: systematic and unsystematic.

Systematic Risk, also called non-diversifiable risk, is risk that cannot be eliminated. It arises from factors which cause the whole market to move up or down, and cannot be eliminated by diversification because it affects all securities. Examples of systematic risk are political or sociological changes that affect all securities. Some of the most common forms of systematic risk are changes in interest rates or inflation.

Unsystematic Risk, also called diversifiable risk can be reduced or eliminated by diversifying your portfolio. Unsystematic risk is risk that is unique to a certain industry, firm, or company. Examples of unsystematic risk include: a company's financial structure, weather and natural disasters, labor strife and a shortage of raw materials. Since unsystematic risk affects a single company or industry, it can be mitigated by investing in many companies across a broad range of industries.

Option positions should be diversified. A major advantage of option purchases is 'truncated risk', whereby your loss is limited to your initial investment yet your profit is virtually unlimited. Diversification will allow you to use truncated risk to its maximum advantage. While some of your positions will inevitably be unprofitable, each profitable trade can offset several unprofitable trades. Option positions should be established among many underlying stocks and indexes in unrelated industries. This gives you diversification, which can help mitigate sector weakness.

In order to trade options, your broker must first approve your account for option trading. There are various levels of option trading and each level has financial requirements that differ from broker to broker:

Level 1 Covered call writing
Level 2 Call and put purchases and covered put writing
Level 3 Spreads (requires margin)

Level 4 Uncovered call and put writing (requires margin)

Level 5 Index option writing (requires margin)

Be sure to ask your broker about their requirements for the level of options you plan to trade. Lastly, before you trade options, regulations require that you read *Characteristics and Risks of Standardized Options* prepared by the Options Clearing Corporation (OCC) and available from your broker.

Types of Orders

Listed below are definitions for a variety of popular orders that may be helpful.

● Market Order

A market order is simply an order without restrictions or limits that guarantees execution but not price. Because it lacks restrictions, it takes precedence over all other types of orders. A market order to buy is executed at the best offering price available, which is normally the "ask" price. A market order to sell is executed at the best bid price available which is normally the "bid" price.

● Limit Order

A limit order is an order in which an investor has placed a restriction or limit on the acceptable purchase or selling price. There are two types of limit orders: a buy limit order and sell limit order. A buy limit order sets the maximum amount an investor is willing to pay to purchase a security or option contract. A sell limit order sets the minimum price that an investor is willing to accept to sell their security or option contract.

● Day Orders

Day orders are only valid for one trading day. If you place the order during market hours, then it will expire at the end of the trading day if it is not executed. If you place a day order after the market close then it will be valid for the next trading day.

● Good Until Canceled Orders (GTC)

Normally each brokerage firm will establish time periods for which GTC orders are valid. Once a GTC order is placed, it will remain open until the option expires, the order itself expires, the order is filled, or the order is cancelled.

● Stop Loss Orders

A stop-loss order is normally used to protect a profit or prevent a further loss if you own a stock and the price of the stock starts to drop. Example: You purchase 100 shares of Microsoft stock at 25 and enter a GTC stop order to sell at 20. As long as Microsoft trades above 20 then the stop order will not be executed. If it trades at 20 or below, however, then the stop order automatically becomes a market order to sell 100 shares of Microsoft at the market. A stop order does not guarantee that you will be filled at the stop price. Using the above example, if Microsoft closes at 21 and opens the next trading day at 19 the stop order will be executed on the open at the best possible price but below the 20 stop-loss price.

Section 2 Quiz

1. Option premiums consist of intrinsic value and _____ value.
   - A. Dividend
   - B. Payout
   - C. Time
   - D. Cash

2. Exxon stock is trading at 70. The Exxon May 65-strike weekly call option is priced at 8 points. The intrinsic value of this call option is ___ points.
   - A. 8
   - B. 3
   - C. 65
   - D. 5

3. The time value of the same Exxon 65-strike call option listed above is ___ points.
   - A. 8
   - B. 3
   - C. 65
   - D. 5

4. A call option is in-the-money when the strike price is _____ the current stock price.
   - A. Less than
   - B. Greater than
   - C. Equal to

5. A put option is out-of-the-money when the strike price is _____ the current stock price.
   - A. Less than
   - B. Greater than
   - C. Equal to

6. Time premium is normally the dollar amount the writer of an option is charging the buyer to assume the price movement risk of the option.
   - A. True
   - B. False

7. As an option's expiration date gets closer, the time value of an option increases.
   - A. True
   - B. False

8. On option expiration day, the only value an option has is its time value.
    A. True
    B. False

9. The most important factor that determines the price of an option is the price of the underlying security relative to the strike price of the option.
    A. True
    B. False

10. Higher volatility usually means higher risk for the option seller and increased prices for option premiums.
    A. True
    B. False

11. Dividends normally increase the value of call options and decrease the value of put options.
    A. True
    B. False

12. Rising interest rates normally decrease the value of call premiums and increase the value of put premiums.
    A. True
    B. False

13. Buying put options is normally a lower risk strategy than selling short stock.
    A. True
    B. False

14. Options offer greater leverage than buying stocks or mutual funds. A 10% move in a stock can translate into a 30% to 60% move in the related option.
    A. True
    B. False

15. One of the biggest differences between purchasing stock and purchasing options is the fact that options are time dependent.
    A. True
    B. False

16. Systematic risk normally can be eliminated with portfolio diversification.
    A. True
    B. False

17. A major advantage of option purchases is truncated risk, which limits your loss to your initial investment but allows for virtually unlimited profits.

         A. True
         B. False

18. Portfolio diversification will allow you to use truncated risk to its maximum advantage.

         A. True
         B. False

19. A market order is an order which an investor has placed a restriction or limit.

         A. True
         B. False

20. A limit order guarantees execution but not price.

         A. True
         B. False

21. A good until cancelled order remains in effect until the option expires, the order itself expires, the order is filled, or the order is cancelled.

         A. True
         B. False

22. A stop loss order guarantees that you will limit your loss to the stop loss price.

         A. True
         B. False

Section 2 Quiz Key

1.	C, Time		12.	B, False
2.	D, 5		13.	A, True
3.	B, 3		14.	A, True
4.	A, Less than		15.	A, True
5.	A, Less than		16.	B, False
6.	A, True		17.	A, True
7.	B, False		18.	A, True
8.	B, False		19.	B, False
9.	A, True		20.	B, False
10.	A, True		21.	A, True
11.	B, False		22.	B, False

Buying and Selling Calls and Puts

There are two ways to invest in options:
- **Buying options**
- **Selling short options**

Buying Options

The goal of buying an option is to 'Buy Low and Sell High'. Buying a call option is a bullish strategy as the value of a call option will increase as the price of the underlying stock increases. Conversely, if the price of the underlying stock decreases then the value of a call option also decreases. Buying calls is a strategy that can be used as an alternative to the outright purchase of the underlying security, giving the purchaser the added benefits of limited risk and increased leverage.

Buying a put option is a bearish strategy as the value of a put option will increase as the price of the underlying stock decreases. Conversely, if the price of the underlying stock increases then the value of a put option will decrease.

The risk for call or put option purchases is limited to the premium paid for the option. The profit potential is not limited.

The price you pay for an option is called the premium. When you buy an option, cash is deducted from your brokerage account to pay for the option premium. One option contract normally controls one hundred shares of the underlying stock. Purchasing an option with a 4.00 point premium would result in $400 being deducted from your brokerage account to pay for the premium (4.00 x 100 shares = $400). If you later sold this option for 6.00 points you would realize a $200 profit.

Buy at 4.00 and sell at 6.00 = 2.00 Profit

Conversely, if you later sell this option for 3.00 points you would realize a $100 loss.

Buy at 4.00 and sell at 3.00 = 1.00 Loss

Buyers of call options profit if the underlying stock increases in price

Buyers of put options profit if the underlying stock decreases in price

Selling Options

The goal of selling (to open) an option is to 'Sell High and Buy Low'. When you sell (to open) an option, cash is credited to your brokerage account. For example, if you sell an option for 6.00 points, $600 will be credited to your account ($6.00 x 100 shares = $600). This is just the opposite of purchasing an option. As noted previously, buying an option for 6.00 points would result in $600 being deducted from your account.

Selling (to open) a call option is a bearish strategy. An investor who sells a call option is also known as the 'writer'. Selling a call is also known as being 'short' a call. The value of a call option declines as the underlying stock decreases in price. Being 'short' a call option generates profits as the call option decreases in value.

If you sell (to open) a call option and the call option subsequently decreases in price then you can 'buy back' to close the short call at a lower price which will result in a profit for the call writer (Sell high and buy low). For example, if you sell (to open) a call option for 5.00 points and then later buy the call back to close for 3.00 points you would realize a 2.00 point profit.

Sell call at 5.00 and then buy back at 3.00 = 2.00 profit

This is a similar concept to 'shorting' a stock. If you short a stock that drops in price and then subsequently buy the stock back at a lower price to close you would realize a profit. For example, if you short IBM stock at 74.25 and subsequently buy the stock back to close at 70.00 you would realize a 4.25 point profit.

Short IBM at 74.25 and buy back at 70.00 = 4.25 profit

If you sell (to open) a call option for 5.00 points and then later buy the call back to close at a higher price let's say 7.00 points you would realize a 2.00 point loss.

Sell call at 5.00 and then buy back to close at 7.00 = 2.00 loss

Selling (to open) a put option is a bullish strategy. An investor who sells a put option is also known as the 'writer'. Selling a put is also known as being 'short' a put. The value of a put option declines as the underlying stock increases in price. If you sell (to open) a put option and the underlying stock subsequently increases in price then you can 'buy back' to close the short put at a lower price which will result in a profit for the put writer. For example, if you sell a put option for 5.00 points and then later buy the put back to close for 3.00 points you would realize a 2.00 point profit.

Sell put at 5.00 and then buy back to close at 3.00 = 2.00 profit.

If you sell (to open) a put option for 5.00 points and then later buy the put back to close at a higher price let's say 7.00 points you would realize a 2.00 point loss.

Sell put at 5.00 and then buy back to close at 7.00 = 2.00 loss

Selling a call option to open profits if the underlying stock decreases in price

Selling a put option to open profits if the underlying stock increases in price

Note: When you buy an option, you can sell the option any time prior to option expiration. When you sell to open an option you can buy to close the option any time prior to option expiration.

Let's review the types of option orders that you would give to your broker (or online) to make sure you understand this important concept.

Order	Result
Buy Call to Open	Establishes Long Call Position
Buy Put to Open	Establishes Long Put Position
Sell Call to Close	Closes Out Long Call Position
Sell Put to Close	Closes Out Long Put Position
Sell Call to Open	Establishes Short Call Position
Sell Put to Open	Establishes Short Put Position
Buy Call to Close	Closes Out Short Call Position
Buy Put to Close	Closes Out Short Put Position

Call Options versus Stock Ownership

It is important to understand the distinction between buying call options and owning stock. Unlike stocks, options have a limited life. If an investor purchases stock and the expected move does not occur with the stock he/she can continue to hold the stock indefinitely. This is not true with options as every option has an expiration date. At expiration a call option has only intrinsic value, which is the difference between its strike price and the current stock price. At expiration a call option is worthless if the stock closes at or below the strike price. Profiting from option purchases depends on your ability to predict both the direction and timing of a move in the price of the underlying stock.

Purchasing an in-the-money call has a higher probability of success than an out-of-the-money call, as there is a reduced requirement for the underlying stock to move in the right direction and a lower breakeven price. Sometimes new option traders will be tempted to buy weekly call options that are out-of-the-money because of the low cost. Everyone loves a bargain but these options are cheap for a reason: the option has little time left until expiration and the strike price and stock price are so far apart that it is highly unlikely that the option will be in the money before expiration day.

At-the-money and out-of-the-money calls have no intrinsic value; their entire price consists of time premium. At expiration, call buyers will lose their entire investment if the stock price is equal to or below the strike price.

If you choose to buy the cheapest options, you must be very precise in timing the move and calling the direction. You can also expect to have a higher percentage of losing trades when purchasing out-of-the money options.

In-the-Money Calls

Buying deep in-the-money call options offers a relatively conservative approach to options investing by giving an options trader more control over the time value and intrinsic value components of the option compared to at-the money and out-of-the-money options.

An important component of a deep in-the-money option is its substantial intrinsic value, which can comprise up to 90 to 95% or more of the total option premium. A major advantage of deep in-the-money options is the significantly lower level of time erosion of your option.

As options move deeper into the money, the amount by which an option's price will change for a one point move in the price of the underlying stock approaches 1.00 or 100% for a call option. This relationship between the price movement for an option compared to the price movement in the underlying security is referred to as an option's Delta. A deep in-the-money option behaves like the underlying stock by making a near point-for-point move with the price change in the underlying security. Therefore, these options are similar to owning the stock but with the advantages options provide:

- leverage resulting from a lower capital requirement
- limited risk
- higher percentage profit potential

Put Purchases

A put option purchase, also known as being long a put, is a bearish position. It gives the purchaser the right but not the obligation to sell the underlying security at a fixed price on or before the expiration. The risk for the purchaser is limited to the premium paid for the put option. The profit potential is not limited. The put purchase strategy benefits from a decrease in the price of the underlying security. Buying puts is a strategy that can be used as an alternative to short selling a stock, giving the purchaser the added benefits of limited risk and increased leverage.

Put Buying Advantages:

- A put purchase is a limited risk alternative to shorting a stock, which is a high-risk strategy

- Put purchases provide leverage without having to use margin

- Put purchases are limited risk but the profit potential is not limited

- Put purchasers do not have to pay dividends on the underlying stock, which is required of short sellers

Summary of Variables for Call and Put Purchases

Variable	Effect on a Call	Effect on a Put
Increase in Stock Price	Increases Call Value	Decreases Put Value
Decrease in Stock Price	Decreases Call Value	Increases Put Value
Higher Strike Price	Decreases Call Value	Increases Put Value
Lower Strike Price	Increases Call Value	Decreases Put Value
Longer Expiration	Increases Call Value	Increases Put Value
Shorter Expiration	Decreases Call Value	Decreases Put Value
Higher Interest Rate	Increases Call Value	Decreases Put Value
Lower Interest Rates	Decreases Call Value	Increases Put Value
Increased Dividends	Decreases Call Value	Increases Put Value
Decreased Dividends	Increases Call Value	Decreases Put Value
Increase in Volatility	Increases Call Value	Increases Put Value
Decrease in Volatility	Decreases Call Value	Decreases Put Value

Section 3 Quiz

1. Buying calls is a strategy that can be used as an alternative to the outright purchase of stock, giving the purchaser the added benefits of limited risk and increased leverage.
   A. True
   B. False

2. At expiration, call buyers will lose their entire investment if the underlying stock closes below the strike price of the call purchased.
   A. True
   B. False

3. The IBM 70-strike call option was purchased for 3 points. IBM stock would have to close at ___ at option expiration for this call purchase to breakeven.
   A. 67
   B. 70
   C. 73
   D. 76

4. In the above example, if IBM stock closes at 80 at option expiration, a ___ point net profit (before commissions) would be realized on the call purchase.
   A. 7
   B. 3
   C. 10
   D. 8

5. Using the same IBM example, the maximum risk for purchasing the 70-strike call option for 3 points would be ___ points.
   A. 7
   B. 10
   C. 3
   D. 73

6. One advantage of purchasing deep in-the-money call options is the significantly lower level of time decay, as most of the option premium is composed of intrinsic value.
   A. True
   B. False

7. IBM stock is currently trading at 77. The IBM 55-strike in-the-money call option is priced at 22.75 points. This call option has __ points of time value.

   A. 22
   B. .75
   C. 22.75
   D. 21.25

8. Purchasing an in-the-money call option has a lower probability of profit than an out-of-the-money call as there is an increased requirement for the underlying stock to move in the right direction.

   A. True
   B. False

9. As options move deeper in-the-money, the amount by which an option's price will change for a one point move in the price of the underlying stock approaches 1.00 or 100%. This is referred to as an option's Delta.

   A. True
   B. False

10. Buying put options is a strategy that can be used as an alternative to short selling a stock, giving the buyer the added benefits of limited risk and increased leverage.

    A. True
    B. False

11. The Mastercard 120-strike weekly put option was purchased for 5 points. Mastercard stock would have to close at __ at option expiration for this put purchase to breakeven.

    A. 120
    B. 125
    C. 130
    D. 115

12. In the above example, Mastercard stock closes at 130 at option expiration. This would result in a __ point _____ for the put purchase.

    A. 10, profit
    B. 10, loss
    C. 5, profit
    D. 5, loss

Section 3 Quiz Key

1. A, True
2. A, True
3. C, 73
4. A, 7 (10 point value – 3 point cost = 7 point profit)
5. C, 3
6. A, True
7. B, .75
8. B, False
9. A, True
10. A, True
11. D, 115
12. D, 5, loss

$4 Million in Option Premium Income

Our brokerage account Transaction Reports that follow show that we collected $4,068,825.32 in option premium over the past five years which resulted in over $67,000 average cash income per month. Brokerage confirmations list the options we sold and the amount of cash that was credited to our brokerage account for each option sale.

Transaction History: Reports

| Transactions | Check Summary | Deposit Summary | Categories | Reports |

Date	Description	Amount
09/18/15	2 AMZN Oct 16 '15 $550 Call(AMZN) AMAZON COM INC COM SH...	$2,524.41
08/20/15	2 AMZN Sep 18 '15 $520 Call(AMZN) AMAZON COM INC COM SH...	$3,402.39
08/11/15	2 GOOGL Sep 11 '15 $690 Call(GOOGL) GOOGLE INC CL A SHO...	$3,750.39
08/10/15	7 NFLX Sep 11 '15 $124 Call(NFLX) NETFLIX INC COM SHORT...	$5,586.47
07/23/15	2 AMZN Aug 21 '15 $470 Call(AMZN) AMAZON COM INC COM SH...	$6,150.34
01/06/15	6 O Feb 20 '15 $50 Call(O) REALTY INCOME CORP COM SHORT...	$587.36
12/11/14	6 O Dec 20 '14 $45 Call(O) REALTY INCOME CORP COM SHORT...	$767.39
12/09/14	6 XLU Dec 20 '14 $46 Call(XLU) UTILITIES SELECT SECTOR ...	$407.37
11/14/14	58 UPRO Jan 15 '16 $120 Call(UPRO) PROSHARES ULTRAPRO S...	$163,507.66
11/14/14	40 FAS Jan 15 '16 $110 Call(FAS) DIREXION DAILY FINANCI...	$96,243.21
11/12/14	42 UPRO Jan 15 '16 $120 Call(UPRO) PROSHARES ULTRAPRO S...	$112,311.32
11/07/14	84 TQQQ Jan 15 '16 $85 Call(TQQQ) PROSHARES ULTRAPRO QQ...	$189,347.04
11/04/14	8 O Nov 22 '14 $45 Call(O) REALTY INCOME CORP COM SHORT...	$1,985.83
11/03/14	25 AAPL Nov 22 '14 $106 Call(AAPL) APPLE INC COM SHORT...	$8,722.60
10/29/14	8 XLP Nov 22 '14 $46.50 Call(XLP) CONSUMER STAPLES SELE...	$217.87
10/29/14	8 XLU Nov 22 '14 $45 Call(XLU) UTILITIES SELECT SECTOR ...	$297.83
10/29/14	7 AMJ Nov 22 '14 $51 Call(AMJ) JPMORGAN ALERIAN MLP IND...	$826.62
10/23/14	20 FAS Jan 15 '16 $100 Call(FAS) DIREXION DAILY FINANCI...	$38,259.74
10/14/14	21 FB Nov 22 '14 $77.50 Call(FB) FACEBOOK INC CL A SHOR...	$6,275.74
10/03/14	8 TWTR Oct 24 '14 $55 Call(TWTR) TWITTER INC COM SHORT...	$1,429.84
09/29/14	8 TWTR Oct 24 '14 $51.50 Call(TWTR) TWITTER INC COM SHO...	$1,981.83
09/24/14	11 FB Oct 18 '14 $80 Call(FB) FACEBOOK INC CL A SHORT...	$1,461.54
09/24/14	10 FB Oct 18 '14 $80 Call(FB) FACEBOOK INC CL A SHORT...	$1,288.31
09/17/14	6 HAL Oct 18 '14 $67.50 Call(HAL) HALLIBURTON CO COM SH...	$795.39
09/17/14	25 AAPL Oct 18 '14 $103.57 Call(AAPL) APPLE INC COM SHO...	$4,526.73
09/16/14	8 TWTR Oct 24 '14 $51.50 Call(TWTR) TWITTER INC COM SHO...	$1,981.79
09/05/14	21 FB Sep 26 '14 $77 Call(FB) FACEBOOK INC CL A SHORT...	$3,801.72
08/29/14	3 GOOGL Sep 20 '14 $585 Call(GOOGL) GOOGLE INC CL A SHO...	$2,228.66
08/26/14	21 FB Sep 05 '14 $74.50 Call(FB) FACEBOOK INC CL A SHOR...	$2,999.84
08/22/14	6 HAL Sep 20 '14 $67.50 Call(HAL) HALLIBURTON CO COM SH...	$807.39
08/22/14	1 GOOGL Sep 20 '14 $600 Call(GOOGL) GOOGLE INC CL A SHO...	$710.22
08/22/14	25 AAPL Sep 20 '14 $102 Call(AAPL) APPLE INC COM SHORT...	$5,251.61
08/14/14	5 AAPL Aug 22 '14 $96 Call(AAPL) APPLE INC COM SHORT...	$988.15
08/13/14	3 GOOGL Aug 29 '14 $580 Call(GOOGL) GOOGLE INC CL A SHO...	$2,989.64
08/07/14	8 FB Aug 16 '14 $72.50 Call(FB) FACEBOOK INC CL A SHORT...	$1,137.85
08/07/14	1 GOOGL Aug 22 '14 $575 Call(GOOGL) GOOGLE INC CL A SHO...	$811.22
08/07/14	6 HAL Aug 22 '14 $67.50 Call(HAL) HALLIBURTON CO COM SH...	$797.36
08/04/14	3 GOOGL Aug 16 '14 $580 Call(GOOGL) GOOGLE INC CL A SHO...	$2,689.65
08/04/14	20 TQQQ Jan 15 '16 $65 Call(TQQQ) PROSHARES ULTRAPRO QQ...	$43,975.67
07/31/14	3 MMM Aug 16 '14 $141 Call(MMM) 3M CO COM SHORT...	$499.68
07/25/14	17 FB Aug 16 '14 $75 Call(FB) FACEBOOK INC CL A SHORT...	$3,569.86
07/25/14	1 GOOGL Aug 16 '14 $600 Call(GOOGL) GOOGLE INC CL A SHO...	$807.22
07/16/14	1 GOOGL Aug 16 '14 $600 Call(GOOGL) GOOGLE INC CL A SHO...	$1,389.20

Transaction History: Reports

Transactions	Check Summary	Deposit Summary	Categories	Reports

Date	Description	Amount
07/16/14	10 AAPL Aug 22 '14 $96 Call(AAPL) APPLE INC COM SHORT...	$3,178.24
07/15/14	9 AAPL Aug 22 '14 $96 Call(AAPL) APPLE INC COM SHORT...	$2,590.03
07/15/14	1 AAPL Aug 22 '14 $96 Call(AAPL) APPLE INC COM SHORT...	$282.23
07/13/14	1 GOOGL Aug 16 '14 $600 Call(GOOGL) GOOGLE INC CL A SHO...	$1,415.20
07/13/14	3 MMM Aug 16 '14 $145 Call(MMM) 3M CO COM SHORT...	$757.68
07/13/14	6 HAL Aug 16 '14 $70 Call(HAL) HALLIBURTON CO COM SHORT...	$1,151.37
06/12/14	20 TQQQ Jan 17 '15 $65 Call(TQQQ) PROSHARES ULTRAPRO QQ...	$24,680.00
05/29/14	20 TQQQ Jan 17 '15 $65 Call(TQQQ) PROSHARES ULTRAPRO QQ...	$21,080.08
05/27/14	20 TQQQ Jan 17 '15 $65 Call(TQQQ) PROSHARES ULTRAPRO QQ...	$19,300.21
05/27/14	12 UPRO Jan 15 '16 $95 Call(UPRO) PROSHARES ULTRAPRO S&...	$30,826.04
05/27/14	5 TQQQ Jan 15 '16 $60 Call(TQQQ) PROSHARES ULTRAPRO QQQ...	$8,831.97
05/27/14	15 TQQQ Jan 15 '16 $60 Call(TQQQ) PROSHARES ULTRAPRO QQ...	$26,563.89
05/27/14	20 TQQQ Jan 15 '16 $65 Call(TQQQ) PROSHARES ULTRAPRO QQ...	$28,680.00
05/21/14	12 UPRO Jan 17 '15 $95 Call(UPRO) PROSHARES ULTRAPRO S&...	$18,910.37
05/13/14	12 UPRO Jan 17 '15 $95 Call(UPRO) PROSHARES ULTRAPRO S&...	$21,346.25
05/13/14	12 UPRO Jan 15 '16 $95 Call(UPRO) PROSHARES ULTRAPRO S&...	$30,346.11
05/13/14	20 FAS Jan 17 '15 $90 Call(FAS) DIREXION DAILY FINANCIA...	$24,460.09
05/12/14	12 UPRO Jan 17 '15 $95 Call(UPRO) PROSHARES ULTRAPRO S&...	$20,566.33
05/09/14	12 UPRO Jan 15 '16 $90 Call(UPRO) PROSHARES ULTRAPRO S&...	$30,226.12
05/08/14	24 LNG Jun 21 '14 $57.50 Call(LNG) CHENIERE ENERGY INC ...	$4,677.45
04/22/14	15 TNA Jan 17 '15 $75 Call(TNA) DIREXION DAILY SMALL CA...	$19,214.05
04/22/14	15 TNA Jan 15 '16 $75 Call(TNA) DIREXION DAILY SMALL CA...	$28,303.78
04/21/14	3 FAS Jan 17 '15 $90 Call(FAS) DIREXION DAILY FINANCIAL...	$3,338.62
04/21/14	7 FAS Jan 17 '15 $90 Call(FAS) DIREXION DAILY FINANCIAL...	$7,792.44
04/21/14	10 FAS Jan 15 '16 $90 Call(FAS) DIREXION DAILY FINANCIA...	$18,467.87
04/14/14	18 HD Jan 17 '15 $75 Call(HD) HOME DEPOT INC COM SHORT...	$8,977.95
04/14/14	20 TJX Jan 17 '15 $55 Call(TJX) TJX COS INC NEW COM SHO...	$11,276.39
04/14/14	36 XLV Jun 21 '14 $55 Call(XLV) HEALTH CARE SELECT SECT...	$6,984.18
04/14/14	4 SSO Jan 17 '15 $100 Call(SSO) PROSHARES ULTRA S&P 500...	$4,016.85
04/14/14	20 FAS Jan 17 '15 $80 Call(FAS) DIREXION DAILY FINANCIA...	$28,695.91
04/11/14	18 LNG Jun 21 '14 $55 Call(LNG) CHENIERE ENERGY INC COM...	$8,707.98
04/11/14	16 SSO Jan 17 '15 $100 Call(SSO) PROSHARES ULTRA S&P 50...	$15,423.36
04/09/14	1 GOLG1 Jun 21 '14 $1130 Call(GOOGL) GOOGLE INC CL A SH...	$5,441.11
04/09/14	6 LNG Jun 21 '14 $55 Call(LNG) CHENIERE ENERGY INC COM ...	$3,587.29
04/04/14	8 SSO Apr 11 '14 $103 Call(SSO) PROSHARES ULTRA S&P 500...	$1,977.81
04/01/14	6 FAS Jan 15 '16 $90 Call(FAS) DIREXION DAILY FINANCIAL...	$13,981.05
04/01/14	3 FAS Jan 15 '16 $90 Call(FAS) DIREXION DAILY FINANCIAL...	$6,975.52
04/01/14	11 FAS Jan 15 '16 $90 Call(FAS) DIREXION DAILY FINANCIA...	$25,678.94
03/28/14	8 SSO Apr 04 '14 $102 Call(SSO) PROSHARES ULTRA S&P 500...	$2,205.81
03/21/14	8 SSO Mar 28 '14 $102 Call(SSO) PROSHARES ULTRA S&P 500...	$2,565.77
03/17/14	4 FAS Jan 15 '16 $45 Call(FAS) DIREXION DAILY FINANCIAL...	$19,568.49
03/17/14	11 FAS Jan 15 '16 $45 Call(FAS) DIREXION DAILY FINANCIA...	$53,952.36
03/14/14	8 SSO Mar 22 '14 $100 Call(SSO) PROSHARES ULTRA S&P 500...	$2,625.81
03/13/14	15 FAS Mar 22 '14 $88 Call(FAS) DIREXION DAILY FINANCIA...	$5,980.35
03/07/14	15 FAS Mar 14 '14 $93 Call(FAS) DIREXION DAILY FINANCIA...	$4,630.39

Transaction History: Reports

Transactions	Check Summary	Deposit Summary	Categories	Reports

Date	Description	Amount
02/21/14	5 FAS Feb 28 '14 $82 Call(FAS) DIREXION DAILY FINANCIAL...	$2,001.09
02/21/14	10 FAS Feb 28 '14 $82 Call(FAS) DIREXION DAILY FINANCIA...	$4,068.20
02/21/14	8 SSO Feb 28 '14 $98 Call(SSO) PROSHARES ULTRA S&P 500 ...	$2,981.80
02/18/14	8 SSO Feb 22 '14 $98 Call(SSO) PROSHARES ULTRA S&P 500 ...	$3,049.77
02/14/14	4 FAS Feb 22 '14 $82 Call(FAS) DIREXION DAILY FINANCIAL...	$1,868.90
02/12/14	11 FAS Feb 22 '14 $82 Call(FAS) DIREXION DAILY FINANCIA...	$4,438.46
02/06/14	15 FAS Feb 14 '14 $74 Call(FAS) DIREXION DAILY FINANCIA...	$8,399.33
02/06/14	8 SSO Feb 14 '14 $90 Call(SSO) PROSHARES ULTRA S&P 500 ...	$3,505.79
01/31/14	15 FAS Feb 07 '14 $78 Call(FAS) DIREXION DAILY FINANCIA...	$6,055.34
01/31/14	8 SSO Feb 07 '14 $93 Call(SSO) PROSHARES ULTRA S&P 500 ...	$2,545.81
01/23/14	15 FAS Jan 31 '14 $84 Call(FAS) DIREXION DAILY FINANCIA...	$6,329.35
01/17/14	13 FAS Jan 24 '14 $87.50 Call(FAS) DIREXION DAILY FINAN...	$5,198.91
01/17/14	2 FAS Jan 24 '14 $87.50 Call(FAS) DIREXION DAILY FINANC...	$794.44
01/17/14	8 SSO Jan 24 '14 $98 Call(SSO) PROSHARES ULTRA S&P 500 ...	$2,989.76
01/10/14	8 SSO Jan 18 '14 $98 Call(SSO) PROSHARES ULTRA S&P 500 ...	$2,949.80
01/10/14	15 FAS Jan 18 '14 $88 Call(FAS) DIREXION DAILY FINANCIA...	$6,314.29
01/02/14	8 SSO Jan 10 '14 $98 Call(SSO) PROSHARES ULTRA S&P 500 ...	$2,645.81
01/02/14	15 FAS Jan 10 '14 $85.50 Call(FAS) DIREXION DAILY FINAN...	$6,434.35
12/26/13	8 SSO Jan 03 '14 $101 Call(SSO) PROSHARES ULTRA S&P 500...	$989.87
12/26/13	15 FAS Jan 03 '14 $90 Call(FAS) DIREXION DAILY FINANCIA...	$2,039.49
12/19/13	8 SSO Dec 27 '13 $97 Call(SSO) PROSHARES ULTRA S&P 500 ...	$1,429.82
12/19/13	15 FAS Dec 27 '13 $84.50 Call(FAS) DIREXION DAILY FINAN...	$3,434.46
12/11/13	8 SSO Dec 21 '13 $95 Call(SSO) PROSHARES ULTRA S&P 500 ...	$1,393.86
12/11/13	15 FAS Dec 21 '13 $81 Call(FAS) DIREXION DAILY FINANCIA...	$3,055.45
12/06/13	15 FAS Dec 13 '13 $82 Call(FAS) DIREXION DAILY FINANCIA...	$2,980.45
12/06/13	8 SSO Dec 13 '13 $96.50 Call(SSO) PROSHARES ULTRA S&P 5...	$1,185.85
12/04/13	15 FAS Dec 06 '13 $82 Call(FAS) DIREXION DAILY FINANCIA...	$2,980.47
11/15/13	30 FAS Nov 22 '13 $81 Call(FAS) DIREXION DAILY FINANCIA...	$4,022.84
11/15/13	16 SSO Nov 22 '13 $96.50 Call(SSO) PROSHARES ULTRA S&P ...	$1,391.66
11/08/13	16 SSO Nov 16 '13 $93.50 Call(SSO) PROSHARES ULTRA S&P ...	$1,451.74
11/07/13	30 FAS Nov 16 '13 $74.50 Call(FAS) DIREXION DAILY FINAN...	$5,128.92
11/01/13	16 SSO Nov 08 '13 $92.50 Call(SSO) PROSHARES ULTRA S&P ...	$1,759.65
10/31/13	30 FAS Nov 08 '13 $76.50 Call(FAS) DIREXION DAILY FINAN...	$5,248.90
10/25/13	16 SSO Nov 01 '13 $92 Call(SSO) PROSHARES ULTRA S&P 500...	$1,647.73
10/24/13	19 FAS Nov 01 '13 $78.50 Call(FAS) DIREXION DAILY FINAN...	$2,930.39
10/24/13	11 FAS Nov 01 '13 $78.50 Call(FAS) DIREXION DAILY FINAN...	$1,688.51
10/18/13	30 FAS Oct 25 '13 $79 Call(FAS) DIREXION DAILY FINANCIA...	$4,532.96
10/18/13	16 SSO Oct 25 '13 $91 Call(SSO) PROSHARES ULTRA S&P 500...	$1,455.66
10/11/13	16 SSO Oct 19 '13 $87 Call(SSO) PROSHARES ULTRA S&P 500...	$1,727.65
10/11/13	30 FAS Oct 19 '13 $72.50 Call(FAS) DIR	$5,372.94

Total Sold Short	**$1,500,120.18**

Transaction History: Reports

| Transactions | Check Summary | Deposit Summary | Categories | Reports |

Date	Description	Amount
09/13/13	30 FAS Sep 21 '13 $70.50 Call(FAS) DIREXION DAILY FINAN...	$3,992.97
09/13/13	16 SSO Sep 21 '13 $85 Call(SSO) PROSHARES ULTRA S&P 500...	$1,887.72
09/06/13	30 FAS Sep 13 '13 $67 Call(FAS) DIREXION DAILY FINANCIA...	$4,052.83
09/06/13	16 SSO Sep 13 '13 $83 Call(SSO) PROSHARES ULTRA S&P 500...	$1,455.66
08/30/13	16 SSO Sep 06 '13 $79.50 Call(SSO) PROSHARES ULTRA S&P ...	$1,899.67
08/30/13	30 FAS Sep 06 '13 $63 Call(FAS) DIREXION DAILY FINANCIA...	$5,218.80
08/27/13	16 SSO Aug 30 '13 $79.50 Call(SSO) PROSHARES ULTRA S&P ...	$1,675.68
08/27/13	30 FAS Aug 30 '13 $63 Call(FAS) DIREXION DAILY FINANCIA...	$4,918.81
08/23/13	16 SSO Aug 30 '13 $82.50 Call(SSO) PROSHARES ULTRA S&P ...	$1,359.68
08/22/13	30 FAS Aug 30 '13 $67.50 Call(FAS) DIREXION DAILY FINAN...	$6,118.96
08/22/13	16 SSO Aug 23 '13 $81 Call(SSO) PROSHARES ULTRA S&P 500...	$1,579.72
08/08/13	16 SSO Aug 17 '13 $85 Call(SSO) PROSHARES ULTRA S&P 500...	$2,539.70
08/07/13	30 FAS Aug 17 '13 $73 Call(FAS) DIREXION DAILY FINANCIA...	$5,968.91
08/02/13	16 SSO Aug 09 '13 $86.50 Call(SSO) PROSHARES ULTRA S&P ...	$1,311.74
08/02/13	30 FAS Aug 09 '13 $76.50 Call(FAS) DIREXION DAILY FINAN...	$4,232.99
07/26/13	30 FAS Aug 02 '13 $75 Call(FAS) DIREXION DAILY FINANCIA...	$4,768.93
07/26/13	16 SSO Aug 02 '13 $85 Call(SSO) PROSHARES ULTRA S&P 500...	$1,579.72
07/19/13	16 SSO Jul 26 '13 $85 Call(SSO) PROSHARES ULTRA S&P 500...	$1,375.74
07/19/13	30 FAS Jul 26 '13 $75.50 Call(FAS) DIREXION DAILY FINAN...	$4,802.98
07/12/13	16 SSO Jul 20 '13 $83.50 Call(SSO) PROSHARES ULTRA S&P ...	$1,711.73
07/12/13	30 FAS Jul 20 '13 $72.50 Call(FAS) DIREXION DAILY FINAN...	$4,322.85
07/05/13	16 SSO Jul 12 '13 $79 Call w(SSO) PROSHARES ULTRA S&P 5...	$1,551.67
07/05/13	30 FAS Jul 12 '13 $66.50 Call w(FAS) DIREXION DAILY FIN...	$4,292.85
06/28/13	16 SSO Jul 05 '13 $78 Call w(SSO) PROSHARES ULTRA S&P 5...	$1,551.67
06/28/13	30 FAS Jul 05 '13 $64.50 Call w(FAS) DIREXION DAILY FIN...	$4,592.98
06/26/13	16 SSO Jun 28 '13 $75 Call w(SSO) PROSHARES ULTRA S&P 5...	$2,715.70
06/25/13	30 FAS Jun 28 '13 $60 Call w(FAS) DIREXION DAILY FINANC...	$5,968.91
06/14/13	8 FAS Jun 22 '13 $65 Call(FAS) DIREXION DAILY FINANCIAL...	$1,289.85
06/14/13	22 FAS Jun 22 '13 $65 Call(FAS) DIREXION DAILY FINANCIA...	$3,565.12
06/14/13	16 SSO Jun 22 '13 $79.50 Call(SSO) PROSHARES ULTRA S&P ...	$1,871.73
06/06/13	16 SSO Jun 14 '13 $77.50 Call w(SSO) PROSHARES ULTRA S&...	$2,699.70
06/06/13	30 FAS Jun 14 '13 $63.50 Call w(FAS) DIREXION DAILY FIN...	$6,868.89
05/31/13	16 SSO Jun 07 '13 $81 Call w(SSO) PROSHARES ULTRA S&P 5...	$1,727.66
05/31/13	30 FAS Jun 07 '13 $69 Call w(FAS) DIREXION DAILY FINANC...	$5,132.98
05/24/13	16 SSO May 31 '13 $81 Call w(SSO) PROSHARES ULTRA S&P 5..	$1,499.67
05/24/13	30 FAS May 31 '13 $67 Call w(FAS) DIREXION DAILY FINANC...	$4,168.94
05/17/13	16 SSO May 24 '13 $82 Call w(SSO) PROSHARES ULTRA S&P 5..	$1,679.66
05/17/13	30 FAS May 24 '13 $69.50 Call w(FAS) DIREXION DAILY FIN...	$4,232.97

Transaction History: Reports

Transactions	Check Summary	Deposit Summary	Categories	Reports	

Date	Description	Amount
05/17/13	30 FAS May 24 '13 $69.50 Call w(FAS) DIREXION DAILY FIN...	$4,232.97
05/09/13	16 SSO May 18 '13 $79 Call(SSO) PROSHARES ULTRA S&P 500...	$1,487.73
05/09/13	30 FAS May 18 '13 $63.50 Call(FAS) DIREXION DAILY FINAN...	$3,662.98
05/03/13	30 FAS May 10 '13 $60.50 Call w(FAS) DIREXION DAILY FIN...	$3,122.99
05/03/13	16 SSO May 10 '13 $77.50 Call w(SSO) PROSHARES ULTRA S&...	$1,439.73
04/26/13	9 FAS May 03 '13 $57.50 Call w(FAS) DIREXION DAILY FINA...	$943.06
04/26/13	21 FAS May 03 '13 $57.50 Call w(FAS) DIREXION DAILY FIN...	$2,251.79
04/26/13	5 SSO May 03 '13 $74.50 Call w(SSO) PROSHARES ULTRA S&P...	$447.14
04/26/13	7 SSO May 03 '13 $74.50 Call w(SSO) PROSHARES ULTRA S&P...	$589.63
04/26/13	4 SSO May 03 '13 $74.50 Call w(SSO) PROSHARES ULTRA S&P...	$340.94
04/22/13	16 SSO Apr 26 '13 $72 Call w(SSO) PROSHARES ULTRA S&P 5...	$1,579.66
04/19/13	30 FAS Apr 26 '13 $53.50 Call w(FAS) DIREXION DAILY FIN...	$3,268.94
04/12/13	7 TNA Apr 20 '13 $43.50 Call(TNA) DIREXION DAILY SMALL ...	$546.64
04/12/13	33 TNA Apr 20 '13 $43.50 Call(TNA) DIREXION DAILY SMALL...	$2,676.70
04/12/13	16 SSO Apr 20 '13 $75 Call(SSO) PROSHARES ULTRA S&P 500...	$1,103.74
04/12/13	30 FAS Apr 20 '13 $57 Call(FAS) DIREXION DAILY FINANCIA...	$3,392.85
04/11/13	16 SSO Apr 20 '13 $76 Put(SSO) PROSHARES ULTRA S&P 500 ...	$1,899.70
04/11/13	30 FAS Apr 20 '13 $58 Put(FAS) DIREXION DAILY FINANCIAL...	$4,168.92
04/11/13	40 TNA Apr 20 '13 $44.50 Put(TNA) DIREXION DAILY SMALL ...	$4,761.25
04/05/13	40 TNA Apr 12 '13 $41 Put w(TNA) DIREXION DAILY SMALL C...	$5,165.12
04/05/13	7 SSO Apr 12 '13 $71.50 Put w(SSO) PROSHARES ULTRA S&P ...	$764.60
04/05/13	9 SSO Apr 12 '13 $71.50 Put w(SSO) PROSHARES ULTRA S&P ...	$988.06
04/05/13	30 FAS Apr 12 '13 $53 Put w(FAS) DIREXION DAILY FINANCI...	$3,752.84
04/04/13	30 FAS Apr 12 '13 $54 Call w(FAS) DIREXION DAILY FINANC...	$3,388.94
04/04/13	16 SSO Apr 12 '13 $72.50 Call w(SSO) PROSHARES ULTRA S&...	$1,323.73
04/04/13	40 TNA Apr 12 '13 $41 Call w(TNA) DIREXION DAILY SMALL ...	$4,201.26
03/28/13	16 SSO Apr 05 '13 $73.50 Put w(SSO) PROSHARES ULTRA S&P...	$1,547.73
03/28/13	20 TNA Apr 05 '13 $89.50 Put w(TNA) DIREXION DAILY SMAL...	$3,776.60
03/28/13	10 FAS Apr 05 '13 $164.50 Put w(FAS) DIREXION DAILY FIN...	$3,184.27
03/28/13	10 FAS Apr 05 '13 $164.50 Call w(FAS) DIREXION DAILY FI...	$3,098.29
03/28/13	16 SSO Apr 05 '13 $73 Call w(SSO) PROSHARES ULTRA S&P 5...	$1,311.74
03/28/13	20 TNA Apr 05 '13 $89.50 Call w(TNA) DIREXION DAILY SMA...	$3,500.64
03/22/13	20 TNA Mar 28 '13 $88 Put w(TNA) DIREXION DAILY SMALL C...	$5,000.51
03/22/13	16 SSO Mar 28 '13 $72 Put w(SSO) PROSHARES ULTRA S&P 50...	$1,583.66
03/22/13	10 FAS Mar 28 '13 $162.50 Put w(FAS) DIREXION DAILY FIN...	$3,788.23
03/22/13	16 SSO Mar 28 '13 $72 Call w(SSO) PROSHARES ULTRA S&P 5...	$1,339.71
03/22/13	20 TNA Mar 28 '13 $87.50 Call w(TNA) DIREXION DAILY SMA...	$4,656.61
03/22/13	10 FAS Mar 28 '13 $162.50 Call w(FAS) DIREXION DAILY FI...	$3,484.27
03/15/13	20 TNA Mar 22 '13 $89.50 Call w(TNA) DIREXION DAILY SMA...	$3,220.55
03/15/13	16 SSO Mar 22 '13 $72 Call w(SSO) PROSHARES ULTRA S&P 5...	$1,247.67

Transaction History: Reports

Transactions	Check Summary	Deposit Summary	Categories	Reports

Date	Description	Amount
03/15/13	10 FAS Mar 22 '13 $168 Call w(FAS) DIREXION DAILY FINAN...	$2,798.25
03/14/13	20 TNA Mar 22 '13 $89 Put w(TNA) DIREXION DAILY SMALL C...	$3,976.63
03/14/13	16 SSO Mar 22 '13 $72.50 Put w(SSO) PROSHARES ULTRA S&P...	$1,323.71
03/14/13	10 FAS Mar 22 '13 $167 Put w(FAS) DIREXION DAILY FINANC...	$3,484.27
03/08/13	16 SSO Mar 16 '13 $71.50 Put(SSO) PROSHARES ULTRA S&P 5...	$1,163.72
03/08/13	16 SSO Mar 16 '13 $71.50 Call(SSO) PROSHARES ULTRA S&P ...	$1,103.67
03/08/13	8 FAS Mar 16 '13 $161.50 Put(FAS) DIREXION DAILY FINANC...	$2,973.79
03/07/13	8 FAS Mar 16 '13 $161 Call(FAS) DIREXION DAILY FINANCIA...	$3,349.78
03/07/13	1 FAS Mar 16 '13 $161 Call(FAS) DIREXION DAILY FINANCIA...	$399.23
03/07/13	1 FAS Mar 16 '13 $161 Call(FAS) DIREXION DAILY FINANCIA...	$398.24
03/07/13	4 TNA Mar 16 '13 $84.50 Put(TNA) DIREXION DAILY SMALL C...	$796.91
03/07/13	16 TNA Mar 16 '13 $84.50 Call(TNA) DIREXION DAILY SMALL...	$2,751.63
03/07/13	4 TNA Mar 16 '13 $84.50 Call(TNA) DIREXION DAILY SMALL ...	$648.93
03/07/13	2 FAS Mar 16 '13 $161.50 Put(FAS) DIREXION DAILY FINANC...	$842.45
03/06/13	16 TNA Mar 16 '13 $83 Put(TNA) DIREXION DAILY SMALL CAP...	$3,499.69
03/05/13	16 SSO Mar 08 '13 $70.50 Put w(SSO) PROSHARES ULTRA S&P...	$939.72
03/05/13	8 FAS Mar 08 '13 $157 Put w(FAS) DIREXION DAILY FINANCI...	$1,985.83
03/01/13	16 TNA Mar 08 '13 $79 Put w(TNA) DIREXION DAILY SMALL C...	$3,311.62
03/01/13	16 TNA Mar 08 '13 $79 Call w(TNA) DIREXION DAILY SMALL ...	$3,019.70
03/01/13	16 SSO Mar 08 '13 $69 Put w(SSO) PROSHARES ULTRA S&P 50...	$1,867.70
03/01/13	16 SSO Mar 08 '13 $68.50 Call w(SSO) PROSHARES ULTRA S&...	$1,455.66
03/01/13	5 FAS Mar 08 '13 $149 Put w(FAS) DIREXION DAILY FINANCI...	$1,742.12
03/01/13	3 FAS Mar 08 '13 $149 Put w(FAS) DIREXION DAILY FINANCI...	$989.67
03/01/13	10 FAS Mar 08 '13 $149 Call w(FAS) DIREXION DAILY FINAN...	$3,142.27
03/01/13	2 FAS Mar 08 '13 $149 Call w(FAS) DIREXION DAILY FINANC...	$620.46
03/01/13	4 FAS Mar 08 '13 $149 Call w(FAS) DIREXION DAILY FINANC...	$1,256.91
02/22/13	16 TNA Mar 01 '13 $79 Put w(TNA) DIREXION DAILY SMALL C...	$3,775.61
02/22/13	12 SSO Mar 01 '13 $68 Put w(SSO) PROSHARES ULTRA S&P 50...	$1,474.74
02/22/13	4 SSO Mar 01 '13 $68 Put w(SSO) PROSHARES ULTRA S&P 500...	$488.90
02/22/13	8 FAS Mar 01 '13 $149 Put w(FAS) DIREXION DAILY FINANCI...	$2,885.79
02/21/13	16 TNA Mar 01 '13 $78 Call w(TNA) DIREXION DAILY SMALL ...	$2,779.63
02/21/13	16 SSO Mar 01 '13 $67 Call w(SSO) PROSHARES ULTRA S&P 5...	$1,707.66
02/21/13	8 FAS Mar 01 '13 $147 Call w(FAS) DIREXION DAILY FINANC...	$2,425.82
02/15/13	16 TNA Feb 22 '13 $81.50 Put w(TNA) DIREXION DAILY SMAL...	$2,379.71
02/15/13	16 TNA Feb 22 '13 $81.50 Call w(TNA) DIREXION DAILY SMA...	$2,303.64
02/15/13	16 SSO Feb 22 '13 $68.50 Put w(SSO) PROSHARES ULTRA S&P...	$1,179.72
02/15/13	16 SSO Feb 22 '13 $68 Call w(SSO) PROSHARES ULTRA S&P 5...	$1,339.71
02/15/13	8 FAS Feb 22 '13 $151.50 Put w(FAS) DIREXION DAILY FINA...	$2,025.83
02/15/13	8 FAS Feb 22 '13 $151 Call w(FAS) DIREXION DAILY FINANC...	$2,101.81

Transaction History: Reports

Transactions	Check Summary	Deposit Summary	Categories	Reports

Date	Description	Amount
02/14/13	4 EDC Mar 16 '13 $110 Put(EDC) DIREXION DAILY EMERGING ...	$2,444.89
02/14/13	4 EDC Mar 16 '13 $108 Call(EDC) DIREXION DAILY EMERGING...	$1,572.91
02/08/13	8 FAS Feb 16 '13 $148 Call(FAS) DIREXION DAILY FINANCIA...	$2,125.81
02/08/13	16 TNA Feb 16 '13 $79.50 Put(TNA) DIREXION DAILY SMALL ...	$3,099.70
02/08/13	16 TNA Feb 16 '13 $79.50 Call(TNA) DIREXION DAILY SMALL...	$2,399.64
02/08/13	16 SSO Feb 16 '13 $68.50 Put(SSO) PROSHARES ULTRA S&P 5...	$1,419.71
02/08/13	16 SSO Feb 16 '13 $68.50 Call(SSO) PROSHARES ULTRA S&P ...	$847.68
02/08/13	8 FAS Feb 16 '13 $147.50 Put(FAS) DIREXION DAILY FINANC...	$2,305.82
02/05/13	4 EDC Feb 16 '13 $108 Call(EDC) DIREXION DAILY EMERGING...	$948.92
01/30/13	16 TNA Feb 08 '13 $76 Put w(TNA) DIREXION DAILY SMALL C...	$3,215.62
01/30/13	16 TNA Feb 08 '13 $76 Call w(TNA) DIREXION DAILY SMALL ...	$3,051.70
01/30/13	16 SSO Feb 08 '13 $67 Put w(SSO) PROSHARES ULTRA S&P 50...	$1,711.66
01/30/13	16 SSO Feb 08 '13 $67 Call w(SSO) PROSHARES ULTRA S&P 5...	$1,183.67
01/30/13	8 FAS Feb 08 '13 $142 Put w(FAS) DIREXION DAILY FINANCI...	$2,365.80
01/30/13	8 FAS Feb 08 '13 $142 Call w(FAS) DIREXION DAILY FINANC...	$2,293.80
01/24/13	16 TNA Feb 01 '13 $77.50 Call w(TNA) DIREXION DAILY SMA...	$2,239.64
01/24/13	16 SSO Feb 01 '13 $67 Call w(SSO) PROSHARES ULTRA S&P 5...	$927.67
01/24/13	8 FAS Feb 01 '13 $144 Call w(FAS) DIREXION DAILY FINANC...	$1,925.81
01/24/13	16 TNA Feb 01 '13 $76 Put w(TNA) DIREXION DAILY SMALL C...	$2,955.70
01/24/13	16 SSO Feb 01 '13 $66.50 Put w(SSO) PROSHARES ULTRA S&P...	$1,419.73
01/24/13	8 FAS Feb 01 '13 $142.50 Put w(FAS) DIREXION DAILY FINA...	$2,265.83
01/23/13	2 EDC Jan 17 '15 $105 Put(EDC) DIREXION DAILY EMERGING ...	$6,890.32
01/23/13	2 EDC Jan 18 '14 $108 Put(EDC) DIREXION DAILY EMERGING ...	$4,990.36
01/18/13	16 TNA Jan 25 '13 $73.50 Call w(TNA) DIREXION DAILY SMA...	$2,015.65
01/18/13	16 SSO Jan 25 '13 $65 Call w(SSO) PROSHARES ULTRA S&P 5...	$1,039.67
01/18/13	8 FAS Jan 25 '13 $136 Call w(FAS) DIREXION DAILY FINANC...	$1,861.81
01/17/13	4 EDC Feb 16 '13 $113 Put(EDC) DIREXION DAILY EMERGING ...	$2,268.89
01/17/13	4 EDC Feb 16 '13 $113 Call(EDC) DIREXION DAILY EMERGING...	$1,872.88
01/17/13	16 TNA Jan 25 '13 $73.50 Put w(TNA) DIREXION DAILY SMAL...	$2,699.70
01/17/13	16 SSO Jan 25 '13 $65.50 Put w(SSO) PROSHARES ULTRA S&P...	$1,579.73
01/17/13	8 FAS Jan 25 '13 $138 Put w(FAS) DIREXION DAILY FINANCI...	$2,393.80
01/16/13	2 EDC Jan 18 '14 $108 Put(EDC) DIREXION DAILY EMERGING ...	$5,230.35
01/15/13	2 EDC Jan 17 '15 $105 Put(EDC) DIREXION DAILY EMERGING ...	$7,330.30
01/11/13	16 TNA Jan 19 '13 $71 Call(TNA) DIREXION DAILY SMALL CA...	$1,983.65
01/11/13	16 SSO Jan 19 '13 $64 Call(SSO) PROSHARES ULTRA S&P 500...	$1,071.67
01/11/13	8 FAS Jan 19 '13 $135 Call(FAS) DIREXION DAILY FINANCIA...	$2,341.80
01/10/13	16 SSO Jan 19 '13 $64.50 Put(SSO) PROSHARES ULTRA S&P 5...	$1,483.66
01/10/13	8 FAS Jan 19 '13 $135.50 Put(FAS) DIREXION DAILY FINANC...	$2,545.83
01/10/13	15 TNA Jan 19 '13 $71 Put(TNA) DIREXION DAILY SMALL CAP...	$2,455.48
01/10/13	1 TNA Jan 19 '13 $71 Put(TNA) DIREXION DAILY SMALL CAP ...	$135.24

Transaction History: Reports

| Transactions | Check Summary | Deposit Summary | Categories | Reports |

Date	Description	Amount
01/04/13	8 TNA Jan 11 '13 $70.50 Call w(TNA) DIREXION DAILY SMAL...	$1,269.86
01/04/13	8 TNA Jan 11 '13 $70.50 Call w(TNA) DIREXION DAILY SMAL...	$1,293.86
01/04/13	16 SSO Jan 11 '13 $63.50 Call w(SSO) PROSHARES ULTRA S&...	$1,071.67
01/04/13	4 FAS Jan 11 '13 $132 Call w(FAS) DIREXION DAILY FINANC...	$1,032.90
01/04/13	4 FAS Jan 11 '13 $132 Call w(FAS) DIREXION DAILY FINANC...	$1,032.90
01/03/13	16 TNA Jan 11 '13 $70 Put w(TNA) DIREXION DAILY SMALL C...	$3,339.69
01/03/13	16 SSO Jan 11 '13 $63 Put w(SSO) PROSHARES ULTRA S&P 50...	$1,419.73
01/03/13	8 FAS Jan 11 '13 $129.50 Put w(FAS) DIREXION DAILY FINA...	$2,465.83
12/31/12	2 EDC Jan 17 '15 $105 Put(EDC) DIREXION DAILY EMERGING ...	$7,710.30
12/31/12	6 FAS Jan 17 '15 $120 Put(FAS) DIREXION DAILY FINANCIAL...	$23,986.89
12/31/12	12 TNA Jan 17 '15 $63 Put(TNA) DIREXION DAILY SMALL CAP...	$27,222.19
12/31/12	2 EDC Jan 18 '14 $108 Put(EDC) DIREXION DAILY EMERGING ...	$5,828.34
12/31/12	8 TNA Jan 04 '13 $63 Call w(TNA) DIREXION DAILY SMALL C...	$1,681.87
12/31/12	21 UPRO Jan 18 '14 $85 Put(UPRO) PROSHARES ULTRAPRO S&P...	$38,195.05
12/31/12	2 EDC Jan 19 '13 $105 Call(EDC) DIREXION DAILY EMERGING...	$1,260.46
12/31/12	4 FAS Jan 04 '13 $120 Call w(FAS) DIREXION DAILY FINANC...	$1,008.91
12/31/12	6 FAS Jan 18 '14 $120 Put(FAS) DIREXION DAILY FINANCIAL...	$17,147.04
12/31/12	12 TNA Jan 18 '14 $60 Put(TNA) DIREXION DAILY SMALL CAP...	$17,622.41
12/27/12	24 TNA Jan 04 '13 $60 Call w(TNA) DIREXION DAILY SMALL ...	$5,013.49
12/27/12	31 SSO Jan 04 '13 $59 Call w(SSO) PROSHARES ULTRA S&P 5...	$3,440.30
12/27/12	12 FAS Jan 04 '13 $115 Call w(FAS) DIREXION DAILY FINAN...	$4,182.76
12/21/12	16 TNA Dec 28 '12 $63 Call w(TNA) DIREXION DAILY SMALL ...	$2,703.67
12/21/12	4 TNA Dec 28 '12 $63 Call w(TNA) DIREXION DAILY SMALL C...	$688.92
12/21/12	4 TNA Dec 28 '12 $63 Call w(TNA) DIREXION DAILY SMALL C...	$664.92
12/21/12	13 SSO Dec 28 '12 $60.50 Call w(SSO) PROSHARES ULTRA S&...	$1,182.07
12/21/12	18 SSO Dec 28 '12 $59.50 Call w(SSO) PROSHARES ULTRA S&...	$2,754.22
12/21/12	2 FAS Dec 28 '12 $120 Call w(FAS) DIREXION DAILY FINANC...	$538.47
12/21/12	8 FAS Dec 28 '12 $120 Call w(FAS) DIREXION DAILY FINANC...	$2,205.86
12/21/12	2 FAS Dec 28 '12 $120 Call w(FAS) DIREXION DAILY FINANC...	$518.47
12/20/12	1 EDC Jan 17 '15 $110 Call(EDC) DIREXION DAILY EMERGING...	$3,012.17
12/20/12	1 EDC Jan 18 '14 $110 Call(EDC) DIREXION DAILY EMERGING...	$2,212.19
12/20/12	2 EDC Jan 19 '13 $105 Call(EDC) DIREXION DAILY EMERGING...	$1,070.46
12/18/12	4 TNA Dec 22 '12 $63 Call(TNA) DIREXION DAILY SMALL CAP...	$448.94
12/18/12	2 TNA Jan 18 '14 $65 Call(TNA) DIREXION DAILY SMALL CAP...	$2,550.43
12/18/12	2 FAS Dec 22 '12 $120 Call(FAS) DIREXION DAILY FINANCIA...	$430.48
12/18/12	1 FAS Jan 17 '15 $120 Call(FAS) DIREXION DAILY FINANCIA...	$3,182.16
12/18/12	2 TNA Jan 17 '15 $64 Call(TNA) DIREXION DAILY SMALL CAP...	$3,590.40
12/18/12	1 FAS Jan 18 '14 $120 Call(FAS) DIREXION DAILY FINANCIA...	$2,271.19
12/17/12	2 TNA Dec 22 '12 $60 Call(TNA) DIREXION DAILY SMALL CAP...	$260.48
12/17/12	2 TNA Dec 22 '12 $60 Call(TNA) DIREXION DAILY SMALL CAP...	$250.48

Transaction History: Reports

Date	Description	Amount
12/17/12	2 TNA Dec 22 '12 $60 Call(TNA) DIREXION DAILY SMALL CAP...	$260.48
12/17/12	2 TNA Dec 22 '12 $60 Call(TNA) DIREXION DAILY SMALL CAP...	$250.48
12/17/12	2 TNA Jan 18 '14 $65 Call(TNA) DIREXION DAILY SMALL CAP...	$2,190.44
12/17/12	2 FAS Dec 22 '12 $116 Call(FAS) DIREXION DAILY FINANCIA...	$340.47
12/17/12	1 FAS Jan 17 '15 $120 Call(FAS) DIREXION DAILY FINANCIA...	$2,918.17
12/17/12	2 TNA Jan 17 '15 $64 Call(TNA) DIREXION DAILY SMALL CAP...	$3,270.41
12/17/12	1 FAS Jan 18 '14 $120 Call(FAS) DIREXION DAILY FINANCIA...	$2,005.19
12/14/12	16 TNA Dec 22 '12 $59 Call(TNA) DIREXION DAILY SMALL CA...	$2,415.68
12/14/12	8 SSO Dec 22 '12 $60 Call(SSO) PROSHARES ULTRA S&P 500 ...	$509.89
12/14/12	9 SSO Dec 22 '12 $59.50 Call(SSO) PROSHARES ULTRA S&P 5...	$795.13
12/14/12	8 FAS Dec 22 '12 $112 Call(FAS) DIREXION DAILY FINANCIA...	$1,665.87
12/13/12	5 SSO Dec 22 '12 $60 Call(SSO) PROSHARES ULTRA S&P 500 ...	$363.19
12/13/12	9 SSO Dec 22 '12 $59.50 Call(SSO) PROSHARES ULTRA S&P 5...	$885.11
12/13/12	3 UPRO Jan 18 '14 $90 Call(UPRO) PROSHARES ULTRAPRO S&P...	$4,543.61
12/12/12	9 SSO Dec 14 '12 $61.50 Call w(SSO) PROSHARES ULTRA S&P...	$354.10
12/12/12	6 UPRO Jan 18 '14 $95 Call(UPRO) PROSHARES ULTRAPRO S&P...	$8,627.24
12/10/12	9 SSO Dec 14 '12 $60 Call w(SSO) PROSHARES ULTRA S&P 50...	$498.09
12/10/12	6 UPRO Jan 18 '14 $90 Call(UPRO) PROSHARES ULTRAPRO S&P...	$8,855.24
12/07/12	16 TNA Dec 14 '12 $58 Call w(TNA) DIREXION DAILY SMALL ...	$2,139.76
12/07/12	8 FAS Dec 14 '12 $112 Call w(FAS) DIREXION DAILY FINANC...	$1,653.87
12/06/12	8 SSO Dec 14 '12 $59.50 Call w(SSO) PROSHARES ULTRA S&P...	$593.88
11/30/12	12 TNA Dec 07 '12 $58 Call w(TNA) DIREXION DAILY SMALL ...	$1,546.77
11/30/12	4 TNA Dec 07 '12 $58 Call w(TNA) DIREXION DAILY SMALL C...	$512.92
11/30/12	8 SSO Dec 07 '12 $60 Call w(SSO) PROSHARES ULTRA S&P 50...	$401.88
11/30/12	8 FAS Dec 07 '12 $107 Call w(FAS) DIREXION DAILY FINANC...	$1,893.86
11/28/12	4 TNA Nov 30 '12 $55.50 Call w(TNA) DIREXION DAILY SMAL...	$368.95
11/28/12	8 FAS Nov 30 '12 $105 Call w(FAS) DIREXION DAILY FINANC...	$1,585.86
11/28/12	2 TNA Jan 17 '15 $60 Call(TNA) DIREXION DAILY SMALL CAP...	$2,990.42
11/28/12	1 FAS Jan 17 '15 $110 Call(FAS) DIREXION DAILY FINANCIA...	$2,705.17
11/28/12	6 UPRO Jan 18 '14 $90 Call(UPRO) PROSHARES ULTRAPRO S&P...	$8,207.25
11/28/12	1 FAS Jan 18 '14 $110 Call(FAS) DIREXION DAILY FINANCIA...	$1,897.19
11/28/12	2 TNA Jan 18 '14 $60 Call(TNA) DIREXION DAILY SMALL CAP...	$2,030.44
11/26/12	4 TNA Nov 30 '12 $54.50 Call w(TNA) DIREXION DAILY SMAL...	$536.94
11/26/12	2 FAS Nov 30 '12 $107.50 Call w(FAS) DIREXION DAILY FIN...	$292.47
11/26/12	1 FAS Jan 17 '15 $110 Call(FAS) DIREXION DAILY FINANCIA...	$2,792.17
11/26/12	1 FAS Jan 18 '14 $110 Call(FAS) DIREXION DAILY FINANCIA...	$1,942.19
11/23/12	8 TNA Nov 30 '12 $54.50 Call w(TNA) DIREXION DAILY SMAL...	$1,125.85
11/23/12	4 FAS Nov 30 '12 $107.50 Call w(FAS) DIREXION DAILY FIN...	$812.94
11/23/12	2 TNA Jan 17 '15 $55 Call(TNA) DIREXION DAILY SMALL CAP...	$3,090.41
11/23/12	2 TNA Jan 18 '14 $55 Call(TNA) DIREXION DAILY SMALL CAP...	$2,470.43
11/19/12	8 TNA Nov 23 '12 $52 Call w(TNA) DIREXION DAILY SMALL C...	$585.89
11/19/12	4 FAS Nov 23 '12 $103 Call w(FAS) DIREXION DAILY FINANC...	$620.92
11/19/12	4 TNA Jan 17 '15 $55 Call(TNA) DIREXION DAILY SMALL CAP...	$6,116.82
11/19/12	2 FAS Jan 17 '15 $110 Call(FAS) DIREXION DAILY FINANCIA...	$5,350.35
11/19/12	4 TNA Jan 18 '14 $55 Call(TNA) DIREXION DAILY SMALL CAP...	$4,388.86
11/19/12	2 FAS Jan 18 '14 $105 Call(FAS) DIREXION D.	$4,084.38
	Total Sold Short	**$692,558.89**

Transaction History: Reports

| Transactions | Check Summary | Deposit Summary | Categories | Reports |

Date	Description	Amount
09/13/13	6 FAS Sep 21 '13 $70.50 Call(FAS) DIREXION DAILY FINANC...	$801.40
09/13/13	8 TNA Sep 21 '13 $59 Call(TNA) DIREXION DAILY SMALL CAP...	$1,269.82
09/06/13	8 TNA Sep 13 '13 $56 Call(TNA) DIREXION DAILY SMALL CAP...	$1,197.82
09/06/13	6 FAS Sep 13 '13 $67 Call(FAS) DIREXION DAILY FINANCIAL...	$795.37
08/30/13	8 TNA Sep 06 '13 $53 Call(TNA) DIREXION DAILY SMALL CAP...	$1,185.83
08/30/13	6 FAS Sep 06 '13 $63 Call(FAS) DIREXION DAILY FINANCIAL...	$1,037.38
08/27/13	6 FAS Aug 30 '13 $63.50 Call(FAS) DIREXION DAILY FINANC...	$827.37
08/27/13	8 TNA Aug 30 '13 $53 Call(TNA) DIREXION DAILY SMALL CAP...	$1,025.84
08/23/13	8 TNA Aug 30 '13 $56.50 Call(TNA) DIREXION DAILY SMALL ...	$949.84
08/22/13	6 FAS Aug 30 '13 $67.50 Call(FAS) DIREXION DAILY FINANC...	$1,247.38
08/22/13	8 TNA Aug 23 '13 $54 Call(TNA) DIREXION DAILY SMALL CAP...	$1,185.85
08/08/13	4 TNA Aug 17 '13 $58 Call(TNA) DIREXION DAILY SMALL CAP...	$788.93
08/07/13	3 FAS Aug 17 '13 $73 Call(FAS) DIREXION DAILY FINANCIAL...	$589.70
08/02/13	3 FAS Aug 09 '13 $76.50 Call(FAS) DIREXION DAILY FINANC...	$446.71
08/02/13	4 TNA Aug 09 '13 $60 Call(TNA) DIREXION DAILY SMALL CAP...	$472.94
07/26/13	4 TNA Aug 02 '13 $58.50 Call(TNA) DIREXION DAILY SMALL ...	$516.94
07/26/13	3 FAS Aug 02 '13 $75 Call(FAS) DIREXION DAILY FINANCIAL...	$475.71
07/19/13	4 TNA Jul 26 '13 $59 Call(TNA) DIREXION DAILY SMALL CAP...	$440.92
07/19/13	3 FAS Jul 26 '13 $75.50 Call(FAS) DIREXION DAILY FINANC...	$485.71
07/12/13	6 FAS Jul 20 '13 $72.50 Call(FAS) DIREXION DAILY FINANC...	$861.40
07/12/13	8 TNA Jul 20 '13 $56.50 Call(TNA) DIREXION DAILY SMALL ...	$989.87
07/05/13	8 TNA Jul 12 '13 $50.50 Call w(TNA) DIREXION DAILY SMAL...	$1,053.84
07/05/13	6 FAS Jul 12 '13 $66.50 Call w(FAS) DIREXION DAILY FINA...	$837.37
06/28/13	8 TNA Jul 05 '13 $48.50 Call w(TNA) DIREXION DAILY SMAL...	$877.87
06/28/13	6 FAS Jul 05 '13 $64.50 Call w(FAS) DIREXION DAILY FINA...	$885.40
06/25/13	6 FAS Jun 28 '13 $60 Call w(FAS) DIREXION DAILY FINANCI...	$1,187.39
06/21/13	8 TNA Jun 28 '13 $46 Call w(TNA) DIREXION DAILY SMALL C...	$1,185.85
06/14/13	8 TNA Jun 22 '13 $49 Call(TNA) DIREXION DAILY SMALL CAP...	$1,061.84
06/14/13	6 FAS Jun 22 '13 $65 Call(FAS) DIREXION DAILY FINANCIAL...	$957.40
06/06/13	8 TNA Jun 14 '13 $47 Call w(TNA) DIREXION DAILY SMALL C...	$1,585.85
06/06/13	6 FAS Jun 14 '13 $63.50 Call w(FAS) DIREXION DAILY FINA...	$1,367.38
05/31/13	6 FAS Jun 07 '13 $69 Call w(FAS) DIREXION DAILY FINANCI...	$1,029.37
05/31/13	8 TNA Jun 07 '13 $49.50 Call w(TNA) DIREXION DAILY SMAL...	$1,173.86
05/24/13	8 TNA May 31 '13 $49 Call w(TNA) DIREXION DAILY SMALL C...	$881.87
05/24/13	6 FAS May 31 '13 $67 Call w(FAS) DIREXION DAILY FINANCI...	$827.37
05/17/13	8 TNA May 24 '13 $50.50 Call w(TNA) DIREXION DAILY SMAL...	$861.87
05/17/13	6 FAS May 24 '13 $69.50 Call w(FAS) DIREXION DAILY FINA...	$903.39
05/09/13	6 FAS May 18 '13 $63.50 Call(FAS) DIREXION DAILY FINANC...	$735.40
05/09/13	8 TNA May 18 '13 $46.50 Call(TNA) DIREXION DAILY SMALL ...	$1,013.86

Transaction History: Reports

Transactions	Check Summary	Deposit Summary	Categories	Reports

Date	Description	Amount
05/03/13	8 TNA May 10 '13 $45.50 Call w(TNA) DIREXION DAILY SMAL...	$781.87
05/03/13	6 FAS May 10 '13 $60.50 Call w(FAS) DIREXION DAILY FINA...	$657.37
04/26/13	8 TNA May 03 '13 $42 Call w(TNA) DIREXION DAILY SMALL C...	$1,045.86
04/26/13	6 FAS May 03 '13 $57.50 Call w(FAS) DIREXION DAILY FINA...	$627.37
04/19/13	6 FAS Apr 26 '13 $53.50 Call w(FAS) DIREXION DAILY FINA...	$639.40
04/19/13	8 TNA Apr 26 '13 $39 Call w(TNA) DIREXION DAILY SMALL C...	$869.84
04/17/13	6 FAS Apr 20 '13 $53 Call(FAS) DIREXION DAILY FINANCIAL...	$587.39
04/17/13	8 TNA Apr 20 '13 $38.50 Call(TNA) DIREXION DAILY SMALL ...	$625.86
04/12/13	2 TNA Apr 20 '13 $43 Call(TNA) DIREXION DAILY SMALL CAP...	$192.46
04/12/13	6 FAS Apr 20 '13 $56.50 Call(FAS) DIREXION DAILY FINANC...	$795.37
04/11/13	6 FAS Apr 20 '13 $58 Put(FAS) DIREXION DAILY FINANCIAL ...	$827.40
04/11/13	8 TNA Apr 20 '13 $44.50 Put(TNA) DIREXION DAILY SMALL C...	$945.85
04/05/13	8 TNA Apr 12 '13 $41 Put w(TNA) DIREXION DAILY SMALL CA...	$1,037.86
04/05/13	6 FAS Apr 12 '13 $53 Put w(FAS) DIREXION DAILY FINANCIA...	$747.40
04/04/13	6 FAS Apr 12 '13 $54 Call w(FAS) DIREXION DAILY FINANCI...	$671.39
04/04/13	8 TNA Apr 12 '13 $41 Call w(TNA) DIREXION DAILY SMALL C...	$833.87
03/28/13	4 TNA Apr 05 '13 $89.50 Call w(TNA) DIREXION DAILY SMAL...	$696.93
03/28/13	2 FAS Apr 05 '13 $165 Call w(FAS) DIREXION DAILY FINANC...	$572.46
03/28/13	2 FAS Apr 05 '13 $164.50 Put w(FAS) DIREXION DAILY FINA...	$600.46
03/28/13	4 TNA Apr 05 '13 $89.50 Put w(TNA) DIREXION DAILY SMALL...	$728.93
03/22/13	2 FAS Mar 28 '13 $162.50 Put w(FAS) DIREXION DAILY FINA...	$744.45
03/22/13	4 TNA Mar 28 '13 $88 Put w(TNA) DIREXION DAILY SMALL CA...	$988.90
03/22/13	4 TNA Mar 28 '13 $88 Call w(TNA) DIREXION DAILY SMALL C...	$828.93
03/22/13	2 FAS Mar 28 '13 $162.50 Call w(FAS) DIREXION DAILY FIN...	$694.45
03/15/13	4 TNA Mar 22 '13 $89.50 Call w(TNA) DIREXION DAILY SMAL...	$704.91
03/15/13	2 FAS Mar 22 '13 $168 Call w(FAS) DIREXION DAILY FINANC...	$554.45
03/14/13	4 TNA Mar 22 '13 $89 Put w(TNA) DIREXION DAILY SMALL CA...	$788.93
03/14/13	2 FAS Mar 22 '13 $167.50 Put w(FAS) DIREXION DAILY FINA...	$722.45
03/08/13	4 TNA Mar 16 '13 $87 Call(TNA) DIREXION DAILY SMALL CAP...	$552.91
03/08/13	2 FAS Mar 16 '13 $163 Put(FAS) DIREXION DAILY FINANCIAL...	$638.45
03/08/13	2 FAS Mar 16 '13 $163 Call(FAS) DIREXION DAILY FINANCIA...	$538.45
03/06/13	4 TNA Mar 16 '13 $83 Put(TNA) DIREXION DAILY SMALL CAP ...	$868.93
03/05/13	2 FAS Mar 08 '13 $157 Put w(FAS) DIREXION DAILY FINANCI...	$490.46
03/01/13	4 TNA Mar 08 '13 $79 Put w(TNA) DIREXION DAILY SMALL CA...	$840.91
03/01/13	4 TNA Mar 08 '13 $79 Call w(TNA) DIREXION DAILY SMALL C...	$748.93
03/01/13	2 FAS Mar 08 '13 $149 Put w(FAS) DIREXION DAILY FINANCI...	$708.45
03/01/13	2 FAS Mar 08 '13 $149 Call w(FAS) DIREXION DAILY FINANC...	$640.46
02/22/13	4 TNA Mar 01 '13 $79 Put w(TNA) DIREXION DAILY SMALL CA...	$916.90
02/22/13	4 TNA Mar 01 '13 $79 Call w(TNA) DIREXION DAILY SMALL C...	$788.93
02/22/13	2 FAS Mar 01 '13 $150 Put w(FAS) DIREXION DAILY FINANCI...	$714.45

Transaction History: Reports

| Transactions | Check Summary | Deposit Summary | Categories | Reports |

Date	Description	Amount
02/15/13	4 TNA Feb 22 '13 $82 Put w(TNA) DIREXION DAILY SMALL CA...	$648.93
02/15/13	4 TNA Feb 22 '13 $81.50 Call w(TNA) DIREXION DAILY SMAL...	$588.91
02/15/13	2 FAS Feb 22 '13 $151.50 Put w(FAS) DIREXION DAILY FINA...	$502.45
02/15/13	2 FAS Feb 22 '13 $151 Call w(FAS) DIREXION DAILY FINANC...	$558.45
02/08/13	2 FAS Feb 16 '13 $148 Call(FAS) DIREXION DAILY FINANCIA...	$530.45
02/08/13	4 TNA Feb 16 '13 $79.50 Put(TNA) DIREXION DAILY SMALL C...	$748.93
02/08/13	4 TNA Feb 16 '13 $79.50 Call(TNA) DIREXION DAILY SMALL ...	$616.91
02/08/13	2 FAS Feb 16 '13 $147.50 Put(FAS) DIREXION DAILY FINANC...	$570.46
02/04/13	1 EDC Jan 17 '15 $115 Put(EDC) DIREXION DAILY EMERGING ...	$4,011.14
02/01/13	1 EDC Jan 18 '14 $115 Put(EDC) DIREXION DAILY EMERGING ...	$2,711.18
01/30/13	4 TNA Feb 08 '13 $76.50 Put w(TNA) DIREXION DAILY SMALL...	$876.91
01/30/13	4 TNA Feb 08 '13 $76 Call w(TNA) DIREXION DAILY SMALL C...	$748.93
01/30/13	2 FAS Feb 08 '13 $142.50 Put w(FAS) DIREXION DAILY FINA...	$566.45
01/30/13	2 FAS Feb 08 '13 $142 Call w(FAS) DIREXION DAILY FINANC...	$600.45
01/24/13	4 TNA Feb 01 '13 $77 Call w(TNA) DIREXION DAILY SMALL C...	$632.91
01/24/13	2 FAS Feb 01 '13 $144 Call w(FAS) DIREXION DAILY FINANC...	$474.45
01/24/13	1 EDC Jan 18 '14 $115 Put(EDC) DIREXION DAILY EMERGING ...	$2,871.17
01/24/13	4 TNA Feb 01 '13 $76 Put w(TNA) DIREXION DAILY SMALL CA...	$748.93
01/24/13	2 FAS Feb 01 '13 $142.50 Put w(FAS) DIREXION DAILY FINA...	$520.46
01/24/13	1 EDC Jan 17 '15 $115 Put(EDC) DIREXION DAILY EMERGING ...	$4,091.14
01/22/13	1 EDC Jan 17 '15 $115 Put(EDC) DIREXION DAILY EMERGING ...	$4,111.14
01/18/13	1 EDC Jan 17 '15 $115 Call(EDC) DIREXION DAILY EMERGING...	$3,022.17
01/18/13	4 TNA Jan 25 '13 $73.50 Call w(TNA) DIREXION DAILY SMAL...	$492.91
01/18/13	2 FAS Jan 25 '13 $136 Put w(FAS) DIREXION DAILY FINANCI...	$470.45
01/18/13	2 FAS Jan 25 '13 $136 Call w(FAS) DIREXION DAILY FINANC...	$442.46
01/17/13	4 TNA Jan 25 '13 $73.50 Put w(TNA) DIREXION DAILY SMALL...	$688.93
01/17/13	1 EDC Jan 18 '14 $115 Put(EDC) DIREXION DAILY EMERGING ...	$2,871.17
01/11/13	2 FAS Jan 19 '13 $135.50 Call(FAS) DIREXION DAILY FINAN...	$538.45
01/11/13	4 TNA Jan 19 '13 $71 Call(TNA) DIREXION DAILY SMALL CAP...	$500.91
01/10/13	4 TNA Jan 19 '13 $71.50 Put(TNA) DIREXION DAILY SMALL C...	$648.93
01/10/13	2 FAS Jan 19 '13 $136 Put(FAS) DIREXION DAILY FINANCIAL...	$610.46
01/08/13	4 TNA Jan 11 '13 $69.50 Put w(TNA) DIREXION DAILY SMALL...	$436.93
01/08/13	2 FAS Jan 11 '13 $131.50 Put w(FAS) DIREXION DAILY FINA...	$382.47
01/04/13	4 TNA Jan 11 '13 $70 Call w(TNA) DIREXION DAILY SMALL C...	$668.93
01/04/13	2 FAS Jan 11 '13 $132 Call w(FAS) DIREXION DAILY FINANC...	$514.45
12/31/12	2 FAS Jan 17 '15 $120 Put(FAS) DIREXION DAILY FINANCIAL...	$7,910.30
12/31/12	4 TNA Jan 17 '15 $65 Put(TNA) DIREXION DAILY SMALL CAP ...	$9,508.72
12/31/12	2 FAS Jan 18 '14 $120 Put(FAS) DIREXION DAILY FINANCIAL...	$5,650.35
12/31/12	4 TNA Jan 18 '14 $60 Put(TNA) DIREXION DAILY SMALL CAP ...	$5,948.80
12/27/12	8 TNA Jan 04 '13 $60 Call w(TNA) DIREXION DAILY SMALL C...	$1,745.84

Transaction History: Reports

| Transactions | Check Summary | Deposit Summary | Categories | Reports |

Date	Description	Amount
12/27/12	4 FAS Jan 04 '13 $115 Call w(FAS) DIREXION DAILY FINANC...	$1,428.92
12/21/12	8 TNA Dec 28 '12 $63 Call w(TNA) DIREXION DAILY SMALL C.	$1,389.84
12/21/12	4 FAS Dec 28 '12 $120 Call w(FAS) DIREXION DAILY FINANC...	$1,152.93
12/14/12	6 TNA Dec 22 '12 $59 Call(TNA) DIREXION DAILY SMALL CAP.	$885.38
12/14/12	2 TNA Dec 22 '12 $59 Call(TNA) DIREXION DAILY SMALL CAP.	$290.47
12/14/12	4 FAS Dec 22 '12 $112 Call(FAS) DIREXION DAILY FINANCIA...	$828.94
12/07/12	2 TNA Dec 14 '12 $58.50 Call w(TNA) DIREXION DAILY SMAL..	$240.48
12/07/12	6 TNA Dec 14 '12 $58 Call w(TNA) DIREXION DAILY SMALL C.	$797.42
12/07/12	4 FAS Dec 14 '12 $112 Call w(FAS) DIREXION DAILY FINANC...	$796.94
12/05/12	2 TNA Jan 18 '14 $60 Call(TNA) DIREXION DAILY SMALL CAP..	$2,410.43
11/30/12	4 TNA Dec 07 '12 $58 Call w(TNA) DIREXION DAILY SMALL C.	$532.92
11/30/12	2 TNA Dec 07 '12 $58 Call w(TNA) DIREXION DAILY SMALL C.	$258.47
11/30/12	4 FAS Dec 07 '12 $107.50 Call w(FAS) DIREXION DAILY FIN...	$888.93
11/27/12	2 TNA Nov 30 '12 $56 Call w(TNA) DIREXION DAILY SMALL C.	$184.48
11/27/12	2 FAS Nov 30 '12 $107.50 Call w(FAS) DIREXION DAILY FIN...	$304.48
11/27/12	1 FAS Jan 17 '15 $114 Call(FAS) DIREXION DAILY FINANCIA...	$2,732.17
11/27/12	1 FAS Jan 18 '14 $110 Call(FAS) DIREXION DAILY FINANCIA...	$2,027.19
11/26/12	2 TNA Jan 17 '15 $58 Call(TNA) DIREXION DAILY SMALL CAP..	$3,270.41
11/23/12	4 TNA Nov 30 '12 $54.50 Call w(TNA) DIREXION DAILY SMAL..	$528.94
11/23/12	2 FAS Nov 30 '12 $107.50 Call w(FAS) DIREXION DAILY FIN...	$406.47
11/23/12	1 FAS Jan 17 '15 $114 Call(FAS) DIREXION DAILY FINANCIA...	$2,672.17
11/21/12	2 TNA Jan 17 '15 $58 Call(TNA) DIREXION DAILY SMALL CAP..	$3,030.42
11/21/12	1 FAS Jan 18 '14 $110 Call(FAS) DIREXION DAILY FINANCIA...	$1,827.19
11/21/12	2 TNA Jan 18 '14 $55 Call(TNA) DIREXI,	$2,310.43

| | Total Sold Short | $167,604.20 |

Transaction History: Reports

Transactions | Check Summary | Deposit Summary | Categories | Reports

Date	Description	Amount
04/27/12	1 ISRG May 19 '12 $585 Call(ISRG) INTUITIVE SURGICAL IN...	$1,115.22
04/27/12	15 WFC May 04 '12 $34 Call w(WFC) WELLS FARGO & CO NEW ...	$284.63
04/27/12	9 SSO May 04 '12 $58 Call w(SSO) PROSHARES ULTRA S&P 50...	$673.17
04/27/12	9 SBUX May 04 '12 $57.50 Call w(SBUX) STARBUCKS CORP CO...	$777.15
04/27/12	8 QQQ May 04 '12 $67 Call w(QQQ) POWERSHARES QQQ TRUST,...	$565.93
04/27/12	1 MA May 04 '12 $460 Call w(MA) MASTERCARD INC CL A SHO...	$1,247.22
04/27/12	12 JPM May 04 '12 $44 Call w(JPM) JPMORGAN CHASE & CO C...	$262.90
04/27/12	1 CMG May 04 '12 $420 Call w(CMG) CHIPOTLE MEXICAN GRIL...	$545.23
04/27/12	15 AIG May 04 '12 $35 Call w(AIG) AMERICAN INTL GROUP I...	$1,289.61
04/27/12	2 AAPL May 04 '12 $605 Call w(AAPL) APPLE INC COM SHORT...	$1,428.45
04/25/12	5 WFC Apr 27 '12 $33 Call w(WFC) WELLS FARGO & CO NEW C...	$238.21
04/25/12	5 SSO Apr 27 '12 $57 Call w(SSO) PROSHARES ULTRA S&P 50...	$153.21
04/25/12	2 SSO Apr 27 '12 $57 Call w(SSO) PROSHARES ULTRA S&P 50...	$82.47
04/25/12	2 SSO Apr 27 '12 $57 Call w(SSO) PROSHARES ULTRA S&P 50...	$72.48
04/25/12	3 SBUX Apr 27 '12 $60 Call w(SBUX) STARBUCKS CORP COM S...	$309.72
04/25/12	3 SBUX Apr 27 '12 $60 Call w(SBUX) STARBUCKS CORP COM S...	$294.72
04/25/12	2 SBUX Apr 27 '12 $60 Call w(SBUX) STARBUCKS CORP COM S...	$196.48
04/25/12	2 SBUX Apr 27 '12 $60 Call w(SBUX) STARBUCKS CORP COM S...	$186.48
04/25/12	1 MA Apr 27 '12 $435 Call w(MA) MASTERCARD INC CL A SHO...	$491.23
04/25/12	1 ISRG Apr 27 '12 $565 Call w(ISRG) INTUITIVE SURGICAL ...	$591.23
04/25/12	1 CMG Apr 27 '12 $410 Call w(CMG) CHIPOTLE MEXICAN GRIL...	$491.23
04/24/12	4 JPM Apr 27 '12 $43 Call w(JPM) JPMORGAN CHASE & CO CO...	$188.96
04/24/12	13 HD Apr 27 '12 $50 Call w(HD) HOME DEPOT INC COM SHOR...	$1,932.09
04/23/12	2 QQQ Apr 27 '12 $65 Call w(QQQ) POWERSHARES QQQ TRUST,...	$130.48
04/23/12	4 AIG Apr 27 '12 $32 Call w(AIG) AMERICAN INTL GROUP IN...	$188.96
04/20/12	15 WFC Apr 27 '12 $33 Call w(WFC) WELLS FARGO & CO NEW ...	$520.62
04/20/12	8 QQQ Apr 27 '12 $66 Call w(QQQ) POWERSHARES QQQ TRUST,...	$557.90
04/20/12	1 PCLN Apr 27 '12 $710 Call w(PCLN) PRICELINE COM INC C...	$1,271.22
04/20/12	1 MA Apr 27 '12 $440 Call w(MA) MASTERCARD INC CL A SHO...	$562.23
04/20/12	12 JPM Apr 27 '12 $43 Call w(JPM) JPMORGAN CHASE & CO C...	$618.89
04/20/12	1 ISRG Apr 27 '12 $575 Call w(ISRG) INTUITIVE SURGICAL ...	$627.23
04/20/12	1 CMG Apr 27 '12 $420 Call w(CMG) CHIPOTLE MEXICAN GRIL...	$802.23
04/20/12	12 AIG Apr 27 '12 $32 Call w(AIG) AMERICAN INTL GROUP I...	$654.88
04/20/12	2 AAPL Apr 27 '12 $590 Call w(AAPL) APPLE INC COM SHORT...	$3,242.41
04/17/12	1 PCLN Apr 21 '12 $720 Call(PCLN) PRICELINE COM INC COM...	$951.22
04/17/12	2 AAPL Apr 21 '12 $600 Call(AAPL) APPLE INC COM SHORT...	$1,990.44
04/17/12	8 QQQ Apr 21 '12 $66 Call(QQQ) POWERSHARES QQQ TRUST, S...	$465.93
04/13/12	10 HD Apr 21 '12 $50 Call(HD) HOME DEPOT INC COM SHORT...	$984.38
04/12/12	10 SSO Apr 21 '12 $57 Call(SSO) PROSHARES ULTRA S&P 500...	$684.41
04/12/12	1 MA Apr 21 '12 $435 Call(MA) MASTERCARD INC CL A SHORT...	$501.23
04/12/12	2 AAPL Apr 21 '12 $630 Call(AAPL) APPLE INC COM SHORT...	$1,790.44
04/12/12	1 PCLN Apr 21 '12 $740 Call(PCLN) PRICELINE COM INC COM...	$1,431.21
04/12/12	8 QQQ Apr 21 '12 $67 Call(QQQ) POWERSHARES QQQ TRUST, S...	$545.93
04/12/12	15 WFC Apr 21 '12 $34 Call(WFC) WELLS FARGO & CO NEW CO...	$899.56
04/12/12	1 CMG Apr 21 '12 $435 Call(CMG) CHIPOTLE MEXICAN GRILL ...	$832.23
04/12/12	12 JPM Apr 21 '12 $45 Call(JPM) JPMORGAN CHASE & CO COM...	$886.88

Transaction History: Reports

Date	Description	Amount
04/12/12	8 AIG Apr 21 '12 $34 Call(AIG) AMERICAN INTL GROUP INC ...	$345.94
04/12/12	8 AIG Apr 21 '12 $33 Call(AIG) AMERICAN INTL GROUP INC ...	$561.93
04/11/12	1 ISRG Apr 21 '12 $550 Call(ISRG) INTUITIVE SURGICAL IN...	$1,234.22
04/05/12	15 WFC Apr 13 '12 $34 Call w(WFC) WELLS FARGO & CO NEW ...	$734.62
04/05/12	10 SSO Apr 13 '12 $58 Call w(SSO) PROSHARES ULTRA S&P 5...	$548.38
04/05/12	8 QQQ Apr 13 '12 $68 Call w(QQQ) POWERSHARES QQQ TRUST,..	$341.91
04/05/12	1 PCLN Apr 13 '12 $755 Call w(PCLN) PRICELINE COM INC C...	$1,137.22
04/05/12	1 MA Apr 13 '12 $440 Call w(MA) MASTERCARD INC CL A SHO...	$576.23
04/05/12	12 JPM Apr 13 '12 $45 Call w(JPM) JPMORGAN CHASE & CO C...	$586.89
04/05/12	10 HD Apr 13 '12 $50 Call w(HD) HOME DEPOT INC COM SHOR...	$808.41
04/05/12	1 CMG Apr 13 '12 $425 Call w(CMG) CHIPOTLE MEXICAN GRIL...	$425.24
04/05/12	2 AAPL Apr 13 '12 $635 Call w(AAPL) APPLE INC COM SHORT...	$1,596.45
03/29/12	15 WFC Apr 05 '12 $34 Call w(WFC) WELLS FARGO & CO NEW ...	$509.63
03/29/12	10 SSO Apr 05 '12 $58 Call w(SSO) PROSHARES ULTRA S&P 5...	$528.39
03/29/12	8 QQQ Apr 05 '12 $68 Call w(QQQ) POWERSHARES QQQ TRUST,..	$245.94
03/29/12	1 PCLN Apr 05 '12 $715 Call w(PCLN) PRICELINE COM INC C...	$1,192.22
03/29/12	12 JPM Apr 05 '12 $46 Call w(JPM) JPMORGAN CHASE & CO C...	$394.90
03/29/12	10 HD Apr 05 '12 $50 Call w(HD) HOME DEPOT INC COM SHOR...	$318.42
03/29/12	1 CMG Apr 05 '12 $420 Call w(CMG) CHIPOTLE MEXICAN GRIL...	$341.24
03/29/12	2 AAPL Apr 05 '12 $615 Call w(AAPL) APPLE INC COM SHORT...	$1,300.46
03/23/12	8 QQQ Mar 30 '12 $67 Call w(QQQ) POWERSHARES QQQ TRUST,..	$349.91
03/23/12	1 PCLN Mar 30 '12 $715 Call w(PCLN) PRICELINE COM INC C...	$1,084.23
03/23/12	12 JPM Mar 30 '12 $45 Call w(JPM) JPMORGAN CHASE & CO C...	$730.89
03/23/12	10 HD Mar 30 '12 $49 Call w(HD) HOME DEPOT INC COM SHOR...	$708.41
03/23/12	1 CMG Mar 30 '12 $415 Call w(CMG) CHIPOTLE MEXICAN GRIL...	$429.24
03/23/12	1 AAPL Mar 30 '12 $600 Call w(AAPL) APPLE INC COM SHORT...	$715.23
03/23/12	1 AAPL Mar 30 '12 $600 Call w(AAPL) APPLE INC COM SHORT...	$991.23
03/22/12	15 WFC Mar 30 '12 $34 Call w(WFC) WELLS FARGO & CO NEW ...	$344.63
03/22/12	10 SSO Mar 30 '12 $58 Call w(SSO) PROSHARES ULTRA S&P 5...	$458.42
03/20/12	1 AAPL Mar 23 '12 $605 Call w(AAPL) APPLE INC COM SHORT...	$791.23
03/16/12	10 HD Mar 23 '12 $49 Call w(HD) HOME DEPOT INC COM SHOR...	$498.42
03/16/12	10 EEM Mar 23 '12 $44 Call w(EEM) ISHARES MSCI EMERGING...	$558.38
03/16/12	1 AAPL Mar 23 '12 $590 Call w(AAPL) APPLE INC COM SHORT...	$1,034.23
03/15/12	15 WFC Mar 23 '12 $34 Call w(WFC) WELLS FARGO & CO NEW ...	$644.62
03/15/12	5 SSO Mar 23 '12 $58 Call w(SSO) PROSHARES ULTRA S&P 50...	$342.19
03/15/12	5 SSO Mar 23 '12 $58 Call w(SSO) PROSHARES ULTRA S&P 50...	$357.19
03/15/12	8 QQQ Mar 23 '12 $67 Call w(QQQ) POWERSHARES QQQ TRUST,..	$261.94
03/15/12	12 JPM Mar 23 '12 $45 Call w(JPM) JPMORGAN CHASE & CO C...	$802.89
03/13/12	5 SSO Mar 17 '12 $57 Call(SSO) PROSHARES ULTRA S&P 500 ...	$138.21
03/13/12	5 EEM Mar 17 '12 $44 Call(EEM) ISHARES MSCI EMERGING MA...	$193.21
03/08/12	15 WFC Mar 17 '12 $31 Call(WFC) WELLS FARGO & CO NEW CO...	$730.60
03/08/12	5 SSO Mar 17 '12 $55 Call(SSO) PROSHARES ULTRA S&P 500 ...	$363.21
03/08/12	8 QQQ Mar 17 '12 $64 Call(QQQ) POWERSHARES QQQ TRUST, S...	$785.93
03/08/12	12 JPM Mar 17 '12 $41 Call(JPM) JPMORGAN CHASE & CO COM...	$442.90
03/08/12	10 HD Mar 17 '12 $48 Call(HD) HOME DEPOT INC COM SHORT...	$428.42
03/08/12	18 AIG Mar 17 '12 $29 Call(AIG) AMERICAN INTL GROUP INC...	$680.32
03/08/12	5 EEM Mar 17 '12 $44 Call(EEM) ISHARES MSCI EMERGING MA...	$238.21

Transaction History: Reports

| Transactions | Check Summary | Deposit Summary | Categories | Reports |

Date	Description	Amount
03/07/12	1 AAPL Mar 17 '12 $530 Call(AAPL) APPLE INC COM SHORT...	$991.23
03/02/12	6 JPM Mar 09 '12 $41 Call w(JPM) JPMORGAN CHASE & CO CO...	$261.45
03/02/12	10 HD Mar 09 '12 $47 Call w(HD) HOME DEPOT INC COM SHOR...	$508.42
03/02/12	1 AAPL Mar 09 '12 $550 Call w(AAPL) APPLE INC COM SHORT...	$666.23
03/01/12	5 SSO Mar 09 '12 $56 Call w(SSO) PROSHARES ULTRA S&P 50...	$267.21
03/01/12	7 QQQ Mar 09 '12 $65 Call w(QQQ) POWERSHARES QQQ TRUST,...	$319.69
03/01/12	6 JPM Mar 09 '12 $41 Call w(JPM) JPMORGAN CHASE & CO CO...	$161.45
03/01/12	5 EEM Mar 09 '12 $45 Call w(EEM) ISHARES MSCI EMERGING ...	$187.21
03/01/12	8 AIG Mar 09 '12 $30 Call w(AIG) AMERICAN INTL GROUP IN...	$229.94
03/01/12	1 AIG Mar 09 '12 $30 Call w(AIG) AMERICAN INTL GROUP IN...	$24.24
03/01/12	9 AIG Mar 09 '12 $30 Call w(AIG) AMERICAN INTL GROUP IN...	$363.18
02/28/12	9 AIG Mar 02 '12 $29 Call w(AIG) AMERICAN INTL GROUP IN...	$237.18
02/24/12	7 QQQ Mar 02 '12 $64 Call w(QQQ) POWERSHARES QQQ TRUST,...	$326.69
02/24/12	10 HD Mar 02 '12 $47 Call w(HD) HOME DEPOT INC COM SHOR...	$344.40
02/24/12	1 AAPL Mar 02 '12 $525 Call w(AAPL) APPLE INC COM SHORT...	$503.24
02/23/12	5 SSO Mar 02 '12 $55 Call w(SSO) PROSHARES ULTRA S&P 50...	$297.21
02/23/12	25 MS Mar 02 '12 $19 Call w(MS) MORGAN STANLEY COM NEW ...	$877.04
02/23/12	6 JPM Mar 02 '12 $38 Call w(JPM) JPMORGAN CHASE & CO CO...	$407.44
02/23/12	6 IWM Mar 02 '12 $83 Call w(IWM) ISHARES RUSSELL 2000 I...	$467.44
02/23/12	5 EEM Mar 02 '12 $44 Call w(EEM) ISHARES MSCI EMERGING ...	$212.21
02/21/12	3 SSO Feb 24 '12 $55 Call w(SSO) PROSHARES ULTRA S&P 50...	$162.72
02/21/12	2 SSO Feb 24 '12 $55 Call w(SSO) PROSHARES ULTRA S&P 50...	$98.48
02/21/12	6 JPM Feb 24 '12 $39 Call w(JPM) JPMORGAN CHASE & CO CO...	$185.45
02/21/12	5 EEM Feb 24 '12 $44 Call w(EEM) ISHARES MSCI EMERGING ...	$178.21
02/17/12	7 QQQ Feb 24 '12 $63 Call w(QQQ) POWERSHARES QQQ TRUST,...	$567.66
02/17/12	25 MS Feb 24 '12 $19 Call w(MS) MORGAN STANLEY COM NEW ...	$1,098.03
02/17/12	6 IWM Feb 24 '12 $83 Call w(IWM) ISHARES RUSSELL 2000 I...	$467.45
02/17/12	10 HD Feb 24 '12 $47 Call w(HD) HOME DEPOT INC COM SHOR...	$554.39
02/17/12	1 AAPL Feb 24 '12 $505 Call w(AAPL) APPLE INC COM SHORT...	$711.23
02/14/12	3 AAPL Feb 18 '12 $500 Call(AAPL) APPLE INC COM SHORT...	$2,299.69
02/14/12	60 XLF Feb 18 '12 $14 Call(XLF) FINANCIAL SELECT SECTOR...	$2,946.47
02/14/12	3 XLF Feb 18 '12 $14 Call(XLF) FINANCIAL SELECT SECTOR ...	$145.73
02/14/12	15 QQQ Feb 18 '12 $63 Call(QQQ) POWERSHARES QQQ TRUST, ...	$580.57
02/14/12	7 HUM Feb 18 '12 $87.50 Call(HUM) HUMANA INC COM SHORT...	$686.66
02/14/12	11 IWM Feb 18 '12 $82 Call(IWM) ISHARES RUSSELL 2000 IN...	$533.65
02/14/12	10 HD Feb 18 '12 $46 Call(HD) HOME DEPOT IN(	
	Total Sold Short	**$82,645.77**

Transaction History: Reports

Date	Description	Amount
04/27/12	8 WFC May 04 '12 $34 Call w(WFC) WELLS FARGO & CO NEW C...	$149.90
04/27/12	5 SSO May 04 '12 $58 Call w(SSO) PROSHARES ULTRA S&P 50...	$382.19
04/27/12	4 SBUX May 04 '12 $57.50 Call w(SBUX) STARBUCKS CORP CO...	$348.96
04/27/12	4 QQQ May 04 '12 $67 Call w(QQQ) POWERSHARES QQQ TRUST,..	$280.97
04/27/12	1 MA May 04 '12 $460 Call w(MA) MASTERCARD INC CL A SHO...	$1,292.22
04/27/12	1 CMG May 04 '12 $420 Call w(CMG) CHIPOTLE MEXICAN GRIL...	$603.23
04/27/12	8 AIG May 04 '12 $35 Call w(AIG) AMERICAN INTL GROUP IN...	$637.93
04/27/12	2 AAPL May 04 '12 $610 Call w(AAPL) APPLE INC COM SHORT...	$1,148.46
04/25/12	2 WFC Apr 27 '12 $33 Call w(WFC) WELLS FARGO & CO NEW C...	$70.48
04/25/12	3 SSO Apr 27 '12 $57 Call w(SSO) PROSHARES ULTRA S&P 50...	$109.73
04/25/12	1 SSO Apr 27 '12 $57 Call w(SSO) PROSHARES ULTRA S&P 50...	$32.23
04/25/12	1 SSO Apr 27 '12 $57 Call w(SSO) PROSHARES ULTRA S&P 50...	$23.24
04/25/12	1 SBUX Apr 27 '12 $60 Call w(SBUX) STARBUCKS CORP COM S...	$101.23
04/25/12	1 SBUX Apr 27 '12 $60 Call w(SBUX) STARBUCKS CORP COM S...	$92.24
04/25/12	1 SBUX Apr 27 '12 $60 Call w(SBUX) STARBUCKS CORP COM S...	$98.23
04/25/12	1 SBUX Apr 27 '12 $60 Call w(SBUX) STARBUCKS CORP COM S...	$89.24
04/25/12	1 QQQ Apr 27 '12 $66 Call w(QQQ) POWERSHARES QQQ TRUST,..	$59.24
04/25/12	1 MA Apr 27 '12 $435 Call w(MA) MASTERCARD INC CL A SHO...	$591.23
04/25/12	1 CMG Apr 27 '12 $410 Call w(CMG) CHIPOTLE MEXICAN GRIL...	$491.23
04/24/12	2 JPM Apr 27 '12 $43 Call w(JPM) JPMORGAN CHASE & CO CO...	$82.48
04/24/12	6 HD Apr 27 '12 $50 Call w(HD) HOME DEPOT INC COM SHORT...	$887.42
04/23/12	2 AIG Apr 27 '12 $32 Call w(AIG) AMERICAN INTL GROUP IN...	$90.48
04/20/12	8 WFC Apr 27 '12 $33 Call w(WFC) WELLS FARGO & CO NEW C...	$281.91
04/20/12	4 QQQ Apr 27 '12 $66 Call w(QQQ) POWERSHARES QQQ TRUST,..	$264.96
04/20/12	1 PCLN Apr 27 '12 $710 Call w(PCLN) PRICELINE COM INC C...	$1,294.22
04/20/12	1 MA Apr 27 '12 $440 Call w(MA) MASTERCARD INC CL A SHO...	$502.23
04/20/12	6 JPM Apr 27 '12 $43 Call w(JPM) JPMORGAN CHASE & CO CO...	$257.45
04/20/12	1 CMG Apr 27 '12 $420 Call w(CMG) CHIPOTLE MEXICAN GRIL...	$627.23
04/20/12	6 AIG Apr 27 '12 $32 Call w(AIG) AMERICAN INTL GROUP IN...	$311.44
04/20/12	1 AAPL Apr 27 '12 $590 Call w(AAPL) APPLE INC COM SHORT...	$1,597.21
04/20/12	1 AAPL Apr 27 '12 $590 Call w(AAPL) APPLE INC COM SHORT...	$1,602.20
04/17/12	1 PCLN Apr 21 '12 $720 Call(PCLN) PRICELINE COM INC COM...	$991.22
04/17/12	2 AAPL Apr 21 '12 $600 Call(AAPL) APPLE INC COM SHORT...	$1,990.44
04/17/12	4 QQQ Apr 21 '12 $66 Call(QQQ) POWERSHARES QQQ TRUST, S...	$228.97
04/12/12	1 MA Apr 21 '12 $435 Call(MA) MASTERCARD INC CL A SHORT...	$481.23
04/12/12	1 AAPL Apr 21 '12 $630 Call(AAPL) APPLE INC COM SHORT...	$891.22
04/12/12	1 PCLN Apr 21 '12 $740 Call(PCLN) PRICELINE COM INC COM...	$1,433.21
04/12/12	4 QQQ Apr 21 '12 $67 Call(QQQ) POWERSHARES QQQ TRUST, S...	$272.97
04/12/12	8 WFC Apr 21 '12 $34 Call(WFC) WELLS FARGO & CO NEW COM...	$429.94
04/12/12	1 CMG Apr 21 '12 $435 Call(CMG) CHIPOTLE MEXICAN GRILL ...	$951.22
04/12/12	6 JPM Apr 21 '12 $45 Call(JPM) JPMORGAN CHASE & CO COM ...	$453.44
04/12/12	4 AIG Apr 21 '12 $34 Call(AIG) AMERICAN INTL GROUP INC ...	$164.97
04/12/12	4 AIG Apr 21 '12 $33 Call(AIG) AMERICAN INTL GROUP INC ...	$276.97
04/05/12	8 WFC Apr 13 '12 $34 Call w(WFC) WELLS FARGO & CO NEW C...	$389.91
04/05/12	5 SSO Apr 13 '12 $58 Call w(SSO) PROSHARES ULTRA S&P 50...	$262.19
04/05/12	4 QQQ Apr 13 '12 $68 Call w(QQQ) POWERSHARES QQQ TRUST,..	$148.96
04/05/12	1 PCLN Apr 13 '12 $755 Call w(PCLN) PRICELINE COM INC C...	$1,148.22

Transaction History: Reports

Date	Description	Amount
04/05/12	1 MA Apr 13 '12 $440 Call w(MA) MASTERCARD INC CL A SHO...	$573.23
04/05/12	6 JPM Apr 13 '12 $45 Call w(JPM) JPMORGAN CHASE & CO CO...	$279.45
04/05/12	5 HD Apr 13 '12 $50 Call w(HD) HOME DEPOT INC COM SHORT...	$377.21
04/05/12	1 CMG Apr 13 '12 $425 Call w(CMG) CHIPOTLE MEXICAN GRIL...	$434.24
04/05/12	1 AAPL Apr 13 '12 $630 Call w(AAPL) APPLE INC COM SHORT...	$1,033.22
03/29/12	8 WFC Apr 05 '12 $34 Call w(WFC) WELLS FARGO & CO NEW C...	$253.91
03/29/12	5 SSO Apr 05 '12 $58 Call w(SSO) PROSHARES ULTRA S&P 50...	$257.21
03/29/12	4 QQQ Apr 05 '12 $68 Call w(QQQ) POWERSHARES QQQ TRUST,...	$112.96
03/29/12	1 PCLN Apr 05 '12 $715 Call w(PCLN) PRICELINE COM INC C...	$1,199.22
03/29/12	6 JPM Apr 05 '12 $46 Call w(JPM) JPMORGAN CHASE & CO CO...	$183.45
03/29/12	5 HD Apr 05 '12 $50 Call w(HD) HOME DEPOT INC COM SHORT...	$147.21
03/29/12	1 CMG Apr 05 '12 $420 Call w(CMG) CHIPOTLE MEXICAN GRIL...	$305.24
03/29/12	1 AAPL Apr 05 '12 $615 Call w(AAPL) APPLE INC COM SHORT...	$605.23
03/23/12	4 QQQ Mar 30 '12 $67 Call w(QQQ) POWERSHARES QQQ TRUST,...	$180.96
03/23/12	1 PCLN Mar 30 '12 $715 Call w(PCLN) PRICELINE COM INC C...	$1,061.23
03/23/12	6 JPM Mar 30 '12 $45 Call w(JPM) JPMORGAN CHASE & CO CO...	$339.45
03/23/12	5 HD Mar 30 '12 $49 Call w(HD) HOME DEPOT INC COM SHORT...	$352.21
03/23/12	1 CMG Mar 30 '12 $415 Call w(CMG) CHIPOTLE MEXICAN GRIL...	$421.24
03/23/12	1 AAPL Mar 30 '12 $600 Call w(AAPL) APPLE INC COM SHORT...	$991.23
03/22/12	8 WFC Mar 30 '12 $34 Call w(WFC) WELLS FARGO & CO NEW C...	$165.94
03/22/12	5 SSO Mar 30 '12 $58 Call w(SSO) PROSHARES ULTRA S&P 50...	$222.19
03/20/12	1 AAPL Mar 23 '12 $605 Call w(AAPL) APPLE INC COM SHORT...	$791.23
03/16/12	5 HD Mar 23 '12 $49 Call w(HD) HOME DEPOT INC COM SHORT...	$242.21
03/16/12	6 EEM Mar 23 '12 $44 Call w(EEM) ISHARES MSCI EMERGING ...	$333.45
03/15/12	8 WFC Mar 23 '12 $34 Call w(WFC) WELLS FARGO & CO NEW C...	$349.94
03/15/12	5 SSO Mar 23 '12 $58 Call w(SSO) PROSHARES ULTRA S&P 50...	$337.19
03/15/12	4 QQQ Mar 23 '12 $67 Call w(QQQ) POWERSHARES QQQ TRUST,...	$128.96
03/15/12	6 JPM Mar 23 '12 $45 Call w(JPM) JPMORGAN CHASE & CO CO...	$363.45
03/08/12	8 WFC Mar 17 '12 $31 Call(WFC) WELLS FARGO & CO NEW COM...	$465.92
03/08/12	5 SSO Mar 17 '12 $55 Call(SSO) PROSHARES ULTRA S&P 500 ...	$363.21
03/08/12	4 QQQ Mar 17 '12 $64 Call(QQQ) POWERSHARES QQQ TRUST, S...	$388.97
03/08/12	6 JPM Mar 17 '12 $41 Call(JPM) JPMORGAN CHASE & CO COM ...	$213.45
03/08/12	5 HD Mar 17 '12 $48 Call(HD) HOME DEPOT INC COM SHORT...	$208.21
03/08/12	9 AIG Mar 17 '12 $29 Call(AIG) AMERICAN INTL GROUP INC ...	$327.18
03/08/12	6 EEM Mar 17 '12 $44 Call(EEM) ISHARES MSCI EMERGING MA...	$287.45
03/02/12	5 SSO Mar 09 '12 $55 Call w(SSO) PROSHARES ULTRA S&P 50...	$417.21
03/02/12	4 QQQ Mar 09 '12 $65 Call w(QQQ) POWERSHARES QQQ TRUST,...	$152.97
03/02/12	6 JPM Mar 09 '12 $41 Call w(JPM) JPMORGAN CHASE & CO CO...	$249.45
03/02/12	5 EEM Mar 09 '12 $45 Call w(EEM) ISHARES MSCI EMERGING ...	$142.21
03/02/12	9 AIG Mar 09 '12 $30 Call w(AIG) AMERICAN INTL GROUP IN...	$322.18
03/01/12	4 WFC Mar 09 '12 $32 Call w(WFC) WELLS FARGO & CO NEW C...	$84.97
02/28/12	5 MS Mar 02 '12 $19 Call w(MS) MORGAN STANLEY COM NEW S...	$113.21
02/28/12	5 AIG Mar 02 '12 $29 Call w(AIG) AMERICAN INTL GROUP IN...	$151.20
02/28/12	4 AIG Mar 02 '12 $29 Call w(AIG) AMERICAN INTL GROUP IN...	$108.97
02/24/12	5 SSO Mar 02 '12 $55 Call w(SSO) PROSHARES ULTRA S&P 50...	$297.21
02/24/12	4 QQQ Mar 02 '12 $64 Call w(QQQ) POWERSHARES QQQ TRUST,...	$164.97

Transaction History: Reports

| | Transactions | Check Summary | Deposit Summary | Categories | Reports | |

Date	Description	Amount
02/24/12	5 HD Mar 02 '12 $47 Call w(HD) HOME DEPOT INC COM SHORT...	$167.21
02/24/12	5 EEM Mar 02 '12 $44 Call w(EEM) ISHARES MSCI EMERGING ...	$257.21
02/23/12	6 JPM Mar 02 '12 $38 Call w(JPM) JPMORGAN CHASE & CO CO...	$407.44
02/23/12	3 IWM Mar 02 '12 $83 Call w(IWM) ISHARES RUSSELL 2000 I...	$229.72
02/21/12	5 SSO Feb 24 '12 $55 Call w(SSO) PROSHARES ULTRA S&P 50...	$248.21
02/21/12	6 JPM Feb 24 '12 $39 Call w(JPM) JPMORGAN CHASE & CO CO...	$185.45
02/21/12	5 EEM Feb 24 '12 $44 Call w(EEM) ISHARES MSCI EMERGING ...	$193.21
02/17/12	4 QQQ Feb 24 '12 $63 Call w(QQQ) POWERSHARES QQQ TRUST,...	$304.96
02/17/12	13 MS Feb 24 '12 $19 Call w(MS) MORGAN STANLEY COM NEW ...	$580.14
02/17/12	3 IWM Feb 24 '12 $83 Call w(IWM) ISHARES RUSSELL 2000 I...	$217.72
02/17/12	3 HD Feb 24 '12 $47 Call w(HD) HOME DEPOT INC COM SHORT...	$177.72
02/17/12	2 HD Feb 24 '12 $47 Call w(HD) HOME DEPOT INC COM SHORT...	$108.48
02/14/12	2 AAPL Feb 18 '12 $500 Call(AAPL) APPLE INC COM SHORT...	$1,530.46
02/14/12	32 XLF Feb 18 '12 $14 Call(XLF) FINANCIAL SELECT SECTOR...	$1,567.62
02/14/12	7 QQQ Feb 18 '12 $63 Call(QQQ) POWERSHARES QQQ TRUST, S...	$266.68
02/14/12	6 HUM Feb 18 '12 $87.50 Call(HUM) HUMANA INC COM SHORT...	$587.42
02/14/12	5 IWM Feb 18 '12 $82 Call(IWM) ISHARES F	$266.21
	Total Sold Short	**$48,735.95**

| | Transactions | Check Summary | Deposit Summary | Categories | Reports | |

Date	Description	Amount
12/09/11	1 GOOG Jan 19 '13 $510 Call(GOOG) GOOGLE INC CL A SHORT...	$14,990.96
12/09/11	7 TJX Jan 19 '13 $57.50 Call(TJX) TJX COS INC NEW COM S...	$7,056.56
12/09/11	1 NOV Jan 19 '13 $50 Call(NOV) NATIONAL OILWELL VARCO I...	$2,661.19
12/09/11	1 HUM Jan 19 '13 $60 Call(HUM) HUMANA INC COM SHORT...	$2,911.19
11/22/11	1 AAPL Jan 19 '13 $270 Call(AAPL) APPLE INC COM SHORT...	$12,920.00
11/21/11	1 MA Jan 19 '13 $260 Call(MA) MASTERCARD INC CL A SHORT...	$11,511.02
11/21/11	5 NOV Jan 19 '13 $50 Call(NOV) NATIONAL OILWELL VARCO I...	$11,537.97
11/21/11	4 HUM Jan 19 '13 $60 Call(HUM) HUMANA INC COM SHORT...	$10,988.74
09/23/11	8 QQQ Sep 30 '11 $54 Call w(QQQ) POWERSHARES QQQ TRUST,	$1,001.93
09/23/11	1 AAPL Sep 30 '11 $405 Call w(AAPL) APPLE INC COM SHORT...	$812.23
09/20/11	3 BIDU Sep 23 '11 $150 Call w(BIDU) BAIDU INC SPON ADR ...	$889.71
09/16/11	10 EEM Sep 23 '11 $41 Call w(EEM) ISHARES MSCI EMERGING...	$454.38
09/16/11	1 AAPL Sep 23 '11 $400 Call w(AAPL) APPLE INC COM SHORT...	$551.23
09/16/11	7 XLE Sep 23 '11 $67 Call w(XLE) ENERGY SELECT SECTOR S...	$840.68
09/16/11	8 QQQ Sep 23 '11 $57 Call w(QQQ) POWERSHARES QQQ TRUST,	$505.94
09/16/11	7 GLD Sep 23 '11 $177 Call w(GLD) SPDR GOLD SHARES SHOR...	$1,568.66
09/16/11	2 GLD Sep 23 '11 $177 Call w(GLD) SPDR GOLD SHARES SHOR...	$450.47
09/16/11	2 GLD Sep 23 '11 $177 Call w(GLD) SPDR GOLD SHARES SHOR...	$450.47
09/16/11	2 GLD Sep 23 '11 $177 Call w(GLD) SPDR GOLD SHARES SHOR...	$450.47
09/09/11	3 BIDU Sep 17 '11 $145 Call(BIDU) BAIDU INC SPON ADR RE...	$1,099.70
09/09/11	7 XLE Sep 17 '11 $65 Call(XLE) ENERGY SELECT SECTOR SPD...	$973.66

Transaction History: Reports

Date	Description	Amount
09/09/11	8 QQQ Sep 17 '11 $53 Call(QQQ) POWERSHARES QQQ TRUST, S...	$929.93
09/09/11	1 AAPL Sep 17 '11 $380 Call(AAPL) APPLE INC COM SHORT...	$566.23
09/09/11	10 EEM Sep 17 '11 $40 Call(EEM) ISHARES MSCI EMERGING M...	$1,124.40
08/07/11	10 UGL Sep 17 '11 $100 Call(UGL) PROSHARES ULTRA GOLD S...	$6,284.30
05/20/11	4 BIDU Jun 18 '11 $135 Call(BIDU) BAIDU INC SPON ADR RE...	$2,248.91
05/20/11	11 UWM Jun 18 '11 $48 Call(UWM) PROSHARES ULTRA RUSSELL...	$1,908.63
05/20/11	7 UGL Jun 18 '11 $79 Call(UGL) PROSHARES ULTRA GOLD SHO...	$1,701.66
05/20/11	9 QLD Jun 18 '11 $92 Call(QLD) PROSHARES ULTRA QQQ SHOR...	$2,235.11
05/20/11	10 SSO Jun 18 '11 $55 Call(SSO) PROSHARES ULTRA S&P 500...	$1,144.36
05/20/11	9 DIG Jun 18 '11 $55 Call(DIG) PROSHARES ULTRA OIL & GA...	$1,974.15
05/05/11	1 AAPL Jan 19 '13 $320 Call(AAPL) APPLE INC COM SHORT...	$7,671.10
04/27/11	10 SSO May 21 '11 $54 Call(SSO) PROSHARES ULTRA S&P 500...	$2,484.31
04/27/11	9 QLD May 21 '11 $92 Call(QLD) PROSHARES ULTRA QQQ SHOR...	$4,485.04
04/26/11	4 BIDU May 21 '11 $150 Call(BIDU) BAIDU INC SPON ADR RE...	$3,988.87
04/25/11	2 EDC Jan 19 '13 $39.35 Call(EDC) DIREXION DAILY EMERGI...	$3,112.42
04/21/11	6 EDC Jan 19 '13 $39.35 Call(EDC) DIREXION DAILY EMERGI...	$9,755.23
04/20/11	2 UGL Oct 22 '11 $72 Call(UGL) PROSHARES ULTRA GOLD SHO...	$1,990.44
04/20/11	5 EEM Jan 19 '13 $48 Call(EEM) ISHARES MSCI EMERGING MA...	$3,598.12
04/19/11	4 BIDU May 21 '11 $145 Call(BIDU) BAIDU INC SPON ADR RE...	$3,988.87
04/19/11	5 EEM Jan 19 '13 $46 Call(EEM) ISHARES MSCI EMERGING MA...	$3,838.11
04/18/11	4 UGL Oct 22 '11 $70 Call(UGL) PROSHARES ULTRA GOLD SHO...	$4,312.86
04/15/11	4 UGL Oct 22 '11 $70 Call(UGL) PROSHARES ULTRA GOLD SHO...	$3,988.87
04/14/11	4 UGL Oct 22 '11 $68 Call(UGL) PROSHARES ULTRA GOLD SHO...	$4,124.87
04/13/11	10 EEM Jan 19 '13 $46 Call(EEM) ISHARES MSCI EMERGING M...	$7,994.20
03/31/11	10 UYM Jan 19 '13 $45 Call(UYM) PROSHARES ULTRA BASIC M...	$18,488.00
03/25/11	1 NOV Jan 19 '13 $70 Call(NOV) NATIONAL OILWELL VARCO I...	$2,078.21
03/23/11	12 NOV Jan 19 '13 $70 Call(NOV) NATIONAL OILWELL VARCO ...	$24,826.36
03/23/11	10 UYM Jan 19 '13 $40 Call(UYM) PROSHARES ULTRA BASIC M...	$19,383.98
03/23/11	1 NOV Jan 19 '13 $65 Call(NOV) NATIONAL OILWELL VARCO I...	$2,355.20
03/21/11	3 AAPL Jan 19 '13 $300 Call(AAPL) APPLE INC COM SHORT...	$25,979.22
03/21/11	18 QLD Jan 19 '13 $67 Call(QLD) PROSHARES ULTRA QQQ SHO...	$49,391.30
03/21/11	17 SSO Jan 19 '13 $42 Call(SSO) PROSHARES ULTRA S&P 500...	$24,122.54
03/21/11	3 SSO Jan 19 '13 $42 Call(SSO) PROSHARES ULTRA S&P 500 ...	$4,223.63
03/21/11	16 DIG Jan 19 '13 $42 Call(DIG) PROSHARES ULTRA OIL & G...	$33,503.13
03/21/11	2 DIG Jan 19 '13 $42 Call(DIG) PROSHARES ULTRA OIL & GA...	$4,214.39
03/21/11	8 BIDU Jan 19 '13 $105 Call(BIDU) BAIDU INC SPON ADR RE...	$30,349.30
03/21/11	5 UYM Jan 19 '13 $40 Call(UYM) PROSHARES ULTRA BASIC MA...	$9,298.01
03/21/11	5 UYM Jan 19 '13 $40 Call(UYM) PROSHARES ULTRA BASIC MA...	$9,353.01
03/21/11	5 CAT Jan 19 '13 $95 Call(CAT) CATERPILLAR INC DEL COM ...	$11,312.97
03/18/11	2 QLD Jan 21 '12 $65 Call(QLD) PROSHARES ULTRA QQQ SHOR...	$4,750.38
03/18/11	3 SSO Jan 21 '12 $41 Call(SSO) PROSHARES ULTRA S&P 500 ...	$3,724.64
03/18/11	3 UWM Jan 21 '12 $36 Call(UWM) PROSHARES ULTRA RUSSELL ...	$3,610.65
03/18/11	1 DIG Jan 21 '12 $44 Call(DIG) PROSHARES ULTRA OIL & GA...	$1,641.21
03/18/11	1 DIG Jan 21 '12 $44 Call(DIG) PROSHARES ULTRA OIL & GA...	$1,632.21
03/17/11	12 NOV Jan 21 '12 $60 Call(NOV) NATIONAL OILWELL VARCO ...	$26,382.33
03/17/11	20 QLD Jan 21 '12 $65 Call(QLD) PROSHARES ULTRA QQQ SHO...	$47,975.79
03/17/11	17 SSO Jan 21 '12 $40 Call(SSO) PROSHARES ULTRA S&P 500...	$21,228.60

Transaction History: Reports

Date	Description	Amount
03/17/11	5 CAT Jan 21 '12 $90 Call(CAT) CATERPILLAR INC DEL COM ...	$9,633.00
03/17/11	20 UWM Jan 21 '12 $35 Call(UWM) PROSHARES ULTRA RUSSELL...	$24,976.24
03/17/11	8 BIDU Jan 21 '12 $100 Call(BIDU) BAIDU INC SPON ADR RE...	$26,385.38
03/17/11	16 DIG Jan 21 '12 $43 Call(DIG) PROSHARES ULTRA OIL & G...	$25,579.28
03/17/11	3 AAPL Jan 21 '12 $270 Call(AAPL) APPLE INC COM SHORT...	$25,639.22
03/03/11	3 UYM Mar 19 '11 $54 Call(UYM) PROSHARES ULTRA BASIC MA...	$322.71
03/03/11	1 UWM Mar 19 '11 $49 Call(UWM) PROSHARES ULTRA RUSSELL ...	$81.24
03/03/11	1 QLD Mar 19 '11 $94 Call(QLD) PROSHARES ULTRA QQQ SHOR...	$164.24
03/02/11	1 BIDU Mar 19 '11 $125 Call(BIDU) BAIDU INC SPON ADR RE...	$159.24
03/02/11	4 SSO Mar 19 '11 $54 Call(SSO) PROSHARES ULTRA S&P 500 ...	$260.94
03/02/11	3 NOV Mar 19 '11 $80 Call(NOV) NATIONAL OILWELL VARCO I...	$601.70
03/02/11	1 DIG Mar 19 '11 $60 Call(DIG) PROSHARES ULTRA OIL & GA...	$159.24
02/17/11	3 UYM Mar 19 '11 $58 Call(UYM) PROSHARES ULTRA BASIC MA...	$482.71
02/17/11	1 BIDU Mar 19 '11 $130 Call(BIDU) BAIDU INC SPON ADR RE...	$412.24
02/17/11	9 QLD Mar 19 '11 $97 Call(QLD) PROSHARES ULTRA QQQ SHOR...	$1,960.09
02/17/11	2 QLD Mar 19 '11 $97 Call(QLD) PROSHARES ULTRA QQQ SHOR...	$424.47
02/16/11	19 UYM Mar 19 '11 $57 Call(UYM) PROSHARES ULTRA BASIC M...	$3,173.41
02/16/11	15 QLD Mar 19 '11 $96 Call(QLD) PROSHARES ULTRA QQQ SHO...	$3,719.46
02/16/11	14 NOV Mar 19 '11 $85 Call(NOV) NATIONAL OILWELL VARCO ...	$2,043.27
02/16/11	42 FAS Mar 19 '11 $36 Call(FAS) DIREXION DAILY FINANCIA...	$4,163.81
02/16/11	21 SSO Mar 19 '11 $55 Call(SSO) PROSHARES ULTRA S&P 500...	$2,583.91
02/16/11	9 DIG Mar 19 '11 $59 Call(DIG) PROSHARES ULTRA OIL & GA...	$1,222.10
02/14/11	28 UWM Mar 19 '11 $49 Call(UWM) PROSHARES ULTRA RUSSELL...	$3,502.53
02/14/11	9 BIDU Mar 19 '11 $130 Call(BIDU) BAIDU INC SPON ADR RE...	$4,309.04
02/14/11	12 DIG Mar 19 '11 $58 Call(DIG) PROSHARES ULTRA OIL & G...	$2,050.80
02/03/11	2 UWM Feb 19 '11 $45 Call(UWM) PROSHARES ULTRA RUSSELL ...	$188.47
02/03/11	3 QLD Feb 19 '11 $90 Call(QLD) PROSHARES ULTRA QQQ SHOR...	$520.70
02/03/11	2 UYM Feb 19 '11 $54 Call(UYM) PROSHARES ULTRA BASIC MA...	$198.47
02/02/11	13 UWM Feb 19 '11 $45 Call(UWM) PROSHARES ULTRA RUSSELL...	$1,438.04
02/01/11	13 UWM Feb 19 '11 $45 Call(UWM) PROSHARES ULTRA RUSSELL...	$1,529.04
01/26/11	2 UWM Feb 19 '11 $45 Call(UWM) PROSHARES ULTRA RUSSELL ...	$202.47
01/26/11	2 SSO Feb 19 '11 $52 Call(SSO) PROSHARES ULTRA S&P 500 ...	$162.47
01/26/11	1 BIDU Feb 19 '11 $110 Call(BIDU) BAIDU INC SPON ADR RE...	$408.24
01/26/11	3 UYM Feb 19 '11 $52 Call(UYM) PROSHARES ULTRA BASIC MA...	$349.71
01/24/11	20 SSO Feb 19 '11 $51 Call(SSO) PROSHARES ULTRA S&P 500...	$2,244.66
01/24/11	2 SSO Feb 19 '11 $51 Call(SSO) PROSHARES ULTRA S&P 500 ...	$214.47
01/24/11	22 DIG Feb 19 '11 $50 Call(DIG) PROSHARES ULTRA OIL & G...	$2,593.13
01/20/11	9 NOV Feb 19 '11 $70 Call(NOV) NATIONAL OILWELL VARCO I...	$1,645.09
01/20/11	6 NOV Feb 19 '11 $70 Call(NOV) NATIONAL OILWELL VARCO I...	$1,101.39
01/20/11	15 XME Feb 19 '11 $68 Call(XME) SPDR S&P METALS & MININ...	$2,830.48
01/20/11	16 UWM Feb 19 '11 $43 Call(UWM) PROSHARES ULTRA RUSSELL...	$2,879.72
01/20/11	9 UWM Feb 19 '11 $43 Call(UWM) PROSHARES ULTRA RUSSELL ...	$1,650.09
01/20/11	9 QLD Feb 19 '11 $88 Call(QLD) PROSHARES ULTRA QQQ SHOR...	$2,212.08
01/20/11	15 QLD Feb 19 '11 $87 Call(QLD) PROSHARES ULTRA QQQ SHO...	$3,899.46
01/20/11	50 FAS Feb 19 '11 $30 Call(FAS) DIREXION DAILY FINANCIA...	$7,953.62
01/20/11	35 EDC Feb 19 '11 $40 Call(EDC) DIREXION DAILY EMERGING...	$7,525.10
01/20/11	3 EDC Feb 19 '11 $40 Call(EDC) DIREXION DAILY EMERGING ...	$649.70

Transaction History: Reports

| Transactions | Check Summary | Deposit Summary | Categories | Reports |

Date	Description	Amount
01/20/11	8 BIDU Feb 19 '11 $105 Call(BIDU) BAIDU INC SPON ADR RE...	$4,261.80
01/20/11	1 BIDU Feb 19 '11 $105 Call(BIDU) BAIDU INC SPON ADR RE...	$521.23
01/20/11	11 UYM Feb 19 '11 $49 Call(UYM) PROSHARES ULTRA BASIC M...	$2,297.55
01/20/11	8 UYM Feb 19 '11 $49 Call(UYM) PROSHARES ULTRA BASIC MA...	$1,665.85
01/12/11	6 XME Jan 22 '11 $70 Call(XME) SPDR S&P METALS & MINING...	$1,253.39
01/12/11	9 UWM Jan 22 '11 $44 Call(UWM) PROSHARES ULTRA RUSSELL2...	$1,335.10
01/11/11	9 FAS Jan 22 '11 $30 Call(FAS) DIREXION DAILY FINANCIAL...	$768.11
01/07/11	9 FAS Jan 22 '11 $30 Call(FAS) DIREXION DAILY FINANCIAL...	$804.11
01/07/11	6 NOV Jan 22 '11 $65 Call(NOV) NATIONAL OILWELL VARCO I...	$1,187.39
01/05/11	9 FAS Jan 22 '11 $30 Call(FAS) DIREXION DAILY FINANCIAL...	$1,290.10
01/05/11	8 BIDU Jan 22 '11 $102 Call(BIDU) BAIDU INC SPON ADR RE...	$3,185.83
01/05/11	2 QLD Jan 22 '11 $83 Call(QLD) PROSHARES ULTRA QQQ SHOR...	$690.46
01/04/11	9 FAS Jan 22 '11 $30 Call(FAS) DIREXION DAILY FINANCIAL...	$966.11
01/03/11	13 QLD Jan 22 '11 $83 Call(QLD) PROSHARES ULTRA QQQ SHO...	$4,531.99
01/03/11	3 AGQ Jan 22 '11 $160 Call(AGQ) PROSHARES ...	$2,932.67

Total Sold Short $764,001.77

| Transactions | Check Summary | Deposit Summary | Categories | Reports |

Date	Description	Amount
12/09/11	1 MA Jan 19 '13 $290 Call(MA) MASTERCARD INC CL A SHORT...	$10,941.03
12/09/11	4 TJX Jan 19 '13 $57.50 Call(TJX) TJX COS INC NEW COM S...	$4,028.90
12/09/11	1 NOV Jan 19 '13 $50 Call(NOV) NATIONAL OILWELL VARCO I...	$2,661.19
12/09/11	1 HUM Jan 19 '13 $60 Call(HUM) HUMANA INC COM SHORT...	$2,911.19
11/22/11	1 AAPL Jan 19 '13 $270 Call(AAPL) APPLE INC COM SHORT...	$12,959.00
11/21/11	3 NOV Jan 19 '13 $50 Call(NOV) NATIONAL OILWELL VARCO I...	$6,949.59
11/21/11	2 HUM Jan 19 '13 $60 Call(HUM) HUMANA INC COM SHORT...	$5,490.38
09/23/11	1 AAPL Sep 30 '11 $405 Call w(AAPL) APPLE INC COM SHORT...	$815.23
09/16/11	7 EEM Sep 23 '11 $40 Call w(EEM) ISHARES MSCI EMERGING ...	$676.68
09/16/11	2 BIDU Sep 23 '11 $150 Call w(BIDU) BAIDU INC SPON ADR ...	$428.48
09/16/11	1 AAPL Sep 23 '11 $400 Call w(AAPL) APPLE INC COM SHORT...	$528.23
09/16/11	4 XLE Sep 23 '11 $67 Call w(XLE) ENERGY SELECT SECTOR S...	$448.97
09/16/11	5 QQQ Sep 23 '11 $57 Call w(QQQ) POWERSHARES QQQ TRUST,...	$258.21
09/16/11	7 GLD Sep 23 '11 $176 Call w(GLD) SPDR GOLD SHARES SHOR...	$1,806.66
09/09/11	2 BIDU Sep 17 '11 $145 Call(BIDU) BAIDU INC SPON ADR RE...	$700.47
09/09/11	4 XLE Sep 17 '11 $65 Call(XLE) ENERGY SELECT SECTOR SPD...	$548.95
09/09/11	5 QQQ Sep 17 '11 $53 Call(QQQ) POWERSHARES QQQ TRUST, S...	$548.18
09/09/11	1 AAPL Sep 17 '11 $380 Call(AAPL) APPLE INC COM SHORT...	$561.23
09/09/11	7 EEM Sep 17 '11 $40 Call(EEM) ISHARES MSCI EMERGING MA...	$756.66
08/07/11	5 UGL Sep 17 '11 $100 Call(UGL) PROSHARES ULTRA GOLD SH...	$3,188.15
05/20/11	2 BIDU Jun 18 '11 $135 Call(BIDU) BAIDU INC SPON ADR RE...	$1,110.46

Transaction History: Reports

Date	Description	Amount
05/20/11	5 UWM Jun 18 '11 $48 Call(UWM) PROSHARES ULTRA RUSSELL ...	$888.20
05/20/11	3 UGL Jun 18 '11 $79 Call(UGL) PROSHARES ULTRA GOLD SHO...	$694.71
05/20/11	4 QLD Jun 18 '11 $92 Call(QLD) PROSHARES ULTRA QQQ SHOR...	$968.94
05/20/11	4 SSO Jun 18 '11 $55 Call(SSO) PROSHARES ULTRA S&P 500 ...	$452.95
05/20/11	4 DIG Jun 18 '11 $55 Call(DIG) PROSHARES ULTRA OIL & GA...	$928.96
05/06/11	1 AAPL Jan 19 '13 $320 Call(AAPL) APPLE INC COM SHORT...	$7,661.10
04/27/11	5 SSO May 21 '11 $54 Call(SSO) PROSHARES ULTRA S&P 500 ...	$1,238.16
04/27/11	4 QLD May 21 '11 $92 Call(QLD) PROSHARES ULTRA QQQ SHOR...	$1,988.91
04/26/11	2 BIDU May 21 '11 $150 Call(BIDU) BAIDU INC SPON ADR RE...	$1,990.44
04/25/11	1 EDC Jan 19 '13 $39.35 Call(EDC) DIREXION DAILY EMERGI...	$1,562.21
04/21/11	4 EDC Jan 19 '13 $39.35 Call(EDC) DIREXION DAILY EMERGI...	$6,512.82
04/20/11	1 UGL Oct 22 '11 $72 Call(UGL) PROSHARES ULTRA GOLD SHO...	$991.23
04/20/11	2 EEM Jan 19 '13 $48 Call(EEM) ISHARES MSCI EMERGING MA...	$1,434.45
04/19/11	3 BIDU May 21 '11 $145 Call(BIDU) BAIDU INC SPON ADR RE...	$2,989.66
04/19/11	3 EEM Jan 19 '13 $46 Call(EEM) ISHARES MSCI EMERGING MA...	$2,299.67
04/18/11	2 UGL Oct 22 '11 $70 Call(UGL) PROSHARES ULTRA GOLD SHO...	$2,168.43
04/15/11	2 UGL Oct 22 '11 $70 Call(UGL) PROSHARES ULTRA GOLD SHO...	$1,950.44
04/14/11	2 UGL Oct 22 '11 $68 Call(UGL) PROSHARES ULTRA GOLD SHO...	$2,058.44
04/13/11	5 EEM Jan 19 '13 $46 Call(EEM) ISHARES MSCI EMERGING MA...	$3,983.11
03/23/11	3 UYM Jan 19 '13 $45 Call(UYM) PROSHARES ULTRA BASIC MA...	$5,149.62
03/23/11	7 NOV Jan 19 '13 $65 Call(NOV) NATIONAL OILWELL VARCO I...	$16,216.34
03/21/11	2 AAPL Jan 19 '13 $280 Call(AAPL) APPLE INC COM SHORT...	$19,284.10
03/21/11	5 QLD Jan 19 '13 $67 Call(QLD) PROSHARES ULTRA QQQ SHOR...	$13,720.91
03/21/11	4 QLD Jan 19 '13 $67 Call(QLD) PROSHARES ULTRA QQQ SHOR...	$11,032.73
03/21/11	10 SSO Jan 19 '13 $42 Call(SSO) PROSHARES ULTRA S&P 500...	$14,088.08
03/21/11	6 DIG Jan 19 '13 $42 Call(DIG) PROSHARES ULTRA OIL & GA...	$12,561.17
03/21/11	3 DIG Jan 19 '13 $42 Call(DIG) PROSHARES ULTRA OIL & GA...	$6,338.59
03/21/11	5 BIDU Jan 19 '13 $105 Call(BIDU) BAIDU INC SPON ADR RE...	$19,076.82
03/21/11	4 UYM Jan 19 '13 $40 Call(UYM) PROSHARES ULTRA BASIC MA...	$7,432.80
03/21/11	3 UYM Jan 19 '13 $40 Call(UYM) PROSHARES ULTRA BASIC MA...	$5,602.61
03/18/11	7 NOV Jan 21 '12 $60 Call(NOV) NATIONAL OILWELL VARCO I...	$16,051.35
03/18/11	11 QLD Jan 21 '12 $65 Call(QLD) PROSHARES ULTRA QQQ SHO...	$26,548.08
03/18/11	10 SSO Jan 21 '12 $41 Call(SSO) PROSHARES ULTRA S&P 500...	$12,384.12
03/18/11	11 UWM Jan 21 '12 $35 Call(UWM) PROSHARES ULTRA RUSSELL...	$13,513.34
03/18/11	5 BIDU Jan 21 '12 $100 Call(BIDU) BAIDU INC SPON ADR RE...	$16,487.87
03/18/11	1 DIG Jan 21 '12 $45 Call(DIG) PROSHARES ULTRA OIL & GA...	$1,561.21
03/18/11	1 DIG Jan 21 '12 $45 Call(DIG) PROSHARES ULTRA OIL & GA...	$1,571.21
03/18/11	1 DIG Jan 21 '12 $45 Call(DIG) PROSHARES ULTRA OIL & GA...	$1,591.21
03/18/11	6 DIG Jan 21 '12 $43 Call(DIG) PROSHARES ULTRA OIL & GA...	$9,887.22
03/18/11	2 AAPL Jan 21 '12 $320 Call(AAPL) APPLE INC COM SHORT...	$10,700.27
03/03/11	1 UYM Mar 19 '11 $54 Call(UYM) PROSHARES ULTRA BASIC MA...	$102.24
03/03/11	2 UWM Mar 19 '11 $49 Call(UWM) PROSHARES ULTRA RUSSELL ...	$170.47
03/03/11	1 DIG Mar 19 '11 $62 Call(DIG) PROSHARES ULTRA OIL & GA...	$113.24
02/17/11	3 DIG Mar 19 '11 $60 Call(DIG) PROSHARES ULTRA OIL & GA...	$418.71
02/16/11	13 UYM Mar 19 '11 $57 Call(UYM) PROSHARES ULTRA BASIC M...	$2,170.02
02/16/11	13 UWM Mar 19 '11 $49 Call(UWM) PROSHARES ULTRA RUSSELL...	$1,767.03
02/16/11	6 BIDU Mar 19 '11 $130 Call(BIDU) BAIDU INC SPON ADR RE...	$2,673.36

Transaction History: Reports

	Transactions	Check Summary	Deposit Summary	Categories	Reports

Date	Description	Amount
02/16/11	15 QLD Mar 19 '11 $96 Call(QLD) PROSHARES ULTRA QQQ SHO...	$3,734.46
02/16/11	9 NOV Mar 19 '11 $85 Call(NOV) NATIONAL OILWELL VARCO I...	$1,294.10
02/16/11	27 FAS Mar 19 '11 $36 Call(FAS) DIREXION DAILY FINANCIA...	$2,756.31
02/14/11	9 DIG Mar 19 '11 $58 Call(DIG) PROSHARES ULTRA OIL & GA...	$1,591.09
01/26/11	5 UYM Feb 19 '11 $49 Call(UYM) PROSHARES ULTRA BASIC MA...	$1,238.16
01/24/11	13 SSO Feb 19 '11 $51 Call(SSO) PROSHARES ULTRA S&P 500...	$1,490.04
01/24/11	13 DIG Feb 19 '11 $50 Call(DIG) PROSHARES ULTRA OIL & G...	$1,529.04
01/20/11	6 NOV Feb 19 '11 $70 Call(NOV) NATIONAL OILWELL VARCO I...	$1,107.39
01/20/11	3 NOV Feb 19 '11 $70 Call(NOV) NATIONAL OILWELL VARCO I...	$551.70
01/20/11	13 UWM Feb 19 '11 $44 Call(UWM) PROSHARES ULTRA RUSSELL..	$1,663.03
01/20/11	15 QLD Feb 19 '11 $89 Call(QLD) PROSHARES ULTRA QQQ SHO...	$3,059.48
01/20/11	30 FAS Feb 19 '11 $30 Call(FAS) DIREXION DAILY FINANCIA...	$4,768.97
01/20/11	24 EDC Feb 19 '11 $40 Call(EDC) DIREXION DAILY EMERGING...	$5,157.56
01/20/11	6 BIDU Feb 19 '11 $105 Call(BIDU) BAIDU INC SPON ADR RE...	$3,339.35
01/20/11	7 UYM Feb 19 '11 $49 Call(UYM) PROSHARES ULTRA BASIC MA...	$1,418.63
01/20/11	1 UYM Feb 19 '11 $49 Call(UYM) PROSHARES ULTRA BASIC MA...	$206.24
01/12/11	4 XME Jan 22 '11 $70 Call(XME) SPDR S&P METALS & MINING...	$832.93
01/12/11	2 UWM Jan 22 '11 $44 Call(UWM) PROSHARES ULTRA RUSSELL2..	$290.47
01/07/11	4 FAS Jan 22 '11 $30 Call(FAS) DIREXION DAILY FINANCIAL...	$352.94
01/07/11	3 NOV Jan 22 '11 $65 Call(NOV) NATIONAL OILWELL VARCO I...	$589.70
01/06/11	16 QLD Jan 22 '11 $85 Call(QLD) PROSHARES ULTRA QQQ SHO...	$3,979.71
01/05/11	9 FAS Jan 22 '11 $30 Call(FAS) DIREXION DAILY FINANCIAL...	$1,281.10
01/05/11	6 BIDU Jan 22 '11 $102 Call(BIDU) BAIDU INC SPON ADR RE...	$2,387.37
01/04/11	9 FAS Jan 22 '11 $30 Call(FAS) DIREXION DAILY FINANCIAL...	$957.11
01/03/11	2 EET Jan 22 '11 $110 Call(EET) PROSHARES ULTRA MSCI EM...	$990.46
01/03/11	1 AGQ Jan 22 '11 $160 Call(AGQ) PROSHAR	

Total Sold Short $396,861.96

Transaction History: Reports

Transactions | Check Summary | Deposit Summary | Categories | Reports

Date	Description	Amount
12/30/10	13 UYM Jan 22 '11 $50 Call(UYM) PROSHARES ULTRA BASIC M....	$3,232.02
12/29/10	6 EET Jan 22 '11 $105 Call(EET) PROSHARES ULTRA MSCI EM...	$3,107.37
12/29/10	6 EET Jan 22 '11 $105 Call(EET) PROSHARES ULTRA MSCI EM...	$2,987.37
12/20/10	8 XME Jan 22 '11 $67 Call(XME) SPDR S&P METALS & MINING...	$1,985.86
12/20/10	9 NOV Jan 22 '11 $64 Call(NOV) NATIONAL OILWELL VARCO I...	$2,235.10
12/20/10	11 UYM Jan 22 '11 $48 Call(UYM) PROSHARES ULTRA BASIC M...	$2,623.56
12/20/10	9 UGL Jan 22 '11 $66 Call(UGL) PROSHARES ULTRA GOLD SHO...	$2,775.09
12/17/10	3 FFIV Jan 22 '11 $140 Call(FFIV) F5 NETWORKS INC COM S....	$2,062.68
12/17/10	3 CRM Jan 22 '11 $140 Call(CRM) SALESFORCE COM INC COM ...	$1,609.69
12/17/10	16 UWM Jan 22 '11 $42 Call(UWM) PROSHARES ULTRA RUSSELL...	$3,099.73
12/17/10	15 SLW Jan 22 '11 $37 Call(SLW) SILVER WHEATON CORP COM...	$3,730.49
12/17/10	9 QLD Jan 22 '11 $82 Call(QLD) PROSHARES ULTRA QQQ SHOR...	$2,730.09
09/21/10	49 SSO Oct 16 '10 $40 Call(SSO) PROSHARES ULTRA S&P 500...	$5,834.50
09/16/10	4 AAPL Oct 16 '10 $270 Call(AAPL) APPLE INC COM SHORT...	$3,988.89
09/15/10	3 AAPL Oct 16 '10 $270 Call(AAPL) APPLE INC COM SHORT...	$2,389.67
09/14/10	25 UGL Oct 16 '10 $55 Call(UGL) PROSHARES ULTRA GOLD SH...	$6,222.81
09/14/10	19 QLD Oct 16 '10 $64 Call(QLD) PROSHARES ULTRA QQQ SHO...	$3,458.44
09/14/10	11 QLD Oct 16 '10 $64 Call(QLD) PROSHARES ULTRA QQQ SHO...	$1,949.56
09/14/10	25 BIDU Oct 16 '10 $90 Call(BIDU) BAIDU INC SPON ADR RE...	$5,301.83
08/20/10	1 SSO Sep 18 '10 $36 Call(SSO) PROSHARES ULTRA S&P 500 ...	$97.22
08/20/10	10 BIDU Sep 18 '10 $84 Call(BIDU) BAIDU INC SPON ADR RE...	$2,618.32
08/20/10	10 BIDU Sep 18 '10 $84 Call(BIDU) BAIDU INC SPON ADR RE...	$2,618.32
08/20/10	1 BIDU Sep 18 '10 $84 Call(BIDU) BAIDU INC SPON ADR REP...	$251.22
08/20/10	4 BIDU Sep 18 '10 $84 Call(BIDU) BAIDU INC SPON ADR REP...	$1,188.93
08/20/10	1 CAT Sep 18 '10 $70 Call(CAT) CATERPILLAR INC DEL COM ...	$161.22
08/19/10	48 SSO Sep 18 '10 $36 Call(SSO) PROSHARES ULTRA S&P 500...	$5,955.25
08/17/10	1 SNDK Sep 18 '10 $45 Call(SNDK) SANDISK CORP COM SHORT...	$187.22
08/17/10	30 QLD Sep 18 '10 $57 Call(QLD) PROSHARES ULTRA QQQ SHO...	$8,968.94
08/17/10	1 EEM Sep 18 '10 $43 Call(EEM) ISHARES MSCI EMERGING MA...	$57.22
08/16/10	1 MWE Sep 18 '10 $35 Call(MWE) MARKWEST ENERGY PARTNERS...	$91.22
08/13/10	1 VMW Sep 18 '10 $80 Call(VMW) VMWARE INC CL A COM SHOR...	$226.22
08/01/10	4 BIDU Aug 21 '10 $85 Call(BIDU) BAIDU INC SPON ADR REP...	$1,188.93
07/26/10	7 SSO Aug 21 '10 $39 Call(SSO) PROSHARES ULTRA S&P 500 ...	$560.65
07/26/10	1 SSO Aug 21 '10 $39 Call(SSO) PROSHARES ULTRA S&P 500 ...	$74.21
07/26/10	6 QLD Aug 21 '10 $61 Call(QLD) PROSHARES ULTRA QQQ SHOR...	$983.41
07/23/10	5 BIDU Aug 21 '10 $80 Call(BIDU) BAIDU INC SPON ADR REP...	$1,278.16
07/22/10	1 VMW Aug 21 '10 $80 Call(VMW) VMWARE INC CL A COM SHOR...	$142.21
07/22/10	9 SSO Aug 21 '10 $38 Call(SSO) PROSHARES ULTRA S&P 500 ...	$731.10
07/22/10	1 SSO Aug 21 '10 $38 Call(SSO) PROSHARES ULTRA S&P 500 ...	$74.21
07/22/10	6 QLD Aug 21 '10 $60 Call(QLD) PROSHARES ULTRA QQQ SHOR...	$1,037.41
07/22/10	5 BIDU Aug 21 '10 $80 Call(BIDU) BAIDU INC SPON ADR REP...	$993.17
07/15/10	1 CAT Aug 21 '10 $67.50 Call(CAT) CATERPILLAR INC DEL C...	$228.21
07/14/10	10 SSO Aug 21 '10 $38 Call(SSO) PROSHARES ULTRA S&P 500...	$1,264.34
07/14/10	6 QLD Aug 21 '10 $60 Call(QLD) PROSHARES ULTRA QQQ SHOR...	$1,367.40
07/14/10	18 EEM Aug 21 '10 $41 Call(EEM) ISHARES MSCI EMERGING M...	$1,886.22
07/13/10	12 QLD Aug 21 '10 $58 Call(QLD) PROSHARES ULTRA QQQ SHO...	$2,838.79
07/13/10	3 AAPL Aug 21 '10 $260 Call(AAPL) APPLE INC COM SHORT...	$2,890.67

Transaction History: Reports

| Transactions | Check Summary | Deposit Summary | Categories | Reports |

Date	Description	Amount
07/09/10	10 BIDU Aug 21 '10 $72.50 Call(BIDU) BAIDU INC SPON ADR...	$4,644.29
07/09/10	17 SSO Aug 21 '10 $36 Call(SSO) PROSHARES ULTRA S&P 500...	$2,825.96
07/09/10	2 SSO Aug 21 '10 $36 Call(SSO) PROSHARES ULTRA S&P 500 ...	$318.46
07/09/10	1 SSO Aug 21 '10 $36 Call(SSO) PROSHARES ULTRA S&P 500 ...	$157.21
07/07/10	1 SNDK Aug 21 '10 $43 Call(SNDK) SANDISK CORP COM SHORT...	$354.21
07/07/10	1 BIDU Aug 21 '10 $70 Call(BIDU) BAIDU INC SPON ADR REP...	$622.20
07/02/10	1 SSO Aug 21 '10 $32 Call(SSO) PROSHARES ULTRA S&P 500 ...	$243.21
07/02/10	1 SDS Aug 21 '10 $38 Call(SDS) PROSHARES ULTRASHORT S&P...	$315.21
06/24/10	1 CPNO Jul 17 '10 $25 Call(CPNO) COPANO ENERGY L L C CO...	$91.21
06/22/10	3 SM Nov 20 '10 $40 Call(SM) SM ENERGY CO COM SHORT...	$2,333.68
06/18/10	2 GLD Dec 18 '10 $115 Call(GLD) SPDR GOLD SHARES SHORT...	$2,534.42
06/18/10	2 AAPL Jan 22 '11 $230 Call(AAPL) APPLE INC COM SHORT...	$11,610.27
06/15/10	2 SNDK Oct 16 '10 $43 Call(SNDK) SANDISK CORP COM SHORT...	$1,856.42
06/15/10	1 SNDK Oct 16 '10 $43 Call(SNDK) SANDISK CORP COM SHORT...	$926.20
06/15/10	1 TIE Sep 18 '10 $20 Call(TIE) TITANIUM METALS CORP COM...	$249.21
06/15/10	3 ESRX Jan 22 '11 $50 Call(ESRX) EXPRESS SCRIPTS INC CO...	$2,273.68
06/14/10	3 XRT Dec 18 '10 $40 Call(XRT) SPDR S&P RETAIL ETF SHOR...	$1,172.70
06/03/10	2 BIDU Jan 22 '11 $60 Call(BIDU) BAIDU INC SPON ADR REP...	$4,594.39
05/28/10	2 AAPL Oct 16 '10 $230 Call(AAPL) APPLE INC COM SHORT...	$8,424.32
04/29/10	3 XRT Dec 18 '10 $43 Call(XRT) SPDR SERIES TRUST S&P RE...	$1,232.69
04/29/10	2 UTX Nov 20 '10 $75 Call(UTX) UNITED TECHNOLOGIES CORP...	$1,056.45
04/23/10	2 IOW Nov 20 '10 $72 Call(IWM) ISHARES TR INDEX RUSSELL...	$1,250.44
04/23/10	2 AAPL Jan 22 '11 $300 Call(AAPL) APPLE INC COM SHORT...	$3,890.40
04/14/10	3 CLF Jan 22 '11 $80 Call(CLF) CLIFFS NATURAL RESOURCES...	$3,208.66
04/14/10	2 AAPL Oct 16 '10 $220 Call(AAPL) APPLE INC COM SHORT...	$7,386.34
04/13/10	3 CLF Oct 16 '10 $65 Call(CLF) CLIFFS NATURAL RESOURCES...	$4,502.64
04/13/10	2 GCZ Dec 18 '10 $108 Call(GLD) SPDR GOLD TRUST GOLD SH...	$2,050.43
04/09/10	2 GPY Oct 16 '10 $165 Call(GS) GOLDMAN SACHS GROUP INC ...	$4,514.39
04/09/10	2 VAA Jan 22 '11 $270 Call(AAPL) APPLE INC COM SHORT...	$3,500.41
04/09/10	4 XQX Jan 22 '11 $80 Call(BUCY) BUCYRUS INTL INC NEW CO...	$3,080.89
04/06/10	8 OYK Jan 22 '11 $65 Call(PRU) PRUDENTIAL FINL INC COM ...	$4,785.81
04/05/10	4 ZJM Jan 22 '11 $50 Call(TCK) TECK RESOURCES LTD CL B ...	$1,892.91
04/05/10	2 SOA Sep 18 '10 $20 Call(SOA) SOLUTIA INC COM NEW SHOR...	$180.46
04/05/10	3 EEM Sep 18 '10 $44 Call(EEM) ISHARES TR INDEX MSCI EM...	$782.70
04/05/10	2 TSX Aug 21 '10 $45 Call(TCK) TECK RESOURCES LTD CL B ...	$1,000.45
04/05/10	1 VAA Jan 22 '11 $270 Call(AAPL) APPLE INC COM SHORT...	$1,579.19
04/05/10	1 VAA Jan 22 '11 $270 Call(AAPL) APPLE INC COM SHORT...	$1,586.18
04/05/10	4 XQX Jan 22 '11 $80 Call(BUCY) BUCYRUS INTL INC NEW CO...	$2,880.90
04/05/10	4 XQX Jan 22 '11 $80 Call(BUCY) BUCYRUS INTL INC NEW CO...	$2,988.89
03/30/10	2 WLT Sep 18 '10 $80 Call(WLT) WALTER ENERGY INC COM SH...	$3,466.42
03/29/10	2 VAA Jan 22 '11 $270 Call(AAPL) APPLE INC COM SHORT...	$2,770.43
03/23/10	20 F Jan 22 '11 $15 Call(F) FORD MOTOR CO SHORT...	$3,696.68
03/23/10	2 ISJ Sep 18 '10 $78 Call(IYT) ISHARES TRUST-DOW JONES ...	$1,012.45
03/23/10	2 F Sep 18 '10 $15 Call(F) FORD MOTOR CO SHORT...	$240.46
03/23/10	2 AJL Jul 17 '10 $210 Call(AAPL) APPLE INC SHORT...	$5,158.40

Transaction History: Reports

Transactions	Check Summary	Deposit Summary	Categories	Reports

Date	Description	Amount
03/23/10	8 OZL Jan 22 '11 $22.50 Call(MRVL) MARVELL TECHNOLOGY G...	$1,961.86
03/23/10	1 OZL Jan 22 '11 $22.50 Call(MRVL) MARVELL TECHNOLOGY G...	$244.20
03/23/10	1 OZL Jan 22 '11 $22.50 Call(MRVL) MARVELL TECHNOLOGY G...	$241.21
03/23/10	2 VAA Jan 22 '11 $260 Call(AAPL) APPLE INC SHORT...	$2,652.43
03/05/10	2 ZYL Jan 22 '11 $65 Call(EWZ) ISHARES INC MSCI BRAZIL ...	$2,434.43
03/05/10	3 XQX Jan 22 '11 $55 Call(BUCY) BUCYRUS INTL INC NEW CO...	$5,321.65
03/04/10	1 UVM May 22 '10 $20 Call(MRVL) MARVELL TECHNOLOGY GROU..	$137.21
03/01/10	1 FWK Sep 18 '10 $150 Put(FXB) CURRENCYSHS BRIT POUND S...	$671.21
03/01/10	3 OFA Jan 22 '11 $63 Call(IWM) ISHARES TR INDEX RUSSELL...	$1,781.69
02/25/10	1 QGJ Apr 17 '10 $25 Call(LINE) LINN ENERGY LLC UNIT LT...	$151.21
02/22/10	2 VSK Jan 22 '11 $80 Call(V) VISA INC COM CL A SHORT...	$2,520.43
02/18/10	4 OQI Jan 22 '11 $70 Call(CREE) CREE INC COM SHORT...	$3,348.90
02/18/10	6 ZJM Jan 22 '11 $40 Call(TCK) TECK RESOURCES LTD CL B ...	$3,389.38
02/18/10	4 OQI Jan 22 '11 $55 Call(CREE) CREE INC COM SHORT...	$6,392.86
02/18/10	4 VGB Jan 22 '11 $36 Call(XRT) SPDR SERIES TRUST S&P RE...	$1,444.93
02/17/10	2 ZJM Jan 22 '11 $35 Call(TCK) TECK RESOURCES LTD CL B ...	$1,554.45
02/17/10	6 ZJM Jan 22 '11 $40 Call(TCK) TECK RESOURCES LTD CL B ...	$3,311.38
02/16/10	2 VAA Jan 22 '11 $170 Call(AAPL) APPLE INC COM SHORT...	$9,592.34
02/16/10	4 OQI Jan 22 '11 $65 Call(CREE) CREE INC COM SHORT	$3,788.90

	Total Sold Short	$267,469.13

Transactions	Check Summary	Deposit Summary	Categories	Reports

Date	Description	Amount
12/30/10	10 UYM Jan 22 '11 $50 Call(UYM) PROSHARES ULTRA BASIC M...	$2,484.32
12/29/10	4 EET Jan 22 '11 $105 Call(EET) PROSHARES ULTRA MSCI EM...	$1,988.92
12/28/10	8 SLW Jan 22 '11 $38 Call(SLW) SILVER WHEATON CORP COM ...	$1,585.87
12/28/10	2 AGQ Jan 22 '11 $160 Call(AGQ) PROSHARES ULTRA SILVER ...	$1,486.45
12/28/10	1 AGQ Jan 22 '11 $160 Call(AGQ) PROSHARES ULTRA SILVER ...	$720.21
12/21/10	5 XME Jan 22 '11 $67 Call(XME) SPDR S&P METALS & MINING...	$1,338.16
12/21/10	6 NOV Jan 22 '11 $64 Call(NOV) NATIONAL OILWELL VARCO I..	$1,787.39
12/21/10	13 UWM Jan 22 '11 $42 Call(UWM) PROSHARES ULTRA RUSSELL..	$3,232.02
12/21/10	2 UYM Jan 22 '11 $48 Call(UYM) PROSHARES ULTRA BASIC MA...	$490.47
12/20/10	6 UYM Jan 22 '11 $48 Call(UYM) PROSHARES ULTRA BASIC MA...	$1,487.40
12/20/10	8 UGL Jan 22 '11 $66 Call(UGL) PROSHARES ULTRA GOLD SHO...	$2,705.85
12/17/10	3 FFIV Jan 22 '11 $140 Call(FFIV) F5 NETWORKS INC COM S...	$2,017.68
12/17/10	3 CRM Jan 22 '11 $140 Call(CRM) SALESFORCE COM INC COM ...	$1,693.69
09/14/10	15 UGL Oct 16 '10 $55 Call(UGL) PROSHARES ULTRA GOLD SH...	$3,730.49
09/14/10	18 QLD Oct 16 '10 $64 Call(QLD) PROSHARES ULTRA QQQ SHO...	$3,168.21
09/14/10	15 BIDU Oct 16 '10 $90 Call(BIDU) BAIDU INC SPON ADR RE...	$3,464.50
09/13/10	18 EEM Oct 16 '10 $43 Call(EEM) ISHARES MSCI EMERGING M...	$2,318.23
09/09/10	4 AAPL Sep 18 '10 $260 Call(AAPL) APPLE INC COM SHORT...	$3,188.90
08/20/10	10 BIDU Sep 18 '10 $84 Call(BIDU) BAIDU INC SPON ADR RE...	$2,618.32
08/20/10	5 BIDU Sep 18 '10 $84 Call(BIDU) BAIDU INC SPON ADR REP...	$1,307.16
08/19/10	30 SSO Sep 18 '10 $36 Call(SSO) PROSHARES ULTRA S&P 500...	$3,689.03

Transaction History: Reports

Transactions	Check Summary	Deposit Summary	Categories	**Reports**

Date	Description	Amount
08/17/10	18 QLD Sep 18 '10 $57 Call(QLD) PROSHARES ULTRA QQQ SHO...	$5,378.17
07/22/10	5 BIDU Aug 21 '10 $80 Call(BIDU) BAIDU INC SPON ADR REP...	$898.17
07/14/10	6 SSO Aug 21 '10 $38 Call(SSO) PROSHARES ULTRA S&P 500 ...	$757.40
07/14/10	2 SSO Aug 21 '10 $38 Call(SSO) PROSHARES ULTRA S&P 500 ...	$256.45
07/14/10	1 SSO Aug 21 '10 $38 Call(SSO) PROSHARES ULTRA S&P 500 ...	$119.21
07/14/10	1 SSO Aug 21 '10 $38 Call(SSO) PROSHARES ULTRA S&P 500 ...	$121.21
07/14/10	6 QLD Aug 21 '10 $60 Call(QLD) PROSHARES ULTRA QQQ SHOR...	$1,367.40
07/14/10	10 EEM Aug 21 '10 $41 Call(EEM) ISHARES MSCI EMERGING M...	$1,064.35
07/14/10	8 EEM Aug 21 '10 $41 Call(EEM) ISHARES MSCI EMERGING MA...	$849.87
07/13/10	12 QLD Aug 21 '10 $58 Call(QLD) PROSHARES ULTRA QQQ SHO...	$2,826.79
07/13/10	3 AAPL Aug 21 '10 $260 Call(AAPL) APPLE INC COM SHORT...	$2,872.67
07/09/10	10 BIDU Aug 21 '10 $72.50 Call(BIDU) BAIDU INC SPON ADR...	$4,644.29
07/09/10	18 SSO Aug 21 '10 $36 Call(SSO) PROSHARES ULTRA S&P 500...	$2,992.19
07/09/10	1 SSO Aug 21 '10 $36 Call(SSO) PROSHARES ULTRA S&P 500 ...	$157.21
07/09/10	1 SSO Aug 21 '10 $36 Call(SSO) PROSHARES ULTRA S&P 500 ...	$155.21
04/23/10	2 AAPL Jan 22 '11 $300 Call(AAPL) APPLE INC COM SHORT...	$3,888.40
04/14/10	3 CLF Jan 22 '11 $80 Call(CLF) CLIFFS NATURAL RESOURCES...	$3,157.66
04/13/10	3 CLF Jan 22 '11 $80 Call(CLF) CLIFFS NATURAL RESOURCES...	$2,989.66
04/09/10	2 VAA Jan 22 '11 $270 Call(AAPL) APPLE INC COM SHORT...	$3,506.41
04/06/10	8 OYK Jan 22 '11 $65 Call(PRU) PRUDENTIAL FINL INC COM ...	$4,785.81
04/05/10	4 XQX Jan 22 '11 $75 Call(BUCY) BUCYRUS INTL INC NEW CO...	$3,596.88
04/05/10	6 ZJM Jan 22 '11 $50 Call(TCK) TECK RESOURCES LTD CL B ...	$2,843.38
04/05/10	2 VAA Jan 22 '11 $270 Call(AAPL) APPLE INC COM SHORT...	$3,164.41
03/29/10	12 VBA Jan 22 '11 $20 Call(BAC) BANK OF AMERICA CORPORA...	$1,722.81
03/29/10	4 OQI Jan 22 '11 $75 Call(CREE) CREE INC COM SHORT...	$3,748.90
03/29/10	6 ZJM Jan 22 '11 $45 Call(TCK) TECK RESOURCES LTD CL B ...	$2,855.39
03/29/10	2 VAA Jan 22 '11 $270 Call(AAPL) APPLE INC COM SHORT...	$2,770.43
03/25/10	4 XQX Jan 22 '11 $75 Call(BUCY) BUCYRUS INTL INC NEW CO...	$3,756.90
03/24/10	4 XQX Jan 22 '11 $75 Call(BUCY) BUCYRUS INTERNATIONAL I...	$3,312.90
03/23/10	3 F Jan 22 '11 $15 Call(F) FORD MOTOR CO SHORT...	$544.71
03/23/10	17 F Jan 22 '11 $15 Call(F) FORD MOTOR CO SHORT...	$3,123.98
03/23/10	10 OZL Jan 22 '11 $22.50 Call(MRVL) MARVELL TECHNOLOGY ...	$2,444.33
03/23/10	1 VAA Jan 22 '11 $260 Call(AAPL) APPLE INC SHORT...	$1,325.20
03/23/10	1 VAA Jan 22 '11 $260 Call(AAPL) APPLE INC SHORT...	$1,332.19
02/18/10	4 OQI Jan 22 '11 $70 Call(CREE) CREE INC COM SHORT...	$3,332.90
02/18/10	8 ZJM Jan 22 '11 $40 Call(TCK) TECK RESOURCES LTD CL B ...	$4,545.84
02/18/10	2 VAA Jan 22 '11 $230 Call(AAPL) APPLE INC COM SHORT...	$3,430.41
02/18/10	1 VAA Jan 22 '11 $230 Call(AAPL) APPLE INC COM SHORT...	$1,716.18
02/18/10	1 VAA Jan 22 '11 $230 Call(AAPL) APPLE INC COM SHORT...	$1,709.19
02/17/10	8 ZJM Jan 22 '11 $40 Call(TCK) TECK RESOURCES LTD CL B	$4,441.84
02/16/10	4 OQI Jan 22 '11 $65 Call(CREE) CREE INC COM SHORT	$3,816.90

	Total Sold Short	**$148,827.47**